ECONOMIC IMPACT OF COLONIAL RULE IN INDIA

Encyclopaedic History of India Series

ECONOMIC IMPACT OF COLONIAL RULE IN INDIA

Dr. Mahesh Vikram Singh
Professor, Deptt. of History
Mahatma Gandhi Kashi Vidyapeeth
Varanasi (UP)

Dr. Brij Bhushan Shrivastava
Head of Deptt., Ancient History, Archeology & Culture
SMMTPG College, Ballia (UP)

CENTRUM PRESS
NEW DELHI-110002 (INDIA)

CENTRUM PRESS
H.O.: 4360/4, Ansari Road, Daryaganj,
New Delhi-110002 (India)
Tel: 23278000, 23261597, 23255577, 23286875
B.O.: No. 1015, Ist Main Road, BSK IIIrd Stage,
IIIrd Phase, IIIrd Block, Bangalore-560085 (INDIA)
Tel: 080-41723429
Email: centrumpress@gmail.com
Visit us at: www.centrumpress.com

Economic Impact of Colonial Rule in India

First Edition, 2011

ISBN 978-93-80836-89-8

PRINTED IN INDIA

Printed at Mehra Offset Press, Delhi

प्रो. विपिन चंद्रा
अध्यक्ष
Prof. Bipan Chandra
Chairman

नेशनल बुक ट्रस्ट, इंडिया
नेहरू भवन
5 इंस्टीट्यूशनल एरिया, फेज़-II, वसंत कुंज, नई दिल्ली-110 070
फोन/ Phone: 011-26121880 फैक्स/ Fax: 011-26121883

NATIONAL BOOK TRUST, INDIA
Nehru Bhawan
5 Institutional Area, Phase II, Vasant Kunj, New Delhi-110 070
ई-मेल / E-mail: chairman@nbtindia.org.in
वेबसाइट / Website: www.nbtindia.org.in

FOREWORD

The term 'history' is derived from the Greek word 'historia' that means knowledge acquired through investigation. Obviously, this knowledge can be correct if the method of investigation is objective and not vitiated by any kind of bias. In other words, if the study of human past is comprehensive and obtained through scientific inquiry, it can provide perspective on the present day problems and help one plan for the future.

A true historian has to identify the sources that can be most useful in a given context. Documents, coins, archaeology, anthropology, geography, travel accounts, oral traditions, mythology and so on can be useful but they can be used only after their veracity is tested and they are critically examined. They should be checked and counter-checked.

Over the centuries, one finds the study and writing of history vitiated by biases. There are numerous instances in which historical data have been distorted to support or oppose certain preconceived ideas and purposes. Strictly speaking such history is just like fiction to accord with preconceived notions and serve some ulterior purposes.

The study of the past has never been static. Conclusions go on changing because of the discovery of new materials and tools of investigation. To give a concrete example, the carbon 14 or radiocarbon dating test has revolutionized the study of civilizations and settlements, especially of prehistoric times, for which written documents, coins, etc. are seldom available. This method has enabled historians to determine more accurately than before the time period of a particular civilization or settlement. This method was discovered only 70 years ago by American scientists.

In our country, excavations brought to light the Indus Valley Civilization and its various features, hitherto unknown. Similarly, no complete text of Kautilya's Arthashastra was available before it was discovered by Shamasastry, the chief of the Mysore Government Oriental Library in the first decade of the last century. Likewise, people's knowledge of the history of the Buddhist period got extended after excavations at Sarnath and the ruins of the Asokan period at Patna. In the future, if the Harappan inscriptions are deciphered, our knowledge of the Indus Valley Civilization will increase enormously. All these instances underline the fact that our knowledge of history is never static and its frontiers go on extending.

In the light of what has been said above the encyclopedic history is going to be of great help to students interested in Indian history. It is comprehensive and as far as possible free from biases. It includes the latest materials, and objective conclusions.

Prof . Bipan Chandra

Professor Emeritus, JNU

Chairman, National Book Trust, India

Contents

Preface

The people of India have had a continuous civilization since 2500 B.C., when the inhabitants of the Indus River valley developed an urban culture based on commerce and sustained by agricultural trade. This civilization declined around 1500 B.C., probably due to ecological changes. During the second millennium B.C., pastoral, Aryan-speaking tribes migrated from the northwest into the subcontinent. As they settled in the middle Ganges River valley, they adapted to antecedent cultures.

The political map of ancient and medieval India was made up of myriad kingdoms with fluctuating boundaries. In the 4th and 5th centuries A.D., northern India was unified under the Gupta Dynasty. During this period, known as India's Golden Age, Hindu culture and political administration reached new heights. Islam spread across the Indian subcontinent over a period of 500 years. In the 10th and 11th centuries, Turks and Afghans invaded India and established sultanates in Delhi. In the early 16th century, descendants of Genghis Khan swept across the Khyber Pass and established the Mughal (Mogul) Dynasty, which lasted for 200 years. From the 11th to the 15th centuries, southern India was dominated by Hindu Chola and Vijayanagar Dynasties. During this time, the two systems—the prevailing Hindu and Muslim—mingled, leaving lasting cultural influences on each other.

The first British outpost in South Asia was established in 1619 at Surat on the northwestern coast. Later in the century, the East India Company opened permanent trading stations at Madras, Bombay, and Calcutta, each under the protection of native rulers. The British expanded their influence from these footholds until, by the 1850s, they controlled most of present-day India, Pakistan, and Bangladesh. In 1857, a rebellion in north India led by mutinous Indian soldiers caused the British Parliament to transfer all political power from the East India Company to the Crown. Great Britain began administering most of India directly while controlling the rest through treaties with local rulers.

In the late 1800s, the first steps were taken toward self-government in British India with the appointment of Indian councillors to advise the British viceroy and the establishment of provincial councils with Indian members; the British subsequently widened participation in legislative councils. Beginning in 1920, Indian leader Mohandas K. Gandhi transformed the Indian National Congress political party into a mass movement to campaign against British colonial rule.

—Authors

1

Introduction

British imperialism was more pragmatic than that of other colonial powers. Its motivation was economic, not evangelical. There was none of the dedicated Christian fanaticism which the Portuguese and Spanish demonstrated in Latin America and less enthusiasm for cultural diffusion than the French (or the Americans) showed in their colonies. For this reason they westernized India only to a limited degree.

British interests were of several kinds. At first the main purpose was to achieve a monopolistic trading position. Later it was felt that a regime of free trade would make India a major market for British goods and a source of raw materials, but British capitalists who invested in India, or who sold banking or shipping service there, continued effectively to enjoy monopolistic privileges. India also provided interesting and lucrative employment for a sizeable portion of the British upper middle class, and the remittances they sent home made an appreciable contribution to Britain's balance of payments and capacity to save. Finally, control of India was a key element in the world power structure, in terms of geography, logistics and military manpower. The British were not averse to Indian economic development if it increased their markets but refused to help in areas where they felt there was conflict with their own economic interests or political security. Hence, they refused to give protection to the Indian textile industry until its main competitor became Japan rather than Manchester, and they did almost nothing to further technical education. They introduced some British concepts of property, but did not push them too far when they met vested interests.

The main changes which the British made in Indian society were at the top. They replaced the wasteful warlord aristocracy by a bureaucratic-military establishment, carefully designed by utilitarian technocrats, which was very efficient in maintaining law and order. The greater efficiency of government permitted a substantial reduction in the fiscal burden, and a bigger share of the national product was available for landlords, capitalists and the new professional classes. Some of this upper class income was siphoned off to the UK, but the bulk was spent in India. However, the pattern of consumption changed as the new upper class no longer kept harems and palaces, nor did they wear fine muslins and damascened swords. This caused some painful readjustments in the traditional handicraft sector. It seems likely that there was some increase in productive investment which must have been near zero in Mughal India: government itself carried out productive investment in railways and irrigation and as a result there was a growth in both agricultural and industrial output. The new elite established a Western life-style using the English language and English schools. New towns and urban amenities were created with segregated suburbs and housing for them. Their habits were copied by the new professional elite of lawyers, doctors, teachers, journalists and businessmen. Within this group, old caste barriers, were eased and social mobility increased.

As far as the mass of the population were concerned, colonial rule brought few significant changes. The British educational effort was very limited. There were no major changes in village society, in the caste system, the position of untouchable, the joint family system, or in production techniques in agriculture.

British impact on economic and social development was, therefore, limited. Total output and population increased substantially but the gain in per capita output was small or negligible. It is interesting to speculate about India's potential economic fate if it had not had two centuries of British rule. There are three major alternatives which can be seriously considered. One would have been the maintenance of indigenous rule with a few foreign enclaves, as in China.

Given the fissiparous forces in Indian society, it is likely that there would have been major civil wars in China in the second half of the nineteenth century and the first half of the twentieth century and the country would probably have split up. Without direct foreign interference with its educational system, it is less likely that India would have developed a modernizing intelligentsia than China because Indian society was less rational and more conservative, and the Chinese had a much more homogeneous civilization around which to build their reactive nationalism. If this situation had prevailed, population would certainly have grown less but the average standard of living might possibly have been a little higher because of the bigger upper class, and the smaller drain of resources abroad. Another alternative to British rule would have been conquest and maintenance of power by some other West European country such as France or Holland. This probably would not have produced results very different in economic terms from British rule. The third hypothesis is perhaps the most intriguing, *i.e.* conquest by a European power, with earlier accession to independence. If India had self-government from the 1880s, after a century and a quarter of British rule, it is likely that both income and population growth would have been accelerated. There would have been a smaller drain of investible funds abroad, greater tariff protection, more state enterprise and favours to local industry, more technical training-the sort of things which happened after 1947. However, India would probably not have fared as well as Meiji Japan, because the fiscal leverage of government would have been smaller, zeal for mass education less, and religious and caste barriers would have remained as important constraints on productivity.

Establishment of a New Westernized Elite

The biggest change the British made in the social structure was to replace the warlord aristocracy by an efficient bureaucracy and army. The traditional system of the East India Company had been to pay its servants fairly modest salaries, and to let them augment their income from private transactions. This arrangement worked reasonably well before the conquest of Bengal, but was inefficient as a way of remunerating the officials of a substantial territorial Empire because (a) too much of the profit went into private hands rather than the Company's coffers, and (b) an overrapacious short-term policy was damaging to the productive capacity of the economy and likely to drive the local population to revolt, both of which were against the Company's longer-term interests. Clive had operated a 'dual' system, *i.e.* Company power and a puppet Nawab. Warren Hastings displaced the Nawab and took over direct administration, but retained Indian officials. Finally, in 1785, Cornwallis created a professional cadre of Company servants who had generous salaries, had no private trading or production interests in India, enjoyed the prospect of regular promotion and were entitled to pensions. All high-level posts were reserved for the British, and Indians were excluded. Cornwallis appointed British judges, and established British officials as revenue collectors and magistrated in each district of Bengal.

From 1806 the Company trained its young recruits in Haileybury College near London. Appointments were still organized on a system of patronage, but after 1833 the Company selected amongst its nominated candidates by competitive examination. After 1853, selection was entirely on merit and the examination was thrown open to any British candidate. The examination system was influenced by the Chinese model, which had worked well for 2,000 years and had a similar emphasis on classical learning and literary competence. The Indian civil service was therefore able to secure high quality people because (a) it was very highly paid; (b) it enjoyed political power which no bureaucrat could have had in England.

In 1829 the system was strengthened by establishing districts throughout British India small enough to be effectively controlled by an individual British official who henceforth exercised a completely autocratic power, acting as revenue collector, judge and chief of police (functions which had been separate under the Mughal administration). This arrangement later became the cornerstone of Imperial administration throughout the British Empire. As the civil service was ultimately subject to the control of the British parliament, and the British community in India was subject to close mutual surveillance, the administration was virtually incorruptible.

The army of the Company was a local mercenary force with 20,000-30,000 British officers and troops. It was by far the most modern and efficient army in Asia. After the Mutiny in 1857, the size of the British contingent was raised to a third of the total strength and all officers were British until the 1920s when a very small number of Indians was recruited. Normally, the total strength of the army was about 200,000. This army was very much smaller than those of Mughal India, but had better training and equipment, and the railway network (which was constructed partly for military reasons) gave it greater mobility, better logistics and intelligence.

The higher ranks of the administration remained almost entirely British until the 1920s when the Indian civil service examinations began to be held in India as well as the UK. In addition, there was a whole hierarchy of separate bureaucracies in which the higher ranks were British, *i.e.* the revenue, justice, police, education, medical, public works, engineering, postal and railway services as well as the provincial civil services. India thus offered highly-paid careers to an appreciable portion of the British middle and upper classes (particularly for its peripheral members from Scotland and Ireland).

From the 1820s to the 1850s the British demonstrated a strong urge to change Indian social institutions, and to Westernize India. They stamped out infanticide and ritual burning of widows (sati). They abolished slavery and eliminated dacoits (religious thugs) from the highways. They legalized the remarriage of widows and allowed Hindu converts to Christianity to lay claim to their share of joint family property. They took steps to introduce a penal code (the code was actually introduced in 1861) based on British law, which helped inculcate some ideas of equality. 'Under his old Hindu law, a Brahmin murderer might not be put to death, while a Sudra who cohabited with a high-caste woman would automatically suffer execution. Under the new law, Brahmin and Sudra were liable to the same punishment for the same offence.

There was a strong streak of Benthamite radicalism in the East India Company administration. James Mill became a senior company official in 1819 after writing a monumental history of India which showed a strong contempt for Indian institutions. From 1831 to 1836 he was the chief executive officer of the E.I.C. and his son John Stuart Mill worked for the Company from 1823 to 1858. Malthus was professor of economics at Haileybury, and the teaching there for future company officials was strongly influenced by Utilitarianism. Bentham himself was also consulted on the reform of Indian institutions. The Utilitarians deliberately used India to try out experiments and ideas (*e.g.* competitive entry for the civil service) which they would have liked to apply in England. The Utilitarians were strong supporters of laissez-faire and abhorred any kind of state interference to promote economic development. Thus they tended to rely on market forces to deal with famine problems, they did nothing to stimulate agriculture or protect industry. This laissez-faire tradition was more deeply embedded in the Indian civil service than in the UK itself, and persisted very strongly until the late 1920s. The administration was efficient and incorruptible, but the state apparatus was of a watchdog character with few development ambitions. Even in 1936, more than half of government spending was for the military, justice, police and jails, and less than 3 per cent for agriculture.

One of the most significant things the British did to Westernize India was to introduce a modified version of English education. Macaulay's 1835 Minute on Education had a decisive impact on British educational policy and is a classic example of a Western rationalist approach to Indian civilization. Before the British took over, the Court language of the Mughals was Persian and the Muslim population used Urdu, a mixture of Persian, Arabic and Sanskrit. Higher education was largely religious and stressed knowledge of Arabic and Sanskrit. The Company had given some financial support to a Calcutta Madrassa (1781), and a Sanskrit college at Benares (1792), Warren Hastings, as governor general from 1782 to 1795 had himself learned Sanskrit and Persian, and several other Company officials were oriental scholars. One of them, Sir William Jones, had translated a great mass of Sanskrit literature and had founded the Asiatic Society of Bengal in 1785. But Macaulay was strongly opposed to this orientalism: "I believe that the present system tends, not to accelerate the progress of truth, but to delay the natural death of expiring errors. We are a Board for wasting public money, for printing books which are less value than the paper on which they are printed was while it was blank; for giving artificial encouragement to absurd history, absurd metaphysics, absurd physics, absurd theology... I have no knowledge of either Sanskrit or Arabic... But I have done what I could to form a correct estimate of their value... Who could deny that a single shelf of a good European library was worth the whole native literature of India and Arabia... all the historical information which has been collected from all the books written in the Sanskrit language is less valuable than what may be found in the most paltry abridgements used at preparatory schools in England."

For these reasons Macaulay had no hesitation in deciding in favour of English education, but it was not to be for the masses: "It is impossible for us, with our limited means to attempt to educate the body of the people. We must at present do our best to form a class who may be interpreters between us and the millions whom we govern; a class of persons, Indian in blood and colour, but English in taste, in opinions, in morals, and in intellect. To that class we may leave it to refine the vernacular dialects of the country, to enrich those dialects with terms of science borrowed from the Western nomenclature, and to render them by degrees fit vehicles for conveying knowledge to the great mass of the population".

Until 1857 it was possible to entertain the view (as Marx did) that the British may eventually destroy traditional Indian society and Westernize the country. But activist Westernizing policies and the attempt to extend British rule by taking over native states whose rulers had left no heirs provoked sections of both the Hindu and Muslim communities into rebellion in the Mutiny of 1857. Although the Mutiny was successfully put down with substantial help from loyal Indian troops including the recently conquered Sikhs, British policy towards Indian institutions and society became much more conservative. The Crown took over direct responsibility and the East India Company was disbanded. The Indian civil service attracted fewer people with innovating ideas than had the East India Company and was more closely controlled from London.

The British forged an alliance with the remaining native princes and stopped taking over new territory. Until the end of their rule about a quarter of the Indian population remained in quasi-autonomous native states. These had official British residents but were fairly free in internal policy, and the effort of Westernization came to a standstill.

The education system which developed was a very pale reflection of that in the UK. Three universities were set up in 1857 in Calcutta, Madras and Bombay, but they were merely examining bodies and did no teaching. Higher education was carried out in affiliated colleges which gave a two-year B.A. course with heavy emphasis on rote learning and examinations. Drop-out ratios were always very high. They did little to promote analytic capacity or independent thinking and produced a group of graduates with a half-baked knowledge of English, but sufficiently westernized to be alienated from their own culture. It was not until the 1920s that Indian universities provided teaching facilities and then only for M.A. students. Furthermore, Indian education was of a predominantly literacy character and the provision for technical training was much less than in any European country. Education for girls was almost totally ignored throughout the nineteenth century. Because higher education was in English, there was no official effort to translate western literature into the vernacular, nor was there any standardization of Indian scripts whose variety is a major barrier to multi-lingualism amongst educated Indians.

Primary education was not taken very seriously as a government obligation and was financed largely by the weak local authorities. As a result, the great mass of the population had no access to education and, at independence in 1947, 88 per cent were illiterate. Progress was accelerated from the 1930s onwards, but at independence only a fifth of children were receiving any primary schooling.

Education could have played a major role in encouraging social mobility, eliminating religious superstition, increasing productivity, and uplifting the status of women. Instead it was used to turn a tiny elite into imitation Englishmen and a somewhat bigger group into government clerks. Having failed to westernize India, the British established themselves as a separate ruling caste. Like other Indian castes, they did not intermarry or eat with the lower (native) castes. Thanks to the British public-school system, their children were shipped off and did not mingle with the natives. At the end of their professional careers they returned home. The small creole class of Anglo-Indians were outcastes unable to integrate into Indian or local British society. The British kept to their clubs and bungalows in special suburbs known as cantonments and civil lines. They maintained the Mughal tradition of official pomp, sumptuary residences, and retinues of servants. They did not adopt the Mughal custom of polygamy, but remained monogamous and brought in their own women. Society became prim and priggish. The British ruled India in much the same way as the Roman consuls had ruled in Africa 2,000 years earlier, and were very conscious of the Roman paradigm. The elite with its classical education and contempt for business were quite happy establishing law and order, and keeping 'barbarians' at bay on the frontier of the raj. They developed their own brand of self-righteous arrogance, considering themselves purveyors not of popular but of good government. For them the word 'British' lost its geographic connotation and became an epithet signifying moral rectitude.

The striking thing about the British raj is that it was operated by so few people. There were only 31,000 British in India in 1805 (of which 22,000 were in the army and 2,000 in civil government). The number increased substantially after the Mutiny, but thereafter remained steady. In 1911, there were 164,000 British (106,000 employed, of which 66,000 were in the army and police and 4,000 in civil government). In 1931, there were 168,000 (90,000 employed, 60,000 in the army and police and 4,000 in civil government). They were a thinner layer than the Muslim rulers had been (never more than 0.05 per cent of the population).

Because of the small size of the administration and its philosophy of minimal government responsibility outside the field of law and order, India ended the colonial period with a very low level of taxation. The British had inherited the Mughal tax system which provided a land revenue equal to 15 per cent of national income, but by the end of the colonial period land tax was only 1 per cent of national income and the total tax burden was only 6 per cent. It is curious that this large reduction in the fiscal burden has passed almost without comment in the literature on Indian economic history. On the contrary, emphasis is usually place on the heaviness of the tax burden, *e.g.* by D. Naoroji and R.C. Dutt. Most of the benefits of the lower fiscal burden were felt by landlords, and were not passed on to the mass of the population. In urban areas new classes emerged under British rule, *i.e.* industrial capitalists and a new bourgeoisie of bureaucrats, lawyers, doctors, teachers and journalists whose social position was due to education and training rather than heredity. In the princely states, the remnants of the Mughal aristocracy continued their extravagances-large palaces, harems, hordes of retainers, miniature armies, ceremonial elephants, tiger hunts, and stables full of Rolls Royces.

Agriculture

The colonial government made institutional changes in agriculture by transforming traditionally circumscribed property rights into something more closely resembling the unencumbered private property characteristic of Western capitalism. The beneficiaries of these new rights varied in different parts of India. The top layer of Mughal property, the jagir, was abolished (except in the autonomous princely states), and the bulk of the old warlord aristocracy was dispossessed. Their previous income from land revenue, and that of the Mughal state, was now appropriated by the British as land tax. However, in the Bengal presidency (*i.e.* modern Bengal, Bihar, Orissa and part of Madras) the second layer of Mughal property rights belonging to Mughal tax collectors (zamindars) was reinforced. All zamindars in these areas now had hereditary status, so long as they paid their land taxes, and their judicial and administrative functions disappeared. In the Mughal period the zamindars had usually kept a tenth of the land revenue to themselves, but by the end of British rule their income from rents was a multiple of the tax they paid to the state. In Bihar, for instance, five-sixths of the total sum levied by 1950 was rent and only one-sixth revenue.

However, zamindars were not really the equivalent of Western landowners. Dominant families in each village remained as their 'tenants-in-chief' and continued to enjoy many of the old customary rights, *i.e.* they could not be evicted, their rights were heritable and their rental payments could not be raised easily. Lower-caste families were usually sub-tenants of the tenants-in-chief, rather than direct tenants of the zamindars. Often there were several layers of tenancy between the actual cultivator and the zamindar. Sub-tenants had less security and less defence against rack-renting than tenants-in-chief. It is worth noting that when zamindari rights were abolished around 1952 and the old zamindar rental income was converted into state revenue, the amount involved was only about 2 per cent of farm income in the relevant areas of India. This suggests that by the end of the colonial period, the zamindars were not able to squeeze as much surplus out of their chief tenants as is sometimes suggested.

The typical zamindari estate at the end of British rule seems to have been very different from that at the end of the eighteenth century. In Bengal the total "number of landowners which did not exceed 100 in the beginning of Hasting's administration in 1772, rose in the course of a century to 154,200". In 1872 there were 154,200 estates of which "533, or 0.34 per cent, only are great properties with an area of 20,000 acres and upwards; 15,747, or 10.21 per cent, range from 500 to 20,000 acres in area; while the number of estates which fell short of 500 acres is no less than 137,920, or 89.44 per cent, of the whole".

Misra attributes this fall in the average size of zamindari properties to the fact that they could be inherited or sold freely, whereas the Mughal state wanted to keep the number small because zamindars had administrative functions under the Mughal Empire. Under the British, transfers became much more frequent, particularly into the hands of money-lenders. The money-lenders are frequently presented as squeezing out poor peasants and tenantry and thus promoting the concentration of wealth, but the evidence of what happened to zamindar estates suggests that village moneylenders may also have helped to break up concentrations of wealth.

In the Madras and Bombay Presidencies, which covered most of Southern India, the British dispossessed many of the old Mughal and Mahratta nobility and big zamindars, and vested property rights and tax obligations in individual 'peasants'. This settlement was known as the ryotwari (peasant tenure) system. However, the term peasant is misleading, because most of those who acquired land titles belonged to the traditionally dominant castes in villages. Lower-caste cultivators became their tenants. Thus there was no change in social structure at the village level, except that the new ownership rights gave greater opportunities for sale and mortgage, and the security of the tenant was less than it had been under the previous system. The change in legal status was limited by several factors. First of all, illiterate peasant did not always understand the new situation, and there were strong social ties in the joint family and the caste panchayats to prevent major deviations from old habits. Secondly, the new administration was rather remote from individual villages (with a district officer responsible for over a thousand villages), and many British administrators had a personal bias in favour of customary tenant rights because by maintaining them they could avoid political trouble. At a later stage, the government itself introduced a good deal of legislation to protect customary rights in response to peasant disturbances. Land policy was, therefore, another instance of British policy of half-westernization. The change from custom to contract was not nearly as sharp as that brought about in Japan by the Meiji land reforms. The British were more concerned with arrangements which would guarantee their revenue and not provoke too much political disturbance rather than in increasing productivity or introducing capitalist institutions. The Utilitarians who dominated the Company from 1820 to 1850 would have liked to push in this direction, but they were displaced at mid-century by the paternalist conservatives of the Imperial raj.

Nevertheless, there were some economic consequences of the new legal situation. Because of the emergence of clear titles, it was now possible to mortgage land. The status of moneylenders was also improved by the change from Muslim to British law. There had been money-lenders in the Mughal period, but their importance grew substantially under British rule, and over time a considerable amount of land changed hands through foreclosures. Over time, two forces raised the income of landowners. One of these was the increasing scarcity of land as population expanded. This raised land values and rents. The second was the decline in the incidence of land tax. Indian literature usually stresses the heavy burden of land tax in the early days of British rule, but the fact that it fell substantially over time is seldom noted. The Mughal land tax was about 30 per cent of the crop, but by 1947 land tax was only 2 per cent of agricultural income. The fall was most marked in Bengal where the tax was fixed in perpetuity in 1793, but it was also true in other areas. As a result of these changes, there was not only an increase in village income but a widening of income inequality within villages. The village squirearchy received relatively higher incomes because of the reduced burden of land tax and the increase in rents; tenants and agricultural labourers may well have experienced a decline in income because their traditional rights were curtailed and their bargaining power was reduced by land scarcity. The class of landless agricultural labourers grew in size under British rule, but modern scholarship has shown that they were not a "creation" of the British. They were about 15 per cent of the rural population at the end of the eighteenth century, and about a quarter of the labour force now.

Although these were important modifications in the village structure, the traditional hierarchy of caste was not destroyed. Income differentials widened, but the social and ritual hierarchy in villages did not change its character. Village society was not egalitarian in Mughal times, and in most cases those whose income rose in the British period were already socially dominant, although there were exceptions. Recent sociological studies, though they indicate changes in the British period, also portray a village hierarchy in the 1940s and 1950s which cannot be very different from that in the Mughal period. We still find a dominant caste of petty landlords, an intermediate group of tenants, village artisans tied by jajmani relationships, a group of low-status labourers, untouchable menials with the whole held together by the same elaborate system of caste.

One might have expected the legal changes introduced by the British to have had a positive effect on efficiency. They removed the class of jagirdars who had no incentive to invest in agriculture, and gave land rights to rural capitalists who could buy and sell land fairly freely and enjoy an increasing portion of the product. Money-lenders helped to root out improvident or inefficient landowners. However, most farmers were illiterate and the government did not provide research or extension services, or encourage the use of fertilizers. Until recently, with the arrival of the tubewell, there were technical limits to the possibility of small-scale irrigation. There were also organizational difficulties in changing technique to improve productivity.

The division of labour in the village and hereditary attitudes to work as a semi-religious ritual rather than a means to improve income were obstacles to change. Furthermore, a good many of the cultivating landowners whose income was increased were relatively poor and used their increased income for consumption rather than investment.

Some of those who were better off probably improved their land or took over waste land, but as religion inculcated the idea that manual labour was polluting, some of them probably worked less. The big zamindars used some of their extra income to develop waste land, but many cultivated a life style rather like the old Mughal aristocracy and had a high propensity to consume.

According to Raychaudhuri, "a zamindar's house with a hundred rooms was not exceptional". Some of the enterprising ones probably transferred their savings out of agriculture into trade and industry or bought their children a western-type education.

Thus the effect of the change was to increase productivity and savings, but not much. During the period of British rule, agricultural production grew substantially in order to feed a population which grew from 165 million in 1757 to 420 million in 1947. The new system of land ownership offered some stimulus to increase output, and there was substantial waste land available for development.

The colonial government made some contribution towards increased output through irrigation. The irrigated area was increased about eightfold, and eventually more than a quarter of the land of British India was irrigated. Irrigation was extended both as a source of revenue and as a measure against famine. A good deal of the irrigation work was in the Punjab and Sindh.

The motive here was to provide land for retired Indian army personnel, many of whom came from the Punjab, and to build up population in an area which bordered on the disputed frontier with Afghanistan. These areas, which had formerly been desert, became the biggest irrigated area in the world and a major producer of wheat and cotton, both for export and for sale in other parts of India.

Apart from government investment in irrigation, there was a substantial private investment, and by the end of British rule private irrigation investment covered nearly 25 million acres of British India. Improvements in transport facilities (particularly railways, but also steamships and the Suez canal) helped agriculture by permitting some degree of specialization on cash crops.

This increased yields somewhat, but the bulk of the country stuck to subsistence farming. Plantations were developed for indigo, sugar, jute and tea. These items made a significant contribution to exports, but in the context of Indian agriculture as a whole, they were not very important. In 1946, the two primary staples, tea and jute, were less than 3.5 per cent of the gross value of crop output.

Thus the enlargement of markets through international trade was less of a stimulus in India than in other Asian countries such as Ceylon, Burma or Thailand.

Little was done to promote agricultural technology. There was some improvement in seeds, but no extension service, no improvement in livestock and no official encouragement to use fertilizer. Lord Mayo, the Governor General, said in 1870, "I do not know what is precisely meant by ammoniac manure. If it means guano, superphosphate or any other artificial product of that kind, we might as well ask the people of India to manure their ground with champagne".

Statistics are not available on agricultural output for the first century and a half of British rule, but all the indications suggest that there was substantial growth. We do not know whether output rose faster or more slowly than population, but it seems likely that the movements were roughly parallel.

For the last half century of British rule, the main calculations of output are those by George Blyn. His first study, which has been widely quoted, was published in 1954 by the National Income Unit of the Indian government and showed only a 3 per cent increase in crop output in British India from 1893 to 1946, *i.e.* a period in which population increased 46 per cent!

His second study, published in 1966 showed a 16.6 per cent increase, and this, too, has been widely quoted, but he also gives a 'modified' series which shows a 28.9 per cent increase. This seems preferable, as the official figures on rice yields in Orissa, which are corrected in his "modified" estimate, seem obviously in error.

However, even Blyn's upper estimate is probably an understatement because he shows a very small increase in acreage.

It is difficult to believe that per capita food output could have gone down as much as he suggests, whilst waste land remained unused.

There has been a very big increase in the cultivated area since independence and it seems likely that the increase in the preceding half century was bigger than Blyn suggests. Therefore, my own estimate of crop output (Appendix B) for 1900-46, uses Blyn's figures on yields but assumes that the cultivated area rose by 23 per cent (Sivasubramonian's figure) rather than by 12.2 per cent (Blyn's figure). My estimate shows agricultural output rising about the same amount as population from 1900 to 1946. However, even this may be too low.

The basic reports on areas under cultivation are those provided by village accountants (patwaris) in areas where land revenue was periodically changed, and by village watchmen (chowkidars) in areas where the land revenue was permanently settled.

There was some incentive for farmers to bribe patwaris to under-report land for tax purposes, and chowkidars are all too often illiterate and drowsy people, who would usually report that things were normal, *i.e.* the same as the year before. There is, therefore, a tendency for under-reporting of both levels and rates of growth in areas covered by statistics, and the areas not covered by statistics were generally on the margin of cultivation and may have had a more steeply rising trend than the average area covered.

Thus Blyn shows no growth in output in Bengal where the chowkidars did the basic reporting. He did not cover the Sindh desert area in which the British built the huge Sukkur barrage in 1932. Blyn was, of course, aware of these difficulties and tried to correct for them as far as possible, but the fundamental problems are not amenable to 'statistical' manipulation but require 'hunch' adjustment. My own conclusion from the evidence available is that agricultural output per head was at least as high at the end of British rule as it was in the Mughal period, and that rural consumption levels were somewhat higher because of the lower tax burden on agriculture, and the smaller degree of wastage which allowed surplus areas to sell their grains.

This slight improvement in standards may have contributed to the expansion in population. However, agricultural yields and nutritional levels at independence were amongst the lowest in the world. Under British rule, the Indian population remained subject to recurrent famines and epidemic diseases. In 1876-78 and 1899-1900 famine killed millions of people. In the 1890s there was a widespread outbreak of bubonic plague and in 1919 a great influenza epidemic.

It is sometimes asserted by Indian nationalist historians that British policy increased the incidence of famine in India, particularly in the nineteenth century. Unfortunately we do not have any figures on agricultural production for this period, and it is difficult to base a judgment merely on catalogues of famine years whose intensity we cannot measure. As agriculture was extended to more marginal land one would have expected output to become more volatile.

But this was offset to a considerable extent by the major improvement in transport brought by railways, and the greater security of water supply brought by irrigation. It is noteworthy that the decades in which famines occurred were ones in which population was static rather than falling. In the 1920s and 1930s there were no famines, and the 1944 famine in Bengal was due to war conditions and transport difficulties rather than crop failure. However, the greater stability after 1920 may have been partly due to a lucky break in the weather cycle rather than to a new stability of agriculture.

British rule reduced some of the old checks on Indian population growth. The main contribution was the ending of internal warfare and local banditry. There was some reduction in the incidence of famine. The death rate was also reduced to some degree by making ritual suicide and infanticide illegal. The British contributed to public health by introducing smallpox vaccination, establishing Western medicine and training modern doctors, by killing rats, and establishing quarantine procedures. As a result, the death rate fell and the population of India grew by 1947 to more than two-and-a-half times its size in 1757.

Industry

Several Indian authors have argued that British rule led to a de-industrialization of India. R.C. Dutt argued, "India in the eighteenth century was a great manufacturing as well as a great agricultural country, and the products of the Indian loom supplied the markets of Asia and Europe. It is, unfortunately, true that the East India Company and the British Parliament, following the selfish commercial policy of a hundred years ago, discouraged Indian manufacturers in the early years of British rule in order to encourage the rising manufactures of England. Their fixed policy, pursued during the last decades of the eighteenth century and the first decades of the nineteenth, was to make India subservient to the industries of Great Britain, and to make the Indian people grow raw produce only, in order to supply material for the looms and manufactories of Great Britain".

R. Palme Dutt, writing forty years later, argued that the process had been continuous:

> *"the real picture of modern India is a picture of what has been aptly called "de-industrialization"-that is, the decline of the old handicraft industry without the compensating advance of modern industry. The advance of factory industry has not overtaken the decay of handicraft. The process of decay characteristic of the nineteenth century has been carried forward in the twentieth century and in the post-war period".*

Nehru, in his popular history is a conflation of the two Dutts, argued that the British deindustrialized India, and that this "is the real the fundamental cause of the appalling poverty of the Indian people, and it is of comparatively recent origin".

There is a good deal of truth in the deindustrialization argument. Mughal India did have a bigger industry than any other country which became a European colony, and was unique in being an industrial exporter in pre-colonial times. A large part of the Mughal industry was destroyed in the course of British rule. However, it is important to understand precisely how this deindustrialization came about and to try to get some idea of its quantitative significance in different periods. Oversimplified explanations, which exaggerate the role of British commercial policy and ignore the role of changes in demand and technology, have been very common and have had some adverse impact on post-independence economic policy.

Between 1757 and 1857 the British wiped out the Mughal court, and eliminated three-quarters of the warlord aristocracy (all except those in princely states). They also eliminated more than half of the local chiefs (zamindars) and in their place established a bureaucracy with European tastes. The new rulers wore European clothes and shoes, drank imported beer, wines and spirits, and used European weapons. Their tastes were copied by the male members of the new Indian 'middle class' which arose to act as their clerks and intermediaries. As a result of these political and social changes, about three-quarters of the domestic demand for luxury handicrafts was destroyed. This was a shattering blow to manufacturers of fine muslins, jewellery, luxury clothing and footwear, decorative swords and weapons. It is not known how important these items were in national income, but my own guess would be that the home market for these goods was about 5 per cent of Mughal national income. The export market was probably another 1.5 per cent of national income, and most of this market was also lost. There was a reduction of European demand because of the change in sartorial tastes after the French revolution, and the greatly reduced price of more ordinary materials because of the revolution of textile technology in England.

The second blow to Indian industry came from massive imports of cheap textiles from England after the Napoleonic wars. In the period 1896-1913, imported piece goods supplied about 60 per cent of Indian cloth consumption, and the proportion was probably higher for most of the nineteenth century. Home spinning, which was a spare-time activity of village women, was greatly reduced. A large proportion of village handloom weavers must have been displaced, though many switched to using factory instead of home-spun yarn. Even as late as 1940 a third of Indian piece goods were produced on handlooms.

The new manufactured textile goods were considerably cheaper and of better quality than hand-loom products, so their advent increased textile consumption. At the end of British rule, there can be no doubt that cloth consumption per head was substantially larger than in the Mughal period. We do not know how big an increase in textile consumption occurred, but if per capita consumption of cotton cloth doubled (which seems quite plausible), then the displacement effect on handloom weavers would have been smaller than at first appears. The handloom weavers who produced a third of output in 1940 would have been producing two-thirds if there had been no increase in per capita consumption. In time, India built up her own textile manufacturing industry which displaced British imports. But there was a gap of several decades before manufacturing started and a period of 130 years before British textile imports were eliminated. India could probably have copied Lancashire's technology more quickly if she had been allowed to impose a protective tariff in the way that was done in the USA and France in the first few decades of the nineteenth century, but the British imposed a policy of free trade. British imports entered India duty free, and when a small tariff was required for revenue purposes Lancashire pressure led to the imposition of a corresponding excise duty on Indian products to prevent them gaining a competitive advantage. This undoubtedly handicapped industrial development. If India had been politically independent, her tax structure would probably have been different. In the 1880s, Indian customs revenues were only 2.2 per cent of the trade turnover, *i.e.* the lowest ratio in any country. In Brazil, by contrast, import duties at that period were 21 per cent of trade turnover. If India had enjoyed protection there is no doubt that its textile industry would have started earlier and grown faster.

The first textile mills were started in the 1850s by Indian capitalists who had made their money trading with the British and had acquired some education in English. Cotton textiles were launched in Bombay with financial and managerial help from British trading companies.

India was the first country in Asia to have a modern textile industry, preceding Japan by twenty years and China by forty years. Cotton mills were started in Bombay in 1851, and they concentrated on coarse yarns sold domestically and to China and Japan; yarn exports were about half of output.

Modern jute manufacturing started about the same time as cotton textiles. The first jute mill was built in 1854 and the industry expanded rapidly in the vicinity of Calcutta. The industry was largely in the hands of foreigners (mainly Scots). Between 1879 and 1913 the number of jute spindles rose tenfold-much faster than growth in the cotton textile industry. The jute industry was able to expand faster than cotton textiles because its sales did not depend so heavily on the poverty-stricken domestic markets. Most of jute output was for export. Coal mining, mainly in Bengal, was another industry which achieved significance. Its output, which by 1914 had reached 15.7 million tons, largely met the demands of the Indian railways.

In 1911 the first Indian steel mill was built by the Tata Company at Jamshedpur in Jharkhand. However, production did not take place on a significant scale before the First World War. The Indian steel industry started fifteen years later than in China, where the first steel mill was built at Hangyang in 1896. The first Japanese mill was built in 1898. In both China and Japan the first steel mills (and the first textile mills) were government enterprises.

Indian firms in industry, insurance and banking were given a boost from 1905 onwards by the swadeshi movement, which was a nationalist boycott of British goods in favour of Indian enterprise. During the First World War, lack of British imports strengthened the hold of Indian firms on the home market for textiles and steel. After the war, under nationalist pressure, the government started to favour Indian enterprise in its purchase of stores and it agreed to create a tariff commission in 1921 which started raising tariffs for protective reasons. By 1925, the average tariff level was 14 per cent compared with 5 per cent pre-war. The procedure for fixing tariffs was lengthy and tariff protection was granted more readily to foreign-owned than to Indian firms, but in the 1930s protection was sharply increased. The government was more willing to protect the textile industry when the threat came from Japan and not the UK. Between 1930 and 1934 the tariff on cotton cloth was raised from 11 to 50 per cent, although British imports were accorded a margin of preference. As a result of these measures, there was considerable substitution of local textiles for imports. In 1896, Indian mills supplied only 8 per cent of total cloth consumption; in 1913, 20 per cent; in 1936, 62 per cent; and in 1945, 76 per cent. By the latter date there were no imports of piece goods. Until the end of the Napoleonic wars, cotton manufactures had been India's main export. They reached their peak in 1798, and in 1813 they still amounted to £2 million, but thereafter they fell rapidly. Thirty years later, half of Indian imports were cotton textiles from Manchester. This collapse in India's main export caused a problem for the Company, which had to find ways to convert its rupee revenue into resources transferable to the UK.

The Company therefore promoted exports of raw materials on a larger scale, including sugar, silk, saltpetre and indigo, and greatly increased exports of opium which were traded against Chinese tea. These dopepeddling efforts provoked the Anglo-Chinese war of 1842, after which access to the Chinese market was greatly widened. By the middle of the nineteenth century opium was by far the biggest export of India, and remained in this position until the 1880s when its relative and absolute importance began to decline.

Another new export was raw cotton, which could not compete very well in European markets against higher quality American and Egyptian cottons, (except during the US Civil War), but found a market in Japan and China. Sugar exports were built up after 1833 when the abolition of slavery raised West Indian production costs, but India had no long-run comparative advantage in sugar exports. Indigo (used to dye textiles) was an important export until the 1890s when it was hit by competition from German synthetic dyes. The jute industry boomed from the time of the Crimean War onwards, when the UK stopped importing flax from Russia. In addition to raw jute (shipped for manufacture in Dundee) India exported jute manufactures. Grain exports were also built up on a sizeable scale, mainly from the newly irrigated area of the Punjab. The tea industry was introduced to India from China and built up on a plantation basis. Tea exports became important from the 1860s onwards. Hides and skins and oil cake (used as animal feed and fertilizer) were also important raw material exports.

Table: Level of Asian Exports f.o.b. 1850-1950

(million dollars)

	1850	1913	1937	1950
Ceylon	5	76	124	328
China	24	294	516	(700)
India	89	786	717	1,178
Indonesia	24	270	550	800
Japan	1	354	1,207	820
Malaya	24	193	522	1,312
Philippines	n.a.	48	153	331
Thailand	3	43	76	304

Figures refer to customs area of the year concerned. In 1850 and 1913 the Indian area included Burma. The comparability of 1937 and 1950 figures is affected by the separation of Pakistan.

Manufactured textile exports form India began to increase in the 1850s when the first modern mills were established. The bulk of exports were yarn and crude piece goods which were sold in China and Japan. As the Chinese and Japanese were prevented by colonial-type treaties from imposing tariffs for manufactured imports they were wide open to Indian goods, and particularly cotton textiles and yarn. Indian jute manufactures were exported mainly to Europe and the USA However, India began to suffer from Japanese competition in the 1890s. Indian yarn exports to Japan dropped sharply from 8,400 tons in 1890 to practically nothing in 1898, and India also suffered from Japanese competition in China. The Japanese set up factories in China after the Sino-Japanese War of 1894-5. Before this, India had supplied 96 per cent of Chinese yarn imports, the UK 4 per cent, and Japan none. Within three years the Japanese were supplying a quarter to Chinese imports, and by 1914 India was exporting less yarn to China than was Japan. During the First World War Japan made further progress in the Chinese market and by 1924 supplied three-quarters of Chinese imports. By 1928 India was exporting only 3 per cent of her yarn output. By the end of the 1930s, Indian exports of yarn to China and Japan had disappeared, piece goods exports had fallen off, and India imported both yarn and piece goods from China and Japan.

Indian exports grew fairly rapidly in the period up to 1913, but their growth was slower than that of most other Asian countries which had a natural resource endowment offering greater opportunities for trade. As a consequence, in 1913, India had a smaller trade per head than most countries except China. Nevertheless, exports were 10.7 per cent of national income, probably a higher ratio than has been reached before or since. Until 1898 India, like most Asian countries, was on the silver standard. In the 1870s the price of silver began to fall and the rupee depreciated against sterling. This led to some rise in the internal price level, but it helped to make Indian exports more competitive with those of the UK, *e.g.* in the Chinese textile market. In 1898, India adopted a gold exchange standard which tied the rupee to sterling at a fixed value of 15 to 1. This weakened her competitiveness vis-a-vis China which remained on a depreciating silver standard, but its potential adverse effects were mitigated because Japan went on to the gold exchange standard at the same time.

During the First World War, when the sterling exchange rate was allowed to float, the rupee appreciated. Unfortunately, when sterling resumed a fixed (and overvalued) parity in 1925, the rupee exchange rate was fixed above the pre-war level. This overvaluation eased the fiscal problems of government in making transfers to the UK and enabled British residents in India, or those on Indian pensions in the UK, to get more sterling for their rupees, but it made it necessary for domestic economic policy to be deflationary (in cutting wages) and greatly hindered Indian exports, particularly those to or competing with China and Japan. As a result, Indian exports fell from 1913 to 1937, a poorer performance than that of almost any other country. At independence exports were less than 5 per cent of national income. If we look at Indian export performance from 1850 to 1950 it was worse than that of any other country in Asia.

The Second World War gave a fillip to Indian industrial output, but there was not much increase in capacity because of the difficulty of importing capital goods and the lack of a domestic capital goods industry.

Many of the most lucrative commercial, financial, business and plantation jobs in the modern sector were occupied by foreigners. Although the East India Company's legally enforced monopoly privileges were ended in 1833, the British continued to exercise effective dominance through the system of 'managing agencies'. These agencies, originally set up by former employees of the East India Company, were used both to manage industrial enterprise and to handle most of India's international trade. They were closely linked with British banks, insurance and shipping companies. Managing agencies had a quasi-monopoly in access to capital, and they had interlocking directorships which gave them control over supplies and markets. They dominated the foreign markets in Asia. They had better access to government officials than did Indians. The agencies were in many ways able to take decisions favourable to their own interests rather than those of shareholders. They were paid commissions based on gross profits or total sales and were often agents for the raw materials used by the companies they managed. Thus the Indian capitalists who did emerge were highly dependent on British commercial capital and many sectors of industry were dominated by British firms, *e.g.* shipping, banking, insurance, coal, plantation crops and jute.

Indian industrial efficiency was hampered by the British administration's neglect of technical education, and the reluctance of British firms and managing agencies to provide training of managerial experience to Indians. Even in the Bombay textile industry, where most of the capital was Indian, 28 per cent of the managerial and supervisory staff were British in 1925 (42 per cent in 1895) and the British component was even bigger in more complex industries. This naturally raised Indian production costs. At lower levels there was widespread use of jobbers for hiring workers and maintaining discipline, and workers themselves were a completely unskilled group who had to bribe the jobbers to get and retain their jobs. There were also problems of race, language and caste distinctions between management, supervisors and workers. The small size and very diversified output of the enterprises hindered efficiency. It is partly for these reasons (and the overvaluation of the currency) that Indian exports had difficulty in competing with Japan.

The basic limitations on the growth of industrial output were the extreme poverty of the rural population, and the fact that a large proportion of the élite had a taste for imported goods or exported their purchasing power. The government eventually provided tariff protection but did not itself create industrial plants, sponsor development banks, or give preference to local industry in allotting contracts. The banking system gave little help to industry and technical education was poor. Most of these things changed when India became independent except the first and most important, *i.e.* the extreme poverty of the rural population which limited the expansion of the 19 market for industrial goods. By the time of independence, large-scale factory industry in India employed less than 3 million people as compared with 12 1/4 million in small-scale industry and handicrafts, and a labour force of 160 million. This may appear meagre, but India's per capita industrial output at independence was higher than elsewhere in Asia outside Japan, and more than half of India's exports were manufactures. British policy was less repressive to local industry than that of other colonial power, and had permitted the emergence of a small but powerful class of Indian entrepreneurs. It should be noted, however, that modern industry was heavily concentrated in Calcutta, Bombay and Ahmedabad. The area which was to become Pakistan had practically no industry at all.

In the last half century of British rule the output of factory industry rose about six-fold (about 4.2 per cent a year) whereas the output of small-scale industry declined. Their joint output rose about two-thirds (1.2 per cent a year), and per head of population, joint output was rising by 0.4 per cent a year. We know that output in the modern factory sector was zero in 1850, and if we assume that small enterprise output grew parallel with population from 1850 to 1900, then total industrial output would have grown by 0.8 per cent a year in this period, or about 0.3 per cent a year per head of population.

Some increase seems plausible in this period of railway development and expanding international trade. It therefore seems possible that in the last century of British rule, per capita output of industrial goods rose by a third. But in the first century of British rule, *i.e.* 1757-1857, it seems certain that industrial output fell per head of population because (a) the home and domestic market for luxury goods was cut so drastically; (b) the home market for yarn and cheap cloth was invaded by foreign competition. Over the whole period of British rule it therefore seems likely that industrial output per head of the population was not significantly changed.

The Economic Burden of Foreign Rule

The major burden of foreign rule arose from the fact that the British Raj was a regime of expatriates. Under an Indian administration, income from government service would have accrued to the local inhabitants and not to foreigners. The diversion of upper-class income into the hands of foreigners inhibited the development of local industry because it put purchasing power into the hands of people with a taste for foreign goods. This increased imports and was particularly damaging to the luxury handicraft industries.

Another important effect of foreign rule on the long-run growth potential of the economy was the fact that a large part of its potential savings were siphoned abroad. This 'drain' of funds from India to the UK has been a point of major controversy between Indian nationalist historians and defenders of the British raj. However, the only real grounds for controversy are statistical. There can be no denial that there was a substantial outflow which lasted for 190 years. If these funds had been invested in India they could have made a significant contribution to raising income levels. The first generation of British rulers was rapacious. Clive took quarter of a million pounds for himself as well as a jagir worth £27,000 a year, but the British did not pillage on the scale of Nadir Shah, who probably took as much from India in one year as the East India Company did in the twenty years following the battle of Plassey (57). They were also shrewd enough to realize that it was not in their long-run interest to devastate the country.

However, British salaries were high: the Viceroy received £25,000 a year, and governors £10,000. The starting salary in the engineering service was £420 a year or about sixty times the average income of the Indian labour force. From 1757 to 1919, India also had to meet administrative expenses in London, first of the East India Company, and then of the India Office, as well as other minor but irritatingly extraneous charges. The cost of British staff was raised by long home leave in the UK, early retirement and lavish amenities in the form of subsidised housing, utilities, rest houses, etc. Under the rule of the East India Company, official transfers to the UK rose gradually until they reached about £3.5 million in 1856, the year before the mutiny. In addition, there were private remittances. In the twenty years 1835-54, India's average annual balance on trade and bullion was favourable by about £4.5 million a year.

During the period of direct British rule from 1858 to 1947, official transfers of funds to the UK by the colonial government were called the "Home Charges". They mainly represented debt service, pensions, India Office expenses in the UK, purchases of military items and railway equipment. Government procurement of civilian goods, armaments and shipping was carried out almost exclusively in the UK. By the 1930s these home charges were in the range of £40 to £50 million a year. Some of these flows would have occurred in a non-colonial economy, *e.g.* debt service on loans used to finance railway development, but a large part of the debt was incurred as a result of colonial wars. Some government expenditure was on imports which an independent government would have bought from local manufacturers. Of these official payments, we can legitimately consider service charges on non-productive debt, pensions and furlough payments as a balance of payment drain due to colonialism.

Table : India's Balance on Merchandise and Bullion, 1835-1967

	Balance in current prices (annual average)	Balance in 1948-9 prices at (£million)	Per capita balance 1948-9 prices (£)
1835-54	4.5	n.a.	n.a.
1855-74	7.3	50.0	0.21
1875-94	13.4	80.0	0.30
1895-1913	16.8	77.6	0.26
1914-34	22.5	59.2	0.19
1935-46	27.9	66.1	0.17
1948-57	-99.9	-97.6	-0.21 (India and Pakistan)
1958-67	-472.7	-384.7	-0.67 (India and Pakistan)

Source: Constant price figures for 1948 onwards deflated by the national income deflator, earlier years by the price index of M. Mukherjee, National Income of India, Statistical Publishing Society, Calcutta, 1969. The Indian surplus is understated, and deficit overstated because imports are recorded c.i.f. and exports f.o.b.

There were also substantial private remittances by British officials in India either as savings or to meet educational and other family charges in the UK. In the inter-war period, these amounted to about £10 million a year, and Naoroji estimated that they were running at the same level in 1887.58 These items were clearly the result of colonial rule. In addition, there were dividend and interest remittances by shipping and banking interests, plantations, and other British investors; to some extent, these were normal commercial transactions, but there was a large element of monopoly profit due to the privileged position of British business in India; and, in many cases, the original assets were not acquired by remitting funds to India but by savings from income earned locally, or by purchase of property on favourable terms, *e.g.* the land acquisitions of plantation companies. About a third of the private profit remittances should therefore be treated as the profits of colonialism.

The total 'drain' due to government pensions and leave payments, interest on nonrailway official debt, private remittances for education and savings, and a third commercial profits amounted to about 1.5 per cent of national income of undivided India from 1921 to 1938 and was probably a little larger before that (59). Net investment was about 5 per cent of national income at the end of British rule, so about a quarter of Indian savings were transferred out of the economy, and foreign exchange was lost which could have paid for imports of capital goods. As a consequence of this foreign drain the Indian balance of trade and bullion was always positive as can be seen in Table 3-3 (60). If we take the table as a rough indicator of the movement in the colonial burden (though not of its absolute level) it would seem that it was biggest around the 1880s. Since independence the picture has been completely reversed and there is now a substantial inflow of resources because of foreign aid.

In spite of its constant favourable balance of trade, India acquired substantial debts. By 1939 foreign assets in India amounted to $2.8 billion, of which about $1.5 billion was government bonded debt and the rest represented direct investment (mainly tea, other plantations and the jute industry).

India did not reduce its foreign debt during the First World War as many other developing countries did. Instead, there were two 'voluntary' war gifts to the UK amounting to £150 million ($730 million). India also contributed one-and-a-quarter million troops, which were financed from the Indian budget. The 'drain' of funds to England continued in the inter-war years because of home charges and profit remittances. There was also a small outflow of British capital.

In the depression of 1929-33, many developing countries defaulted on foreign debt or froze dividend transfers, but this was not possible for India. The currency was kept at par with sterling and devalued in 1931, but the decisions were based on British rather than Indian needs. Furthermore, the salaries of civil servants remained at high level, and the burden of official transfers increased in a period of falling prices.

During the Second World War, India's international financial position was transformed. The UK had enormous military expenditures for its own troops in India and also financed local costs of allied troops under Lease-Lend arrangements. Indian war finance was much more inflationary than in the UK and prices rose threefold, so these local costs of troop support were extremely high in terms of sterling, as the exchange rate remained unchanged. As a result, India was able to liquidate $1.2 billion of pre-war debt and acquired reserve assets of $5.1 billion, ending the war a large net creditor. These new assets and the disappearance of the colonial drain gave a formidable boost to post-war development policy.

Conclusions

There has been a good deal of controversy amongst statisticians about the rate of growth of income in India in the colonial period. The argument is politically coloured and the statistics are poor. For the last fifty years of British rule there is enough statistical information to make rough estimates of the growth of national income. My own estimates, which are based largely on work by Blyn and Sivasubramonian, show no increase in per capita income over the years 1900-46 (see Appendix B). Other observers have estimates which show some growth over this period as well as in the period from 1857. Although I think my estimates are the best available, I have enough scepticism about the basic agricultural data to believe that the other estimates could be right for the wrong reasons and that there may have been some rise in per capita income from 1857 to 1947.

There are no estimates for the movement in income from Clive's conquest to the Mutiny, but there could not have been much net progress in real income per head before the development of railways, modern industry, irrigation and the big expansion in international trade, and there are reasons for thinking that there was some decline. From the beginning of British conquest in 1757 to independence, it seems unlikely that per capita income could have increased by more than a third and it probably did not increase at all. In the UK itself there was a tenfold increase in per capita income over these two centuries. The most noticeable change in the economy was the rise in population from about 170 million to 420 million from 1757 to 1947. However, there were some significant changes in social structure and in the pattern of output. The social pyramid was truncated because the British lopped off most of the top three layers of the Mughal hierarchy, *i.e.* the Mughal court, the Mughal aristocracy and quasi-autonomous prices (a quarter of these survived), and the local chieftainry (zamindars who survived in about 40 per cent of India). In place of these people the British installed a modern bureaucracy which took a smaller share of national income. The newcomers had a more modest life-style than the Mughals, but siphoned a large part of their savings out of the country and provided almost no market for India's luxury handicrafts. The modern factory sector which they created produced only 7.5 per cent of national income at the end of British rule and thus did little more than replace the old luxury handicrafts and part of the village textile production.

The British reduced the tax squeeze on agriculture and turned warlords into landlords, but the new order had little dynamism. A good deal of the old fuzziness about property rights remained, and landlords were still largely parasitic. The bigger zamindars copied the Mughal lifestyle by maintaining hordes of retainers and huge mansions, the smaller landowner's ambition was to stop working and enhance his ritual purity by establishing a seedy gentility. Very little incentive was provided for investment and almost nothing was done to promote technical change in agriculture. At the bottom of society the position of sharecropping tenantry and landless labourers remained wretched. In urban areas a new Westernized 'middle class' of Indians emerged and became the major challenge to the British Raj.

The social structure around 1938. Some of the figures are based on detective work and hunches and should be regarded as well-informed guesses rather than firm estimates. However, the table illustrates the orders of magnitude involved and, as these are often misunderstood, there is some justification for tabulating them. It can be seen that the British were a very thin layer at the top of society but they took about 5 per cent of national income. Their allies, the native princes and zamindars, took about 3 per cent. Eight per cent is a sizeable proportion for the ruling class but, under the Mughal regime, the equivalent group collected 15 per cent of national income in taxes and spent most of it on their own consumption. Immediately under this group were two new indigenous classes-capitalists and professionals-who became the dominant elite in independent India. They were relatively larger in number and probably had a bigger share of national income than their counterparts under the Mughals, *i.e.* the shroffs (indigenous urban bankers), merchants, qazis and pandits (lawyers), hakims (indigenous doctors), etc.

There were also changes in the lower class in the non-village economy. At the end of British rule there were 3 million factory workers making cheap textiles and jute sacking, whose Mughal predecessors had worked on muslins and silks, and a million railway workers who had no earlier counterpart. This lower-class urban group was probably bigger than in Mughal times, because they had displaced some of the village artisans.

Within village society the social structure was probably similar to that in Mughal India, with the two top economic groups corresponding to the old dominant castes, the next group to peasant castes, and the bottom group consisting largely of untouchable. The main difference from the Mughal economy is that village proprietors and tenants-in-chief were no longer heavily squeezed by taxation and their share of national income had probably increased. Thus the main gainers from the British regime (apart from the British) were the so-called 'middle' class of Indian capitalists and professionals, and the village squirearchy. Most of these were high caste Hindus though the Parsis and Sikhs did fairly well. The main losers were the Muslims who had formed the major part of the Mughal aristocracy, officer corps, lawyers, and artisans in the luxury handicrafts.

Temporary Settlement

Temporary Settlement of revenue lands not included in permanent settlement. The Permanent Settlement of 1793 did not include all the lands of Bengal within its operations. Many revenue estates settled on temporary basis. The temporary settlement lands were of two categories: lands held by proprietors but not under the permanent settlement law and khas lands or lands held not by private proprietors but by the government.

Temporary settlement of proprietary lands under the law of the permanent settlement all Zamindars, talukdars and other landholders were entitled to engage themselves as proprietors, fix land revenue and enjoy other privileges for ever. But many zamindars refused to engage because they could not accept the assessment of revenue on their estates and allowed them to be managed by government with ten percent malikana or proprietary allowance. These were vested estates which government managed on behalf of the respective proprietors. In this category of land, there was a settlement of land revenue, and not of land itself. The revenue assessment of the proprietary estates was variable. The government policy was to raise the revenue level of these estates by progressive increase in assessment. The district collector, as settlement officer, used to conduct periodical revenue survey of these estates and revise the rates of assessment in the light of the survey.

The management of privately owned temporarily settled estates was governed by Regulation VII of 1822, Regulation IX of 1833, and some other special acts. Under these laws a proprietor was always free to come under the fold permanent settlement if they accepted the assessment fixed by government. Since 1772, government had been resuming the invalid lakhiraj lands and brought them into rental. The law recognised the holders of resumed lakhiraj lands as proprietors and they were also free to engage themselves under the rules of the permanent settlement, but they were required to accede to the revenue demanded by government. The estates of proprietors unwilling to accept the assessment were managed, subject to payment of malikana to proprietors, by government under temporary settlement system.

Government estates to this class of land belonged mainly the wastelands. The permanent settlement regulations extended only to estates of zamindars and other actual proprietors as they existed in 1793. Every estate had extensive wastelands waiting for cultivation. These were duly recognised as integral parts of the original zamindaris. But there were zones, especially jungle lands, in which the area of waste was so large that no claim was ever made, not even by squatters.

The districts of Chittagong, Sylhet, Khulna and Bakerganj were full of such unclaimed lands. The government declared those lands as public estates. The estates purchased by the government at public auctions in the absence of bona fide bidders were also added to government estates. Islands and chars formed in rivers or on the seashore-not being accretions by alluvion to existing estates, were declared as government estates. Lands escheated in default of revenue payment or absence of legal heirs were also publicly taken over as government estates. Originally, it was a government policy to settle the revenue lands of the said descriptions on permanent settlement basis if the terms offered by government were accepted by the incumbent. But within ten years of the operations of the permanent settlement, it became clear to the government that the permanent settlement was not yielding the results expected from the system. The idea of permanent settlement was thus abandoned for the rest of British India. Even in Bengal it was resolved not to transfer normally the government estates to private ownership under permanent settlement.

Land ownership thus devolved in Bengal on two parties by and large-private landholders and government. The government estates were leased out to farmers who held the estates on temporary settlement basis. The lease period was not uniformly followed for all estates. It ranged from minimum five years to maximum hundred years depending on the circumstances and situations of individual estates. The district settlement officer was empowered by the Regulations of 1822-23 to settle the khas estates to the best advantage of the government. In safeguarding the interest of government the settlement officer sometimes sold government estates to private ownership on permanent settlement basis.

Management : The district collector, in the capacity of a settlement officer, was the authority of government held estates. Conducting periodical revenue survey of government estates was a legal necessity. Formerly, estate boundaries were always notional. The revenue surveys resulted for the first time in the clear demarcation of estates, adjustment of boundary disputes, fixing and recording of rents, recording rights and interests in the soil and many other features, which had great impact on the management of zamindari lands as well. To extend the benefits of these measures to permanently settled estates as well, the government resolved to undertake thakbast (boundary) and revenue surveys in the zamindari estates also. The General Survey Act (Bengal Act V 1875) and the Bengal Tenancy Act of 1885 made provisions for conducting survey and settlement operations in all permanent and temporary settlement estates. These operations had far reaching impact on the agrarian relations.

Consequent upon these operations the rights of various interests in land were ascertained and established. The establishment of rights in land affected the rent level. Zamindars found it difficult to enhance rent at will. The survey and settlement operations revealed that the rent level of temporarily settled estates was generally much higher than that of the zamindari estates and that the raiyats were more eager to operate in zamindari estates than in the government ones. The impersonal character of temporarily settled estates under government made the raiyats exposed to distress at times of calamities and loss of crops.

Temporary settlement in the Sundarbans All zamindars and talukdars adjacent to the Sundarbans were allowed to lay their claims on lands they could reclaim and bring under cultivation. They enjoyed this freedom until the 'Waste Land Rules' were applied in 1825. Under these rules all lands claimed and occupied by the neighbouring proprietors during the period from 1790 to 1825 were recognised as zamindari rights under the permanent settlement and the tracts beyond the boundaries of zamindari as khas or government property. The government tried to dispose of the wastelands on temporary settlement basis. Any landholder, capitalist or raiyat, who came to reclaim the Sundarban wastelands was granted settlement free of rent for ten years initially and the rent levied was nominal.

Under the Wastelands Rules of 1853 and 1863, all holders of estates of the Sundarbans area were given freedom to engage as proprietors under permanent settlement or as leaseholders under temporary settlement rules. The reclaimers preferred temporary settlement, which allowed them to pay revenue at graduated rates. Under the wastelands rules of 1879, the term of the original lease under temporary settlement was fixed at forty years, and subsequently, settlement was to be renewed with new assessment of revenue after every thirty years.

The maximum area of grant was restricted to 5,000 bighas (or 669 hectares), the minimum being 200 hectares. Farmers were required not to scatter cultivation all over the area of the land, but proceed regularly through the blocks. The leases conferred a hereditary and transferable occupancy right. Thus with the change of superior right for sale or default, the occupancy right at peasant level was to continue unaffected by such change. The Wasteland Rules 1879 and Bengal Tenancy Act 1885 were the guiding manuals for the temporary settlement of lands until 1951 when the permanent settlement and all other type of settlements were abolished in favour of actual raiyats declared as malik or proprietor under the East Bengal State Acquisition Act, 1951. [Sirajul Islam].

2

The Drain of Wealth Theory

The Drain of Wealth theory is a set of perspective that developed in the latter half of nineteenth century and reflected the adverse impact of economic colonisation of India by British imperialism. This concept was systematically initiated by Dadabhai Naoroji in 1867 and further analysed and developed by others, most notably- M.G. Ranade, R.C. Dutt and William Digby. Others also contributed, notably, G.V. Joshi, G. Subramaniya Iyer, G.K. Gokhale, P.C. Ray and many others. This formed an issue of much excitement among the political workers and the different streams of anti imperial movements in India would consider this as the basis and rationale on which they needed to severe their political relation with Britain.

The entire range of political issues was dissected as an omnibus critique of the imperial rule. Whether it be the Gandhians or the Leftists or the Revolutionaries, this Drain of Wealth thesis was acceptable by them all. Interestingly, this Drain of Wealth though an economic critique was not a Marxist critique. Indian Marxists added their own perspective later on and derived much of the issues from the observations of Marx in the Capital and other writings on India. Also, it was developed prior to emergence of any systematic anti imperial political movement in the country.

The Drain of Wealth approach also got popularity as a reaction to the supposed benevolence of British rule that many British scholars and administrators would speak about. This difference in approach can be classified as nationalist (or anti-imperialist) school and the imperialist school. Scholars who critiqued the nationalist approach included L.C.A. Knowles and V. Anstey. This imperialist school is now more popularly called the Cambridge School and it views the economic dimensions of British rule favourably and the imperialist process as beneficial to the colony. This debate has further aggravated with micro studies and newer analysis. This essay would take a perspective that tries to correlate the issues of economics, commerce and technology within the framework of economic relations deriving out of colonial India and imperial Britain.

British Power in India

The British East India Company (EIC) was a monopoly company and received charter of its operation from the sovereign, the company itself was an extended arm of the sovereign. Though such trade companies cannot be given the canopy of the sovereign as some scholars have argued, but it was a delegated power that was assigned by the charter. And because of the monopoly aspect, it can even be argued that these European companies were not just for trade but also an extended arm of their respective governments either directly or indirectly fulfilling the goals of their government vis-a-vis their rival nation-states in Europe. Though it was a private company, in the framework of mercantilism, the British EIC could even be termed a government enterprise. Apart from the Charters, this was particularly true from the times of Regulating Act (1773) onwards, when the British government came to have an important say in the affairs of the EIC.

From India's point of view, it was Plassey (1757) that became most significant. It was here that EIC came to have trappings of a territorial power. After battle of Buxar (1764), it also took control over the Diwani rights (right to collect land revenue) of the province of Bengal. This arrangement continued under the system of Dual Government (1765-72) that was introduced by Clive. Finally under Hastings, the EIC took over complete control of administration (1772).

Components of Drain

The Drain of Wealth from India took different forms over the period of time. Over time, the nature of British rule evolved from that of a merchant company to that of a sovereign and structure of trade from monopoly trade to free trade. The profit making interests of EIC gradually got subsumed to the requirements of industrialisation in Britain. Consequently the nature of drain also kept transforming. It started with the case of EIC, using the territorial revenue to buy goods from Bengal (late 18th century) and selling them in Europe to make its profit. The territorial revenue was enhanced considerably in the very initial years of the EIC's rule. "In the last year of administration of the last Indian ruler of Bengal, in 1764-65, the land revenue realised was £817,000. In the first year of Company's administration, in 1765-6, the land revenue realised in Bengal was £1,470,000. By 1771-2, it was £2,341,000, and by 1775-6 it was £2,818,000. The land revenue was finally fixed under scheme of Permanent Settlement of Lord Cornwallis in 1793, when it was fixed at £3,400,000. Such usage of territorial revenue in buying the goods was considered 'investment' in Bengal. Thus the money farmed in Bengal ended up in Europe as a form of tribute. Adam Smith would write on EIC as, "...the mercantile company which oppresses and domineers in the East Indies...". The EIC would enrich itself without adding anything as investment and make the profit for itself.

The 1770s was a period of famine for Bengal, and it was aggravated by such exaggerated demands by the EIC. It is interesting to note what Abbe Raynal wrote relating to the Bengal famine of 1770-71. According to him, the chief agent of the East India Company and the Council of Calcutta 'kept locked up in their magazine a part of the harvest, and carried on the most odious and the most criminal of all monopolies'. And despite of that, the company continued to increase the land revenue. And if all this was not enough, the EIC even manipulated the value of currency to its advantage by undervaluing and over pricing its currency. This happened in the way whereby the EIC would "struck gold rupees to the amount of about 15 million nominal value but which represented in fact only 9 million, so that four-tenths or something more was alloy". All these also led to decline in the standard of living of the people, 'especially marked in the diminution of consumption of ghee, oil, salt and sugar that were cheap formerly relatively to both money and cereals'.

Before the British, land itself was not an economic resource- 'the ruler and the villager were interested principally in the use of land and neither was worried about its ownership'. The EIC introduced the component of ownership in land. This was coupled with various experiments for tax collection that replaced the customary dues. In Bengal a series of experiments were initiated and different theoretical justifications were given to legitimise such systems. Warren Hastings (1772-85) assumed that all land belonged to the sovereign, leading to a system of farming of revenues by auctioning the revenue collection to the highest bidder. This led to havoc in the Bengal countryside. If the old zamindar failed to get the lands in the auctions, he would be turned out from his estates. These auctions were for farming of revenues, and did not give ownership rights to the winning bidder. If the bidder failed to collect the EIC determined high land revenue from the cultivator, the bidder would be turned out. This led to institutional plunder of the farmlands. The system failed and led to misery and depopulation. The land revenues failed, however, in spite of the utmost coercion. In a minute of September 18, 1789, Lord Cornwallis remarked, "I may safely assert that one-third of the Company's territory in Hindustan is now a jungle inhabited only by wild beasts."

Cornwallis on his appointment took a completely different view of the issue. His view was that it was the zamindar and not the sovereign who was the proprietor of the land. This concept formed the basis of the Permanent Settlement. Interestingly enough while the Utilitarians would speak of a competitive society and individual rights, in case of India, James Mill would propose that in India's case, the "State should remain as the landlord and that each peasant should hold directly from the State as its tenant." Rather than going into the ideological debates concerning rent etc., like those of Ricardo, Malthus and others that were in some ways influential in India's context, lets continue with our narrative.

The land revenue system emerged as a consequence of experiments. Three systems of land revenue emerged in different parts of British territory in India-Permanent Settlement (or Zamindari), ryotwari and Mahalwari. But whatever be the legitimising credo, the tax on the land went on continuous increase. Very often subsuming the economic rent and leading to a situation of less than subsistence for the farmers. Under the Permanent Settlement, this meant fragmentation of land and creation of multiple intermediaries. Usually, the large estate would be partitioned into chain of multiple intermediaries leading to fragmentation of land to the extent that "by the late nineteenth century 88.5% of the 110,456 permanently settled estates of Bengal and Bihar were less than 500 acres in size" This also meant that the actual producers were too oppressed and burdened with the revenue demands that they could not go for improvements. And on the other hand, it also created a hierarchy of rentiers who would be dependent on the revenue derived from the primary producers. This led to a situation where the entrepreneurial spirit was institutionally destroyed. This meant that a middle class could not come up as the society was divided into chain of revenue rentiers and cultivators.

In the ryotwari areas, under the experimentation of Munroe, the British itself extracted the surplus directly from the farmers. This problem was sought to be rectified on the basis of traditions of common ownership of land in the Mahalwari system that was introduced in the northern provinces. However, being badly administered it led to similar problems for the cultivators. By the Saharanpur Rules of 1855 the Government demand was limited to one-half of rental but it was later interpreted to mean one-half of 'the prospective and potential' rental of estates. This meant that if an estate had a rental of £ 1000 a year, then the claim of government could be £ 600 on the ground that the rental might rise to £ 1200 in the coming year. This issue got further compounded by the additional tax burden on the people on other heads of government like education, post offices etc.

Consequences to such experiments were disastrous. In Zamindari areas, agricultural production suffered and agricultural prices fell. Cultivators were unable to pay revenue, thus leading to large number of land alienation. It also meant that very often the cultivators were ejected from their lands. But now as land itself had become a commodity, the cultivators unlike previous times, could not find new land to re-settle. There was an increasing incidence of famines and to a large extent the famine was consequence of EIC policy.

In ryotwari areas, since the cultivators were under heavy tax burden, they had to resort to loans from local money-lenders and thus fall into further penury. In such case, in areas like Madras province, the price of land declined so that it was not seen as a profitable investment avenue. But when the over-assessment was reduced in the latter half of 19th century, similar to the Zamindari areas, the Madras cultivator would often hire out his land (Dharma Kumar, 1965). While in areas of Deccan, because of inability of ryots (cultivators) to pay back the debt led to alienation of land by the money-lenders. This was particularly perceptible in the post 1860 cotton boom phase, when the international cotton prices crashed consequent to the end of American Civil War. Cultivators would be going into indebtedness in other areas as well, like that in Punjab.

Another important aspect of the economic exploitation was the process of de-industrialisation. Certain western scholars find that the de-industrialisation did not happen. The process of de-industrialisation encompassed a vaster spread than just decline of traditional handicrafts and increasing exports of raw materials. This was intricately linked to the area of technology and issues of foreign capital and foreign investment in India, particularly from the latter half of the 19th century. The rural artisans under increasing pressure of coercive tactics used by EIC were giving up their traditional crafts, and this was a continuous process since the latter half of the 18th century. This was further aggravated by the monopolising nature of EIC that would monopolise these trades and force the artisans to work for the company on coercive terms. This meant that the artisans were to leave their independent work and come under their employment through a process of coerced outsourcing in terms of agreement that was beneficial only to the EIC. This process was mediated by the requirements of the imperial country and by the penetration of the western technology and the Manchester goods into the interior countryside. Such thing however did not happen through a free competition. Instead, the process was catalysed through the use of political power that the company commanded. In a letter dated March 17, 1769, the EIC directors desired the encouragement to manufacture of raw silk and discouragement to manufactured silk products. H.H. Wilson, History of British India, remarks, "It was stated in evidence (in 1813) that the cotton and silk goods of India up to the period could be sold for a profit in the British market at a price from 50% to 60% lower than those necessary to protect the latter by duties of 70% and 80% on their value, or by positive prohibition. Had this not been the case, had not such prohibitory duties and decrees existed, the mills of Paisley and Manchestor would have been stopped in their outset, and could scarcely have been again set in motion, even by the power of steam. They were created by the sacrifice of the Indian manufacture."

Such dispossessed craftsmen added to the queue of cultivator class. Amiya Bagchi in a paper "De-industrialisation in Gangetic Bihar", 1809-1901, comparing the Buchanan-Hamilton surveys and census figures of 1901, finds that the craft employment in the districts under study of Bihar, contracted from 18.6% to 8.5% in the given time period. There was also a significant fall in the number of cotton spinners and weavers.

Consequently, pressure on land increased. This meant an increasing pressure on the unremunerative land (due to the land revenue pressures). This led to a situation of steady economic decline of the countryside. De-industrialisation led to decline in manufacturing of value added cotton and silk finished products. India, which had earlier been exporter of finished products, now became an exporter of raw cotton and other raw materials (by early 19th century) and importer of British industry manufactured clothes. Much of this process had already taken place before the 1850s. Between 1815 and 1832, the value of Indian cotton goods exported fell from £ 1.3 million to below £ 100,000. In the same period, the value of English cotton goods imported into India rose from £ 26,000 to £ 400,000. As R. Palme Dutt puts it, "While machine-made cotton goods ruined the weavers, machine made twist ruined the spinners". This process happened in various different products whether it be silk, woollen goods, iron, pottery, glass or paper.

If the drain had not taken place and the imbalance in the economic structures had not been introduced, it was well possible that areas like manufacturing and processing would have improved than what it actually remained. This would have been mediated by the process of capital formation that would have added to the economic activity of the country. Instead, this capital was siphoned off through various structures of economy that was tilted to serve the imperial interest.

This also meant ruralisation of the economy. As the value added industries were being systematically finished, India lost her manufacturing base. Rather than being an exporter, it now became an importer of British manufacture. And in return India paid with the raw materials in form of food grains. Such a process is also evident from the increase in percentage of population dependent on agriculture. Between 1891 and 1921, the percentage of population dependent on agriculture increased from 61.1 to 73 percent.

But most important aspect of de-industrialisation was technological impoverishment-both real and potential. The 'two great events, the Industrial Revolution and the process of colonisation, took place almost simultaneously. Perhaps they had a cause and effect relationship'. This related to sectors like shipping, railways, telegraph, and technical education, among others. It was technology that made colonisation feasible and cheap. But the emergence of technology as an application for use was a consequence deriving out of imperial exploitation of colonial resources. This input of the western technology was directly related to forced decline of the technology that had developed in India and was in competition with British technology. In case of shipping, 'If the Braudelian judgment is extended to the Indian Ocean shipping, surely, Indian ships were the equal of European'. The only difference being that the European ships were also weapons of war and used guns to further their economic interests. Throughout the 18th century and the initial part of 19th century, there was concerted move by lobbyists and authorities in England to protect British shipping rights. In 1814, a Select Committee headed by Robert Peel recommended restrictions of Indian ships and sailors. The finale happened to be the Registry Act of 1815 that proved disastrous for the Indian shipping. The Registry Act imposed a 15% duty on ships built in India. It further ruled that the goods from the south and east of Cape of Good Hope should come only in British ships. Moreover, the Mariners would have to be British (three-fourth of crew or seven per hundred tons) and only those ships were to be allowed to London port whose master was British. And Indian sailors were not deemed British. The steam ships using coal were introduced in India only by 1830s. It is transparent that it was the imperial policy and not superiority of industrial revolution that led to decline of Indian shipping. Not pulled down by imperial policy, Indian shipping could have survived and technologically developed as it happened in other sovereign countries of Europe, Asia and America.

Railway was an area that was linked both with technological development of industrial revolution in Britain as well as export of foreign capital to India. However, the investment of foreign capital in India was only apparent and not real. The burden of funding was shifted over to India through a system of guaranteed interest rate regime whereby dividend was paid to the private companies even if there were no profits. It was 'private investment at public risk' There was also much wasteful construction and operational expenditure that were done.

In the whole scheme of things, there was an ongoing debate regarding comparative merit of canals for irrigation vis-a-vis the railways system-'preference was given to railways that facilitated British trade with India, and not to canals which would have benefited Indian agriculture'. By the mid 19th century, the financiers of England were in look for a safe place for their investment and they found it in the form of investment in railways. William N. Massey, Finance Minister of India under Lawrence and Mayo would understand the issue as-"All the money came from the English capitalist, and so long as he was guaranteed 5 per cent on the revenues of India, it was immaterial to him whether the funds that he lent were thrown into the Hooghly or converted into brick and mortar....the East India Railway cost...are the most extravagant works that were ever undertaken".

The nature of investment in railways is quite a giveaway of how such foreign capital became another source of Drain of Wealth from India. All railway investments were given sovereign guarantee for profit by the Government of India. Railways were an extravagant project that was undertaken by British by guaranteeing assured profit from territorial revenues. The equipments for the project was imported from England. This meant that ancillary industries that usually take shape when such huge industry comes up at a place, did not take shape in India and in the nearly a century before 1947, only 700 locomotives came to be built in India. The higher posts in railways were reserved for the British and by 1921, only 10% Indians were in railways. This meant two things that the money received by the British manpower would go out of India as part of the invisible transfer, it also meant that the Indians would remain excluded from the association with technological know-how. This was despite the fact that in the ultimate analysis, their own money generated through revenues was financing it. Moreover, railways itself became a source of further penetration of the British goods to the interior-which had till now been relatively free from the influence of Manchester goods. This led to further disruption of the village economy and decline in local crafts.

The tariff policies were discriminatory-Indian goods were levied higher tariffs than the British goods. From the technological angle, the early introduction of railways had an unfavourable influence in terms of inability to absorb later developments of railway technologies. Ian Derbyshire speaks of railways being " equipped with expensively superfluous bull and double-headed rails, and laid out an anachronistic broad gauge.

India's railways were also built at a time when constructional technologies were crude". However, India did not receive the benefits of development of railways because of the absence of the backward linkages of such development. These advantages were being reaped by the British industry in Britain. While the railway finances were a drag on Indian taxpayer, the comparative interests that would have been useful in terms of investment in agriculture was not appreciated.

There was a skewing of public policy whereby the imperial interests led to creation of distorted priorities. "£ 225,000,000 were spent on railways, resulting not in a profit, but in a loss of £ 40,000,000 to the Indian taxpayer up to 1900. And so little were the interests of Indian agriculture appreciated that only £ 25,000,000 were spent on irrigation works up to 1900. Moreover, even in technological terms, India did not derive much benefit, as transfer of railway technology in complicated processes did not happen. The technology that was made available to India was of low-tech areas of railways like those of way levelling, while in "the more complex activities of plate-laying, tunnelling and bridge-building, western working technologies were never transferred undiluted". Besides, railways also served the imperial military purpose of quick movement of army from one place to another and in penetration into the areas of local princely kingdoms that were theoretically independent with treaty arrangements with the British. But as the British wished to have a foothold on those areas as well, what better than the railway network that would pass through these areas. Interestingly enough the railways network touched only the strategic areas or areas important to British from commercial point.

The area of technical education was also neglected. Arun Kumar, notes that "Japan began engineering education under British guidance in 1873 and within 30 years, nine technical institutions teaching civil engineering, shipbuilding, electrical engineering, mining and metallurgy were in existence. By 1903, the Tokyo Engineering College had a staff of 24 professors, 24 assistant professors and 22 lecturers. In the US, MIT was established in 1865, and by 1906 had 306 teachers. Within 50 years it had produced thousands of graduates-6,248 with bachelor's degrees, 290 with master's degrees and 29 with doctorates. In India, where engineering education was introduced much earlier (in 1847), 100 years after its founding, the most prestigious institution, Roorkee college still had only three professors, six assistant professors and 12 lecturers." This was primarily because, engineering was linked to the colonial objectives that sought to make India a resource of raw materials (for Britain) and deny it any basis for industrial development.

The issue of imperial interests did not just rest within the confine of conquest, but equally into the issues of technological impoverishment. In this regard it is useful to quote Clark & Feenstra (2001), "...by 1910... incomes per capita began to diverge sharply between an advanced group of economies, and an underdeveloped world whose most important members were India and China...Why did income per capita decline in poor countries such as India and China relative to the advanced economies such as the US since 1800? We argue that the overwhelmingly cause was a decline in the relative efficiency of utilisation of technology in these countries relative to the more successful economies such as Britain and the USA." It is quite obvious of who was in-charge of utilisation of technology in India from 1800 onwards and how these impacted on the various issues of economy including, but not exclusively to the per-capita income!

Similarly, development of telegraph was also shaped by the 'political and military necessities'. All these areas of technology and economy was symbiotically related with each other, where institutionally created deficiencies tended to impact each of these fields in a system-wide manner. This meant that the technology from Britain also served the political needs, and not just the requirements of economy or commerce from the imperial perspective. These technologies (like railways and telegraph) were a prime instrument in quelling revolts and for troop movement. While the political decisions led to decline of indigenous technology, western technology itself became a political tool of thwarting potentials of development of indigenous technology. Both reinforcing each other and increasing the stranglehold of imperialism on the colony. In this regard, Bipin Chandra has commented, "...actual British capital investment in India was rather small, and if guaranteed investments in railways and public debt were excluded, virtually negligible, or that even of this capital very little had gone into modern industries...there was no recognition of the fact that even the foreign-owned capital in India was not imported from Britain but was generated within India and that India was throughout this period a net exporter of capital".

A major critique of the drain by the Nationalists was built around the issue of invisibles. This formed the core of the drain theory of the Nationalists. This related to the transfer of money from India on several accounts like-home charges (expenses of Indian Government in Britain). This included the money that was charged on India for maintenance of offices like that of Secretary of State in England. Also were included the transfer of money on account of salaries, pensions and savings sent to Britain by Britishers living in India; remittances of profits by merchants; dividend to the shareholders of the EIC from the coffers of the territorial revenue of the country.

While the Charter Act, 1833 deprived the company of its monopolist trader status, the entire burden was shifted on to the territorial revenue of the country. While this may be understood in some respect as successor power-arrangement inheriting the liabilities, what defies understanding is that the Act would also make provision for the shareholders of EIC, who were promised 10 ½% as annual dividend for a further period of fifty years. And as a compensation for its loss of trading interests, EIC was offered a lump sum of 90 million pound sterling. This way, "The Charter Act of 1833 provided for an annual dividend of £ 630,000 to be paid to the shareholders of the Company out of the Indian revenues till 1874. In 1874, the loan of £4.5 million was raised to redeem the stock at a premium of 100 percent."

In the gradual way in which the Britain developed the bureaucracy and the superstructure of government in India, the most significant thing was that Indians were nearly denied participation in the higher positions of civil bureaucracy and the army. G.K. Gokhale's deposition to Royal Commission on Expenditure (1895-97), (based on Parliamentary return of May 1892) regarding the personnel in the high offices clearly delineates this anomaly.

				total salaries in thousand of rupees of		
	natives	**eurasians**	**europeans**	**natives**	**eurasians**	**europeans**
civil dept	55	10	1211	947	151	25,274
military	1	1	854	12	11	13,268
public works	3	4	239	33	45	3,415
incorporated local funds	1	-	9	10	-	113
	60	15	2313	1002	207	42,070

The money on these heads gradually got transferred out from India, without India deriving any benefit-except political subjugation on these heads. This drain took the form of excess of exports over imports. These exports were consequent to the changed pattern of international trade that was now being conducted from India. Instead of India exporting finished goods, India had now become an exporter of raw materials that fed the expanding operations of the British industries. "According to the nationalist calculations, this drain amounted to one-half of government revenues, more than the entire land revenue collection, and over one-third of India's total savings."

This would by 20th century as well add into its heads interests on foreign capital, banking commissions, freight and passenger carriage etc. These were transferred via the trading structure and financial system. This was consequent to the peculiar form of trading and financial institutions that developed by the early 20th century. Britain owned the shipping, banking, insurance, and the different agencies through which the trade was conducted. This system functioned via the managing agency system. These were agencies that would provide a one-stop solution to all trading requirements. These Agencies had become powerful in their own right and charged high commission and share of profits. These commission and other remittances went directly to British coffers, Sumit Sarkar writes that under managing agency system "the tendency was at best towards creating capitalist enclaves under foreign control which really inhibited the development of the rest of the economy"

Another important area of change in the economic system, brought about by imperialism was commercialisation of agriculture. This involved conversion of farms into areas of production for raw materials for distant lands. Most important of these was of-course cotton production. Another important area related to the plantations that had indigo, tea, jute, tobacco, etc. Tea and jute were monopolised by European planters. Indigo was introduced as a measure to substitute calicos, whose import to England was being opposed by the Cotton lobbyists. The European planters forced indigo plantation on local farmers. In most of the cases, this meant that the cultivators were forced to assign a certain part of their fields to indigo cultivation in consideration of a forced contract. The farmers were forced, against their will, to take small amount of loans and bound into a contract. However, this did not mean that the cost of cultivation was being borne by the European planter. All the equipments, livestock etc. were those that were used by the cultivator for his own use. So, this also meant that in real terms there was not any net addition to the ancillary economic activity. This can as well be seen as a situation in which the European Planter was using the resources of the native without actually putting in the investment in land or equipment. And if the cultivator protested, the officials and the courts supported the European planters. The Charter Act of 1833 gave the Europeans rights in ownership of land and full freedom of contract.

Similarly in the tea plantations, the Europeans would get many concessions in form of large tracts of land at nominal prices, concessions in taxation and powers akin to criminal justice. Assam wasteland rules provided for grant of land upto 3000 acres per holder as freehold property exempt from land tax. Act 13 of 1859 and Inland Immigration Act of 1882 made breach of contract a criminal offence and authorised the tea planters to arrest a run away labourer without any warrant.

Commercialisation led to dependence on the foreign market increased and the risk of fluctuation that was inherent was to be finally borne by the cultivators. This is fairly demonstrated by the Deccan Agrarian disturbances of 1870s. In this, the demand for cotton during the 1860s from India increased because of the ensuing civil war in USA. During these prosperity years, the government also revised the revenues taking these prosperity year statistics to be the standard. But since the cotton boom was temporary, the prices crashed after the civil war in USA was over. This led to complete desperation in the Deccan cotton belt. As these were the ryotwari areas of direct settlement, the cultivators had to take loans from local money-lenders to pay their revenue demand. All these led to increased control of money-lenders on the cultivators' lands. All these led to considerable distress and disturbances. At one level this would seem a fairly innocuous working of the market principles. But at another level, this was caused by the kind of economic structures that the imperial government had introduced in the country.

The commercialisation of agriculture was largely meant for foreign market and consequently led to neglect of production of food crops. The estimates of D. Thorner reveal the following figures:

Indices of average output of food and commercial crops	Area under Food crops	Area under Commercial crops	Estimates of gross production of foodgrains (million tons)
Avg. of 1893-1896	100	100	73.9
Avg. of 1906-1916	99	126	74.0
Avg. of 1926 to 1936	94	171	60.6
Avg. of 1936 to 1946	93	185	60.3

Three things become fairly clear-One, the avenues of value addition had been systematically removed from the country. Two, the money that were going out on various heads had they remained in the country, then they could create a ripple effect in the economy and lead to expansion of the economy. Three, an expanding economy with capital accumulation would induce technological innovations in the system. This was not happening, because the wealth that was being drained out was adding into the economic expansion of the imperialist country. This also made it possible for Britain to absorb technologies into its economic processes. This also had the effect of increasing the power of the imperial nation. The colony itself was deriving no benefit out of its own resources that it was generating.

The nature of economic relation between India and Britain was also undergoing continuous modifications. This was prompted by the changing requirements of Britain for its progressing industrialisation. Consequently by Charter of 1813, the monopoly status of EIC with regard to India came to an end. Within twenty years, by the 1833 charter, even the trading status of EIC with regard to India came to an end, and it remained only a territorial agent of British sovereign. Such changes opened up India to free trade regime and newer areas of drain.

This was most achieved through the route of tariff differentiation. Tariff discrimination had come into existence early in the first half of the nineteenth century. "In the parliamentary enquiry of 1840 it was reported that while British cotton and silk goods imported into India paid a duty of 3 ½ per cent and woollen goods 2 per cent, Indian cotton goods imported into Britain paid 10 per cent, silk goods 20 per cent and woollen goods 30 per cent." The drain was most visible in growing export surplus by which the home charges and other remittances was transferred to Britain.

The army itself was another factor of this drain. The defence expenditure by the colonial regime in India was far higher in ratio than that in England. By 1904-5 the figure had reached 51.9 percent of the expenditure of the government of India that was in sharp contrast to the amount spent on this head by Britain itself. The reason was quite obvious. India was spending this amount for Britain and not for itself. Army from India was used in distant foreign expeditions ranging from China to Middle East to Africa to Europe-and all these had no bearing with India, but only with the imperial interests of Britain. Now while the army would fight for the imperial interests in far off lands-that only served the imperial interests of Britain, the cost of such wars was borne by the Government of India, whose ultimate burden fell on the people of India. To the Royal Commission on Expenditure (1895-97) Lord

Northbrook would say, "The English Government were put to very considerable cost, and we thought that India would be put to a small cost, and we thought she might very well pay the small cost of the troops sent to Suez.

However, the operation became very extended, and it ended in the expedition from India becoming a large expedition. The whole cost was I think £ 1,700,000 and the ultimate arrangement made between the two Governments, the Government of India and the Government of England, was that India pay £ 1,200,000, and England paid £ 500,000." While Henry Brackenbury would say, "The strength of the army in India is calculated to allow of a powerful field army being placed on or beyond the Indian frontier, in addition to the obligatory garrisons required for keeping order in India...The foreign policy of India is directed entirely from England by her Majesty's Government, and it is part of British foreign policy generally. The object of British foreign policy generally, I believe is to secure British rule over British Empire...I cannot but feel that Britain's interest in keeping India under British rule is enormous. India affords employment to thousands of Britons; India employs millions of British capital...Therefore it seems to me that India, being held by Great Britain, not only for India's sake, but also for Great Britain's sake, Great Britain should pay a share of the expenditure for this purpose..." The army was also skewed in its personnel policies. Indians were not recruited for the higher jobs. They served only the lower levels.

Why was the Drain a Drain?

Whenever there is an economic exchange, the exchange takes place at parity. This parity is based on certain norms acceptable to the parties involved in the exchange. Many times, the exchange may be unequal. Some of this can be derived from positions like the power that is exercised by a monopolist. Many times, this unequal exchange can even be negative where one party would use its privileged position to dictate terms of exchange. But all this relates to a situation that takes into account 'ceteris-paribus'.

In contrast to this, there are situations, where one party to exchange would use its privileged position and extra-situational variables (particularly political factors) to induce changes in the structure of economy itself. This change of structure leads to the situation where the exchange transcends that of an unequal exchange. The exchange transforms into a system of continuous one-way flow of resources. This transfer of resources is without any benefit to one side. This leads to a situation of drain and exploitation. The structures are not only geared so as to benefit the recipient on a continuous basis, but are also controlled by the beneficiary by use of policy mechanism and administrative action.

This had impact on various dimensions of political economy. Its economic consequences included increasing poverty, occupational shift from craft to agriculture, stagnant per capita income, declining population, de-urbanisation, and also harm to potential economic development. This harm to potential economic development led to creation of Dependency in the future. Such Dependency is also visible in various third world economies, and continues in the situation of the current Globalisation. Such issues of economic drain could even be seen in the context of countries colonised in Africa. Eventhough such themes were discussed in African countries, there seems that a systematic theorisation did not take place in the African context prior to independence movements in its various countries. Much of the debate took place on such issues in the context of Dependency theoretical framework later on during the decades of sixties. However, in India, which had been longer in the colonised setup and this theorisation and realisation of hard Economics was more systematically written, it formed the ground on which the freedom movement could have firm foundation. However, apart from this, even in the colonial context of America vis-a-vis Britain there existed such issues like goods could be sold only to English merchants, and foreign goods could be bought only after paying duties at English ports. However, America fought and won its independence much earlier and escaped the creation of such exploitative structures. In India's case, the colonial period was much overdrawn and led to creation of such structures of economic drain. The point to note is that such issues could emerge in any context of imperial-colonial relations. It is existence of such structures that creates an imperial-colonial relation that provides benefits to only one of them. If such structure would exist even in absence of a formal control over territories, even then such issues would come up, though such aspects are beyond the scope of this essay.

Imperial Issues and Economic Consequences

Britain in India was the significant central power. It was significant, because it exercised more powers of direct centralised control than it was ever possible earlier. It was central, because even the princely states that were theoretically independent were peripheral to the emerging and ensuing political scene. At no time earlier was government organised with so technical efficiency. Use of technology and work methods and organisational skills were central to the exercise of this efficiency. This technical efficiency of a government run by bureaucracy was geared to the imperial interests and was totally ignorant and unaccountable to the native country and the people. Many Eurocentric commentators have remarked on the positives of British rule. However, I would argue that this technical efficiency was reflection of organisational efficiency. The technological efficiency did not exist in the first place, but was rather a derivative of such an interaction through the imperial enterprise.

Firstly, at political level, the sovereign did not reside in India and did not have any accountability to the people. It may be argued that even the monarchs of India were not accountable to the people. But the basic difference was that while the monarchs of India could be overthrown by revolts such could not be done to the sovereign thousands of miles away. On the other hand, all the money that was going out to Britain would remain in India and get reinvested in the economy. This was not happening in case of India in its colonised condition. Also, the foreign sovereign in this case was a bulwark of the reactionary forces in the country. This is visible from treaties of Subsidiary Alliance that protected the native rulers of Indian States from external and internal enemies. Imperialism thus worked as a bulwark against any kind of revolution or as a denial of democratic aspirations of the people as well.

Secondly, some scholars have argued that the drain was a charge for administrative services. This is simply incongruous, based on assumption that India did not have any administrative system or any rules prior to EIC. EIC only introduced a newer form of rules displacing the older system. It would be wrong to assume that rules of the older system were not rational. But in this context what is important is that if India had not come into the net of imperialism, the wealth that got drained away to the imperial country would have remained within and contributed to economic progress and innovation. Prabhat Patnaik has rightly argued that, '...India, whose economic structure was not dissimilar to Japan's could if left alone have conceivably followed the latter's example, but their very exposure to European capitalism sabotaged this prospect'.

Thirdly, imperialism in India was diffuse to a great extent through policies like Subsidiary Alliance, Doctrine of Lapse etc. British imperialism in India worked through the institutions that it had created. This included the economic structures, the legal system and medium of education. The way the non-economic variables were geared to requirements of imperialism can be gauged through objectives of education as laid down by British policy. Macaulay in his minute of education (2-2-1835), regarding English as a medium of instruction for education said, "We must at present do our best to form a class who may be interpreters between us and the millions whom we govern, a class of persons Indian in blood and colour, but English in tastes, in opinions, in morals and in intellect".

It is interesting to note that even after more than a century of introduction of English as a medium of education, the literacy level in India was abysmally low. And not all of who were literate were of the English medium. This meant that the potential for development of human resources and human capital was also stymied. The education system could not emerge in the right direction. The education system that the British introduced in India was no different than the traditional liberal system of India, the only difference was that this time this was in the English medium and non-religious in nature. It continued to have the generalist non-technical orientation of earlier times.

Fourthly, a related issue is that of westernisation/ modernisation. Often it is argued that modernisation of values and mode of living was a consequence of British rule. This is only partly true. If we analyse the major reform movements, we would find that most of these reform movements of 19th and 20th century that attempted to modernise the society took place as an internal regeneration process. As K.N. Panikkar has observed, "It was not just an attempt at religious revival and glorification, but an intellectual inquiry into the past, embracing almost every field of social, cultural and political endeavour...to suggest that the present was not an index of what Indians were capable of. Implicit in this was the assumption that regeneration and restructuring of the existing cultural complex was necessary pre-requisites for the realisation of this potential. Hence the Indian mind increasingly turned inward." Most of the time, the British were hostile to such movements and played a reactionary role, particularly after 1857. And more often than not, these progressive reform movements in some ways or other provided the philosophical inspiration to the freedom struggle. But even such a process was not devoid of the economic idiom and recognised the need of economic regeneration of the country.

These above two issues can be said to be important in the context that there was an inherent recognition of the economic dimension of society and that India was not just 'spiritual' as is often thought of in the western myth making of India. This combined with the fact that gradually there would have emerged a stream of technical education in the country had it not come under the imperial folds. This issue can also be related to the issue of proto-industrialisation. It is considered by Historians that India had a situation of proto-industrialisation that resembled similar developments in England relating to methods and organisation of production, at the same period of time during the centuries prior to industrial revolution in Britain. [As an aside, sometimes I feel that going by the nature of active manufacturing and trade that existed in the sub-continent, it seems as if this was the place where materialism was born; infact an active spiritual activity could only exist when there would be funds to subsidise such activities.]

Fifthly, the question in regard to economic betterment is, to what extent could India have improved on its condition, if the factor of British imperialism was not there. This relates both to the economic dimensions as well as the industrial dimensions. For sure, the drain would not have occurred. India's ability to translate this wealth into one of international competitiveness would have depended on to what extent could Indian technologies have improved (and also innovated) by the capital accumulation and continued to compete or even challenge the goods of industrial revolution. It was more likely that India could have gone the way of industrialisation akin to one found in other countries of Europe- this was because, India already had the proto-industrial, entrepreneurial and commercial setup. And in a competitive economic situation, increase in population would have meant that as in countries like France and Germany, it would have encouraged adoption of the technologies that had transformed Britain. However, British involvement in India led to a situation where due to various reasons of economic impoverishment, it also impacted on the population trends that remained either stagnant or even showed declining tendencies.

Equally valid question is that could Britain continue with its industrial revolution in absence of subsidised raw materials from its colony? Wouldn't have Britain needed to buy those raw materials in a competitive market, if the market would have worked according to the laws of demand and supply? And in such case could it bear the costs of translating the technological innovation into factory production? When we think of industrial revolution, we need to segregate the scientific know-how to that of commercial product that involves translating that science into technology that has commercial application or utility is an economic environment of the market.

It was here what we call the 'industrial revolution', where the factories would need to function within the ambit of the market with large-scale production that goes beyond the serendipity of scientific innovation. This transformation of science, to that of technological application, was a direct development largely deriving from political subjugation of the colony. The political factor was too important in deciding the economic fortunes and the trajectory of development, than the purely technological or economic factor.

To put it in a more understandable manner-in our times, we have many environmental friendly technologies, or more precisely scientific know-how. But these currently have no use. This is because their manufacturing costs are prohibitive and consequently their market is either non-existent or extremely limited (who wouldn't wish to have a electric fuelled car or be happy with sea water converted to potable water?) What actually transforms the future technologies to current technology? Is it just the technology per se? Now a similar analogy holds for Britain if it had not undertaken the imperial enterprise. Development of technology is no guarantee for its success in the market place. If the raw material like cotton was not available cheaply, or political tariff differentials were not used, the presence or absence of technology would have hardly been a significant variable for the Lancashire manufacturers. Burns et al point out that, "The English possessed a merchant marine capable of transporting goods across the world, and a navy practised in the art of protecting its commercial fleets...English entrepreneurs and technicians responded to the compulsion by revolutionising the production of cotton textile goods. Although far less cotton goods were made in eighteenth century England than wool...Tariff prohibiting the importation of East Indian cottons, imposed by Parliament to stimulate the sale of woollen goods, had instead served to spur the manufacture of domestic cotton.".

One advantage leads to another. So we get a highly subsidised manufacturing base that was driven by cheap raw materials from the colony. The other dimension of this is equally relevant. The colony worked as a captive market for those manufactured textiles and later on other products like the railways. If such were not available, then the whole business would have again faced tremendous difficulties, hardly worth the trouble to keep running the revolution, if it was not paying enough. It is after all the market that decides the manufacture not the other way round. It is hardly useful to think that a non-colonised India would have preferred imported cotton goods over its own domestic production when such cotton goods even without machine technology (and despite of the tariff restrictions & the process of de-industrialisation) could hold on their own in Britain till the early 19th century. Left to itself, it is quite possible that the trajectory of industrial development in Britain would have followed a slower path as was followed by others. In the larger context of imperial-colonial relations, it also explains why the countries of South, the erstwhile colonies, would be poor despite their resources and raw materials. Imperialism thus has deep economic implications that adversely affect all facets of life by creation of enduring unequal structures.

Drain of Wealth during British Raj

Whenever the issue of economic exploitation and the "Drain of Wealth" during the 200 years of British colonial rule comes up, the one rebuttal from western historians is that there is scant evidence to prove it. To bolster the argument, the point is then made that Indian historians are nationalist, biased (sometimes as a consequence) and do not pay attention to figures and statistical evidence.

In my analysis of this topic, I have therefore, relied heavily on recent research by Western historians and tried to draw conclusions based on that.

Even by the accounts of western historians, the positive impact of British rule, which PM Sh. Man Mohan Singh had so pointedly mentioned during his speech at Oxford in July '05, is questionable.

The "drain of wealth" from India to Britain during the two centuries of colonial rule was very real, very substantial and there are strong reasons to believe that India may have looked significantly different (and far better) economically and socially had it not been for the two centuries of British rule.

The beginning of this period can probably be traced back to the Battle of Plassey. As Prof. Richards writes in the introduction to his paper "Imperial Finance Under the East India Company 1762-1859", "On June 23,1757, Robert Clive, commanding a small force of East India Company professional troops, defeated and killed Siraju-ud-daula, the ruling Nawab of Bengal, on the battlefield of Plassey. The battle marked a significant turning point in world history, for it permitted the English East India Company to gain control over the rich resources of the Mughal successor state in north-eastern Bengal and Bihar. ...This was the starting point for a century-long process of British conquest and dominion over the entire Indian sub-continent and beyond."

To help grasp the full extent of this exploitation, I have split my analysis into five parts. In Part 1, I look at the tax regime and the burden of administrative machinery. In Part 2, I try to get behind the assertion that the British contributed much to the improvement of education and public works in India. In Parts 3 and 4, I look at unfair trade practices and the drain of wealth. In the final part, I have tried to summarize the impact of these 200 years of servitude.

Taxes and Administrative Burden

In their recent research on de-industrialisation in India, Profs. Williamson and Clingingsmith mention that while the maximum revenue extracted by the Mughals as high as 40%, this paled in comparison to the effective tax rate in the early years of colonial rule: "as central Mughal authority waned, the state resorted increasingly to revenue farming...(raising) the effective rent share to 50% or more..."

Further, "There is no reason to believe that when the British became rulers of the successor states the revenue burden declined (pg 7)".

After initial attempts at revenue farming, Company officials aggressively introduced new taxes in an attempt to reduce their dependence on agrarian production, thus worsening the tax burden on the common man.

As Prof. Richards points out in his paper (Ref 1), "Land revenue continued to be the mainstay of the regime until the end of British rule in India, but its share of gross revenues was far less than under the Mughal emperors...To a larger degree, however, new taxes not imposed by the Mughals accounted for land revenue's declining share. Company officials began early to diversify their tax base so that the new regime was not so overwhelmingly dependent upon agrarian production. "

In his research on the subject, Prof. Maddison mentions the burden imposed by the administrative machinery of the State: "...British salaries were high: the Viceroy received £25,000 a year, and governors £10,000...From 1757 to 1919, India also had to meet administrative expenses in London, first of the East India Company, and then of the India Office, as well as other minor but irritatingly extraneous charges. The cost of British staff was raised by long home leave in the UK, early retirement and lavish amenities in the form of subsidised housing, utilities, rest houses, etc."

Prof. Richards mentions that although the Company "raised their revenue demands in each territory ... to the highest assessments made by previous Indian regimes" they were still insufficient to "meet the combined administrative, military and commercial expenses of the Company"

Spending on Education and Public Works

Although there is a prevalent myth around British contribution to development if education and infrastructure in India, in reality, the situation was quite different.

Prof. Maddison writes that as late as 1936, the bulk of government expenditure was focused more on ensuring the stability of the empire than anything else: "Even in 1936, more than half of government spending was for the military, justice, police and jails, and less than 3 per cent for agriculture.

Amidst all the paraphernalia of the "Raj", public works and social expenditure was completely forgotten. As Prof. Richards notes"...the Company allocated negligible funds for public works, for cultural patronage, for charitable relief, or for any form of education....(confining) its generosity to paying extremely high salaries to its civil servants and military officers. Otherwise parsimony ruled."

The following excerpt from Prof. Maddison's essay squarely debunks the notion that the British did a lot for education and were conscious of the wealth of ancient knowledge-some of which was still extant at the time. The contempt that Macaulay felt towards the knowledge and wisdom of ancient Hindus is evident from this quote: "We are a Board for wasting public money, for printing books which are less value than the paper on which they are printed was while it was blank; for giving artificial encouragement to absurd history, absurd metaphysics, absurd physics, absurd theology... I have no knowledge of either Sanskrit or Arabic... But I have done what I could to form a correct estimate of their value... Who could deny that a single shelf of a good European library was worth the whole native literature of India and Arabia... all the historical information which has been collected from all the books written in the Sanskrit language is less valuable than what may be found in the most paltry abridgements used at preparatory schools in England."

Unsurprisingly, "The education system which developed was a very pale reflection of that in the UK. Three universities were set up in 1857 in Calcutta, Madras and Bombay, but they were merely examining bodies and did no teaching. Drop-out ratios were always very high. They did little to promote analytic capacity or independent thinking and produced a group of graduates with a half-baked knowledge of English, but sufficiently Westernised to be alienated from their own culture.

> *"...the great mass of the population had no access to education and, at independence in 1947, 88 per cent were illiterate... at independence only a fifth of children were receiving any primary schooling."*
>
> *Education was used as a tool "...to turn a tiny elite into imitation Englishmen and a somewhat bigger group into government clerks."*

If we turn our eyes to other areas of development, the picture does not improve. In spite of agriculture being-by far-the most significant part of the economy, "Little was done to promote agricultural technology. There was some improvement in seeds, but no extension service, no improvement in livestock and no official encouragement to use fertilizer. Lord Mayo, the Governor General, said in 1870, "I do not know what is precisely meant by ammoniac manure. If it means guano, superphosphate or any other artificial product of that kind, we might as well ask the people of India to manure their ground with champagne".

In his analysis of the various charges and expenses that the Company incurred, Professor Richards mentions how Company officials were extremely wary of any public works spending uinless it was for projects of direct use to the state.

The following sentences are instructive and effectively blast the myth that the British did lasting good by building modern infrastructure in India: "The Company even failed to repair and maintain roads, river embankments, and bunded storage tanks for irrigation that had been the responsibility of earlier regimes. When, in 1823, the Governor General in Council decided to devote a portion of anticipated surplus revenues to works of public improvement, the Court of Directors rejected this proposal. When, the Directors learned of heavy expenditures on buildings in the mid 1820's, they wrote to the Governor General to condemn this extravagance."

Monopoly and Unfair Trade Practices

To comprehend the extent of "unfair" trade norms, just one example would suffice (excerpted from this excellent essay: "The Colonial Legacy-Myths and Popular Beliefs") "As early as 1812, an East India Company Report had stated "The importance of that immense empire to this country is rather to be estimated by the great annual addition it makes to the wealth and capital of the Kingdom....." Few would doubt that Indo-British trade may have been unfair-but it may be noteworthy to see how unfair. In the early 1800s imports of Indian cotton and silk goods faced duties of 70-80%. British imports faced duties of 2-4%! As a result, British imports of cotton manufactures into India increased by a factor of 50, and Indian exports dropped to one-fourth! A similar trend was noted in silk goods, woollens, iron, pottery, glassware and paper...millions of ruined artisans and craftsmen, spinners, weavers, potters, smelters and smiths were rendered jobless and had to become landless agricultural workers."

The monopoly on trade in salt and opium was an important mainstay of the Company's finances. Prof. Richards notes that "Together opium and salt produced on average 18.9 percent of gross revenues. In last fifteen years of Company rule their share climbed to 25.1 percent, as opium became one of the most valuable commodities sold in world commerce." Prof. Richards has noted Edmund Burke's report that accompanied the Select Committee of Parliament meetings in 1782-1783 to investigate the Company's affairs. To quote Edmund Burke:

> *"But at, or very soon after, the Acquisition of the Territorial Revenues to the English Company...a very great Revolution took place in Commerce as well as in Dominion;....From that Time Bullion was no longer regularly exported by the English East India Company to Bengal, or any part of Hindustan;.... A new Way of supplying the Market of Europe by means of the British Power and Influence, was invented; a Species of Trade (if such it may be called) by which it is absolutely impossible that India should not be radically and irretrievably ruined...".*

This is how the pernicious system worked: "A certain portion of the revenues of bengal has been for many years set apart, to be employed in the purchase of good for exportation to England,

and this is called the investment, the greatness of this investment has been the standard by which the merit of the Company's principal servants has been generally estimated; and this main cause of the impoverishment of India has generally been taken as a measure of its wealth and prosperity.... This Export from India seemed to imply also a reciprocal Supply, which the trading capital employed in these productions was continually strengthened and enlarged. But the payment of a tribute, and not a beneficial commerce to that country, wore this specious and delusive Appearance."

The Drain of Wealth

However, the high taxes, the heavy burden of state, the neglect of education and public works and unfair trade practices were only the tip of the iceberg. The most damning evidence of British exploitation was the irrefutable "drain of wealth" that took place over the period of two centuries.

Prof. Williamson and Clingingsmith have noted that "between 1772 and 1815 there was a huge net financial transfer from India to Britain in the form of Indian goods. The "drain resulting from contact with the West was the excess of exports from India for which there was no equivalent import" included "a bewildering variety of cotton goods for re-export or domestic [consumption], and the superior grade of saltpeter that gave British cannon an edge"

Javier Cuenca Esteban estimates these net financial transfers from India to Britain reached a peak of £1,014,000 annually in 1784-1792 before declining to £477,000 in 1808-1815." However, even there high figures are significantly lower than the estimates by Prof. John Richards (cited later in this essay).

Like all other commentators, Maddison too has mentioned the debilitating effect of the drain of funds from India: "Another important effect of foreign rule on the long-run growth potential of the economy was the fact that a large part of its potential savings were siphoned abroad. This 'drain' of funds from India to the UK has been a point of major controversy between Indian nationalist historians and defenders of the British Raj. However, the only real grounds for controversy are statistical. There can be no denial that there was a substantial outflow which lasted for 190 years. If these funds had been invested in India they could have made a significant contribution to raising income levels."

The total 'drain' due to government pensions and leave payments, interest on non-railway official debt, private remittances for education and savings, and a third commercial profits amounted to about 1.5 per cent of national income of undivided India from 1921 to 1938 and was probably a little larger before that... about a quarter of Indian savings were transferred out of the economy, and foreign exchange was lost which could have paid for imports of capital goods. Separately, Dadabhai Naoroji estimated the economic costs and drain of resources from India to be at least at 12m per annum. Here is an extract from one of his essays, "The Benefits of British Rule, 1871"

Materially: The political drain, up to this time, from India to England, of above, 500,000,000, at the lowest computation, in principal alone...The further continuation of this drain at the rate, at present, of above, 12,000,000 per annum, with a tendency to increase." Prof. Richards mentions in his research that: "Between 1757 and 1859... ....Officials of the East India Company... tapped the productive people and resources of Bengal and the eastern Gangetic valley to fund the protracted military campaigns necessary to conquer India. Over the same century, these same resources also supplied the wherewithal for a century-long transfer of wealth from India to Great Britain...."

> *"...Burke estimated that in the four years ending in 1780 the investment averaged no less than one million sterling and "commonly Nearer Twelve hundred thousand pounds". This was the value of the goods sent to Europe "for which no Satisfaction is made". The transfer continued without interruption and with formal approval from Parliament."*

3

India's De-industrialisation in the 18th and 19th Centuries

Introduction

The idea that India suffered de-industrialisation during the 19th century has a long pedigree. The image of skilled weavers thrown back on the soil was a powerful metaphor for the economic stagnation Indian nationalists believed was brought on by British rule. However, whether and why de-industrialisation actually happened in India remains open to debate. Quantitative evidence on the overall level of economic activity in 18th and 19th century India is scant, let alone evidence on its breakdown between agriculture, industry, and services. Most of the existing assessments of de-industrialisation rely on very sparse data on employment and output shares. Data on prices are much more plentiful, and this paper offers a new (price dual) assessment of de-industrialisation in 18th and 19th century India supported by newly compiled evidence on relative prices. A simple model of de-industrialisation links relative prices to employment shares. We think the paper sheds new light on whether and when de-industrialisation happened, whether it was more or less dramatic in India than elsewhere, and what its likely causes were.

The existing literature primarily attributes India's de-industrialisation to Britain's productivity gains in textile manufacture and to the world transport revolution. Improved British productivity, first in cottage production and then in factory goods, led to declining world textile prices, making production in India increasingly uneconomic (Roy 2002). These forces were reinforced by declining sea freight rates which served to foster trade and specialisation for both Britain and India. As a result, Britain first won over India's export market and eventually took over its domestic market as well. This explanation for de-industrialisation was a potent weapon in the Indian nationalists' critique of colonial rule (see *e.g.* Dutt 1906/1960, Nehru 1947). The historical literature suggests a second explanation for de-industrialisation in the economic malaise India suffered following the dissolution of Mughal hegemony in the 18th century. We believe the turmoil associated with this political realignment ultimately led to aggregate supply-side problems for Indian manufacturing, even if producers in some regions benefited from the new order.

Like the first, a third explanation for India's de-industrialisation also has its roots in globalisation forces: India's commodity export sector saw its terms of trade relative to textiles improve significantly in the late 18th century and it drew workers away from textiles. We will argue that these explanations are complementary and that each makes a contribution to our overall understanding of India's de-industrialisation experience.

Before proceeding to our argument and evidence, we first offer a precise definition of de-industrialisation and elaborate on its likely causes. We develop some initial intuition using a simple 2-good 3-factor framework. Suppose an economy produces two commodities: agricultural goods, which are exported, and manufactured goods, which are imported.

Suppose it uses three factors of production: labour, which is mobile between the two sectors; land, which is used only in agriculture; and capital, which is used only in manufacturing. Further suppose that this economy is what trade economists call a "small country" that takes its terms of trade as exogenous, dictated by world markets. Given these assumptions, de-industrialisation can be defined as the movement of labour out of manufacturing and into agriculture, either measured in absolute numbers (what we call strong de-industrialisation), or as a share of total employment (what we call weak de-industrialisation). While de-industrialisation is easy enough to define, an assessment of its short and long run impact on living standards and GDP growth is more contentious and hinges on the root causes of de-industrialisation. One possibility is that a country deindustrialises because its comparative advantage in the agricultural export sector has been strengthened by productivity advance on the land at home or by increasing openness in the world economy, or both. Under this scenario, GDP increases in the short-run. If productivity advance on the land is the cause, nothing happens to the terms of trade unless the small country assumption is violated, in which case they deteriorate. If increased openness is the cause, the country enjoys an unambiguous terms of trade improvement as declining world trade barriers raise export prices and lower import prices in the home market. Whether real wages also increase depends on the direction of the terms of trade change and whether the agricultural good dominates workers' budgets. Whether GDP increases in the long run depends on whether industry generates accumulation and productivity externalities that agriculture does not. If industrialisation is a carrier of growth-as most growth theories imply-then de-industrialisation could lead to a growth slowdown and low-income equilibrium that gives the idea of de-industrialisation its power in the historical literature. A second possibility is that a country deindustrialises due to a deterioration in home manufacturing productivity and/or competitiveness. In this case, and still retaining the small country assumption, nothing happens to the terms of trade, but real wages and living standards will deteriorate, and so will GDP. The economic impact of de-industrialisation from this source is unambiguous.

In order to make this theoretical framework flexible enough to handle the causes of de-industrialisation we believe most important, we need to add a non-tradable grain sector. The three sectors considered in the rest of the paper are: agricultural commodity exports, which are tradable on world markets and include industrial intermediates (such as raw cotton and jute) and high-value consumer goods (such as opium and tea); manufacturing, which is primarily textiles and metal products and is also tradable; and grains, which are non-tradable and include rice, wheat and other food staples.

We will build up our account of India's de-industrialisation as follows. In Section 2 we present a theoretical narrative of India's de-industrialisation experience, drawing on evidence from the historical literature. Section 3 reviews existing attempts to measure India's de-industrialisation. We then present a simple general equilibrium model of de-industrialisation in Section 4 to formalize our predictions about relative prices and their relationship to employment shares. Section 5 presents three price series-commodity agricultural exports (pC), manufactured textiles (pT) and non-tradable grains (pG), three intrasectoral terms of trade series-pC/pT, pC/pG and pT/pG, three wage series-the grain wage, the own-wage in the import competing sector, and the own-wage in the export sector, and the external terms of trade. We will then assess this evidence in relation to the theoretical narrative and model, and also compare the relative price experience of India with its primary competitor during this period, England. Section 6 compares India's deindustrialising terms-of-trade shocks with those from other parts of the periphery, and section 7 concludes.

A Narrative Account of India's De-industrialisation

Our narrative account of India's de-industrialisation embraces the three contending de-industrialisation hypothesis, and traces the roots of de-industrialisation well back into the 18th century. Two continent-wide political changes ground our understanding of India's 18th century: The dissolution of the Mughal empire into a constellation of small successor states followed after a time by the initial phase of reintegration of these states under the East India Company. Historians have long thought that India saw an overall economic decline during the 18th century, following the collapse of Mughal authority. This proposition has recently become controversial, and we will stake out our position in favour of it below.

We believe the dissolution of Mughal hegemony affected manufacturing through several channels.

The first was a reduction in overall agricultural productivity. Reduced agricultural productivity would be reflected in an increase of the price of grain, the key non-tradable, and therefore in the relative price of non-tradeables to tradables (such as textiles). To the extent that grain was the dominant consumption good for workers and that the grain wage was close to subsistence, this negative productivity shock should have put upward pressure on the nominal wage in cotton spinning and weaving. Cotton textile wages started from a low nominal but high real base in the mid-18th century (Parthasarathi 1998; Allen 2001). Competitiveness in textile manufacturing is negatively related to the own real wage w/pT, the nominal wage divided by the price of textiles. Declining textile prices and rising nominal wages put downward pressure on "profits" from both below and above. If India experienced it, an increase in the own wage in textiles would have hurt the competitive edge India had relative to its 18th century competitors in third-country export markets, such as the booming Atlantic economy. A decline in 18th century agricultural productivity in India suggests that even before factory-driven technologies appeared between 1780 and 1820, Britain was already beginning to wrest away from India its dominant grip on the world export market for textiles.

We are not the first to exploit the connection between labour productivity in pre-industrial agriculture, nominal wages in manufacturing, and the resulting competitiveness in world markets for manufactures. Alexander Gerschenkron (1962) and W. Arthur Lewis (1978: chp. 2) have both used the argument to good effect in explaining why low productivity in agriculture helps explain the absence or delay of industrial revolutions. More recently, Prasannan Parthasarathi (1998) has argued that while low nominal wages in precolonial and early colonial India gave it the edge in world textile markets, living standards for labour in the south of India were just as high as that in the south of England. Indian productivity was higher in foodgrain production, and thus foodgrain prices were lower.

Historians have traditionally viewed India's 18th century as a dark era of warfare, political chaos, and economic decline sandwiched between stable and prosperous Mughal and British hegemonies. This view has been vigorously challenged by the most recent generation of Indian historians, who have emphasised the continuities between the earlier Mughal and later British states and the constellation of small successor states that emerged with the ebbing of Mughal power (*e.g.* Alam 1986, Bayly 1983, Marshall 1987). The largest of these successor states were the former Mughal provinces of Bengal, Awadh, Benaras, and Hyderabad. There were many smaller ones as well. Their rulers were former provincial governors, Mughal officials, and other men powerful enough to assert de facto sovereignty. They collected the land revenue, sometimes using a modification of the old Mughal system, but submitted less and less of it to Delhi in favour of building up their own armies and courts.

While it has been widely accepted that the successor states provided a greater degree of political continuity and stability than was previously thought to have existed, no consensus has been reached about the implications of this fact for overall course of the continental Indian economy in the 18th century. Marshall (2003) brings together contributions from the contending scholars and provides a useful overview. Where the 18th century economy is concerned, some see the literature on the successor states as a useful corrective but believe the overall picture is one of decline. Others believe the traditional view to be fully overturned and view the 18th century as a period of continued growth, despite the ebbing of Mughal hegemony. Two key differences between these scholars concern first, the implications of the emergence of a new prosperity for the principal towns and middle classes of the successor states and second, the degree of centralisation and stability provided by the Mughal regime before its collapse, and thus the relative effect of the subsequent decentralisation of power.

We tend to agree with the position that sees an aggregate economic decline following the dissolution of a strong empire into contending states. We believe that the more optimistic narrative tends to place too much emphasis on the prosperity of a few areas and groups, such as the towns of the successor states and their middle classes, and too little emphasis on the evidence for decline in the rural areas and peripheries of these states.

Even in an era of aggregate economic decline, we would expect local booms to result from the diversion of land revenue flows from Delhi to the big towns of the successor states, where the new rulers and their revenue farmers lived. Moreover, the rural, agricultural sector was overwhelmingly dominant in the 18th century Indian economy, so it is the course of that sector which largely dictated the course of the overall economy, not what happened in the towns. The optimistic narrative also seems to overly discount the strength of the Mughal empire and the economically favourable stability it brought. The Mughal state shows evidence of having achieved a high level of centralisation and control of revenue sources. Revenue realisation per cultivated acre was as high in remote provinces as in the centre. Examination of the careers of Mughal revenue officials shows that provincial postings were of virtually the same duration (about two and a half years) all over the empire, suggesting that remote provinces were well integrated into the imperial machinery (Habib 2003). There do not appear to have been many Mughal officials who were in reality local potentates. An imperial regime powerful enough to extract 40 percent of the economic surplus from distant provinces must have also insured peace and security, which in turn must have been favourable for agricultural investment and productivity.

Our evidence for an overall 18th century economic decline begins with an examination of unskilled wages in grain units, which are a good measure of the overall level of economic activity in a largely agricultural economy. Figure 1 presents three grain-wage series, two from North India and one from South India, from Radhakamal Mukerjee (1939) and Stephen Broadberry and Bishnupriya Gupta (2005). This figure shows a suggestive long-run decline in grain wages beginning in the last decades of the 17th century and continuing until late in the 18th century. We believe it is important to realize that even though the wage and price data for early modern India is thin, it provides us with one of the few indicators of the condition of ordinary people and the aggregate economy that is easily compared across time. We believe a number of features of the transition of political authority from the Mughal empire to the successor states provide further evidence supporting an overall economic decline, and moreover one that resulted from reduced agricultural productivity. We find Christopher Bayly's view of 18th century north India particularly compelling, as it is shows how urban prosperity coexists with aggregate agricultural decline (Bayly 1983).

As central Mughal authority waned, the state resorted increasingly to revenue farming, and the practice became even more widespread in the successor states. This served to raise the effective rent share to 50 percent or more, greater than the 40 percent maximum said to have been extracted by the Mughal state (Raychaudhuri 1983: 17; Bayly 1983, 10). "With revenue assessment geared to 50 per cent or more, in contrast to China's 5 to 6 per cent, the Indian peasant had little incentive to invest labour or capital" (Raychaudhuri 1983: 17). The economics is familiar to development economists, economic historians, and observers of modern agrarian backwardness: The lower the share of output received by the peasant, the less incentive he has to be productive, to carefully monitor the crop, to invest in land, and to remain in place rather than fleeing. Scattered evidence suggests in some locations the rent burden may have been quite extreme (Bayly 1983, 42). In the Rohilla state north of Delhi, cultivators were stripped of their land rights entirely and reduced to direct dependence. Under the savak system in north Awadh, cultivators received as little as one sixth of the produce and their wives and children were required for corvee for a large part of the year. The Sayyids of Moradabad employed the batai system in which they "appropriated all 'save a bare subsistence' from the cultivators and invaded the villages for several months a year with bullock teams, armed retainers, and weighmen to secure the best portion of the crop." Productivity must have suffered as a result of the increased rent burden. Tapan Raychaudhuri claims the grain prices "increased by 30 percent or more in the 1740s and 1750s" as a result (Raychaudhuri 1983: 6). There is no reason to believe that when the British became rulers of the successor states the revenue burden declined. Initially at least, British revenue officials saw slack in the existing system more often than not, and increased the revenue burden.

Rulers of the successor states also engaged in territorial disputes, and it is possible that the increased rent burden reflected military expenses. These wars drew key resources out of agriculture and also led to the destruction of capital.

> *"Endemic local warfare...and the collapse of local aristocracies had effects which were inimical to agricultural production...Cultivation was driven back from the roads by the passage of marauding armies who sometimes deliberately destroyed walls and irrigation tanks" (Bayly 1983, 70).*

Areas at the edges of successor states were particularly prone to agricultural decline, perhaps because these were the areas most affected by territorial disputes, both between states and between local strongmen, who in remote areas were relatively free to plunder their neighbours. Bayly describes "large penumbras of agricultural decline, particularly in the northwest" (1983, 76). However, Bayly believes that increases in input prices were even more significant than the withdrawal of some areas from cultivation.

> *"More important, warfare withdrew both men and animals from agriculture...Recruitment into armies, the consolidation of population into defensive centres, and general migration...contributed to a patchy and local decline in cultivated area. Draught animals determined the extent of cultivation even more than human labour, and there is scattered evidence of a great dearth of animal power in north central India" (Bayly 1983, 70-1).*

A dearth of animal power would certainly have led to less efficient cultivation techniques and increased prices. Cultivators who relied on the bullocks owned by others would have been particularly vulnerable to fluctuations in their availability due to warfare. To cite an example, when Ahmed Shah Durrani invaded India from the northwest in 1759, bullock hire rates between Benares and Patna, a route nearly 600 km from the furthest extent of the fighting, increased by 500 percent (Bayly 1983, 68). This suggests the agricultural economy was operating on very inelastic regions of the supply and/or demand curves for these key inputs, which is suggestive of a shortage. Political fragmentation and warfare also disrupted India's major internal trade routes, and likely increased transport costs and insurance. Since most long distance transport was by bullock, the scarcity of bullock power resulting from warfare would have increased transport costs. Irfan Habib (2003) also presents fragmentary evidence that insurance rates may have gone up during the 18th century. We therefore find Holwell's claim that the dissolution of the Mughal empire led to "a scarcity of grains in all parts, [and] the wages of labour [were] greatly enhanced" as credible, even if other aspects of the traditional view of 18th century India have been discredited (Holwell 1766-1767, cited in Raychaudhuri 1983: 6). This presumed rise in nominal wages would have slowly eroded the long-standing source of Indian 17th and 18th century competitiveness in foreign textile markets, long before Britain flooded those markets with factory-made products, and declining agricultural productivity in India must have been at the heart of it. After 1800, Indian "textile exports ... could not withstand the competition of English factory-produced cottons in the world market" (Moosvi 2002: 341).

Even if we had good data on Indian employment and output in the 18th century, de-industrialisation effects could be hard to see because between 1772 and 1815 there was a huge net financial transfer from India to Britain in the form of Indian goods. The "drain resulting from contact with the West was the excess of exports from India for which there was no equivalent import" (Furber 1948: 304), including "a bewildering variety of cotton goods for re-export or domestic [consumption], and the superior grade of saltpeter that gave British cannon an edge" (Cuenca Esteban 2001: 65). Indian textiles were at this time an important vehicle by which Britons repatriated wealth accumulated in India to England, increasing demand for them. Javier Cuenca Esteban estimates these net financial transfers from India to Britain reached a peak of £1,014,000 annually in 1784-1792 before declining to £477,000 in 1808-1815 and-£77,000 in 1816-1820 (Cuenca Esteban 2001: Table 1, line 20).

However, at their peak in 1784-1792, these net Indian transfers still amounted to less than 2 percent of British industrial output (Deane and Cole 1967: Table 37, 166, using 1801 "manufacture, mining, building"). As a share of Indian industrial output, these net transfers were probably about the same. Thus, while a secular fall in the "drain" after the 1784-1792 peak must have served to speed up the pace of de-industrialisation in early 19th century India by reducing demand for Indian textiles, the effect could not have been big. There must have been other fundamentals at work that mattered far more. Around the beginning of the 19th century, the fundamental economic dynamic underlying de-industrialisation in India changed from agricultural productivity decline taking place at home to globalisation shocks induced by events abroad. Globalisation is the most popular explanation for India's de-industrialisation in the literature, and is an important component of the historiography of colonial India constructed by the Indian nationalists. For example, Jawaharlal Nehru's classic Discovery of India (1947) argued that India became progressively ruralised in the 19th century owing to the destruction of artisanal employment by British factory-made goods. Nehru laid the blame squarely on colonial economic policy, which almost entirely eschewed tariff protection and did nothing to help nurture Indian industry (Nehru 1947: 247-53). Similar arguments can be found in the work of the 19th century nationalist Dadabhai Naoroji, the pioneering Indian economic historian R.C. Dutt, and the Marxist historian D.D. Kosambi. The economic logic underlying the de-industrialisation-through-globalisation hypothesis is that rapid productivity advance in European manufacturing-led by Britain-lowered the relative price of textiles, metal products and other manufactures in world markets. The European industrial leaders shared those productivity gains with the rest of the world as augmented world supplies of manufactures lowered world prices. Having defeated India in its export markets, "after 1813 Lancashire invaded India as well" (Moosvi 2002: 341). Cheap British factorymade yarn and cloth took away India's local market from her own producers. India experienced de-industrialisation over the half century following 1810 due to terms-of-trade shocks in its favour. The relative price impact of the unbalanced productivity performance is best illustrated by trends in Britain's terms of trade.

According to Albert Imlah, they fell by 40 percent over the four decades between 1801-1810 and 1841-1850 (Mitchell and Deane 1962: 331). That is, the price of British exports (manufactures) fell dramatically compared with that of its imports (industrial intermediates, food and other primary products). India's textile producers-already well integrated into the world textile market-faced a big negative price shock on that score alone. Failing to keep up with the factory-based productivity growth achieved abroad, the Indian textile industry took the price hit, became less profitable, and de-industrialisation ensued. As if this were not enough, the foreign-productivity-induced negative price shock was reinforced by another powerful global event. Trade barriers between India and her foreign markets declined, particularly due to the transport revolution (Shah Mohammed and Williamson 2004) but also due to tariff policy. The relative supply price of manufactures in India was driven down still further, and it was driven down even more compared with Indian exports, since overseas transport improvements served to raise export prices in the home market. These world market integration trends served to create "Dutch disease" effects in India: The import-competing sectors slumped, the export sectors boomed, and de-industrialisation was reinforced. The decline in world textile prices caused by British productivity advance made textile production in India less attractive relative to Britain. It also contributed to a shift in the terms of trade between India's own textiles and agricultural commodity export sectors, a shift reinforced by booming world demand for Indian agricultural commodities. This shift alone would have caused a decline in the relative employment in textiles. The most important agricultural commodities for India in the first half of the 19th century were opium, raw cotton, raw silk, and sugar, and they were a growing fraction of India's exports. By 1811, they accounted for 57 percent of India's exports by value compared to 33 percent for cotton piecegoods (Chaudhuri 1983). The role played by the terms of trade in reallocating resources to commodity agriculture is noted in the literature on the commercialisation of Bengali agriculture in the late 18th century (Chowdhury 1964), but it has not yet been a part of the de-industrialisation debate.

In sum, our view is that the long run sources of India's de-industrialisation were both the globalisation price shocks due to European productivity advance in manufacturing (and the induced demand for industrial intermediates such as cotton and indigo) plus the negative productivity shocks to Indian agriculture induced by the earlier Mughal decline. We do not see these foreign and domestic effects as competing. They were both at work, and they reinforced each other, although each had its most important influence in different epochs.

Measuring India's De-industrialisation

Inputs, Outputs, and De-industrialisation

Despite its importance for Indian historiography, there have been only four attempts to measure India's 19th century de-industrialisation experience owing to the dearth of statistical sources. We believe we are the first to apply relative price evidence to the de-industrialisation question, and by doing so the first to offer evidence, tentative though it may be, about de-industrialisation in the 18th century. Tirthankar Roy (2000) offers a useful survey of the existing evidence, starting with this big fact: It seems likely that the share of the work force engaged in industry was quite a bit higher in 1800 (probably 15-18 percent) than it was in 1900 (about 10 percent). In the strictest sense, therefore, strong de-industrialisation appears to have taken place over the 19th century. However, the literature insists on some qualifications to this big de-industrialisation fact. First, many workers who gave up industry over the century were working only part-time. Second, the import of machine-made goods only helps explain the demise of textiles. Third, while there was a fall in textile employment, there was a rise in employment in indigo, opium, and saltpeter. Finally, cheaper imported cloth would have benefited consumers. All of these qualifications make good sense.

The first evidence supporting strong de-industrialisation was offered more than a half century ago by Colin Clark (1950). Clark published tabulations of the 1881 and 1911 Census of India showing that the share of the Indian workforce in manufacturing, mining, and construction declined from 28.4 to 12.4 percent from 1881 to 1911, implying dramatic de-industrialisation in the late 19th century. Daniel Thorner (1962) reexamined the Census data and convincingly argued that the tabulations used by Clark were misleading. His revised estimates show that the sectoral employment structure was stationary after 1901, with only a very small decline in male non-agricultural employment between 1881 and 1901. Thorner used these revisions to convincingly make two important points: first, if there was a major shift out of industry and into agriculture, it occurred before 1881, not after; and second, if de-industrialisation occurred after 1881, it was on a very modest scale, and all of it took place before 1901.

Peter Harnetty would appear to agree, although he was speaking of the Central Provinces in the 1860s, after our century of interest starting roughly with 1750. Harnetty says (1991: 460): "The combination of high food prices and cheap cloth imports had a depressing effect on the local industry."

The literature also argues that cheaper imported yarn would have reduced the production costs facing handloom weavers, thus making them more competitive. Since cheaper European factory-produced yarn would have lowered the production costs not just for Indian handloom weavers but for weavers the world around, it is not clear how this made Indian weavers more competitive with imported cloth. The third attempt to measure de-industrialisation looks to the early 19th century, closer to the years which anecdotal evidence has always suggested were those of most dramatic de-industrialisation. Amiya Bagchi (1976a, 1976b) examined evidence on handloom spinning and other traditional industry in Gangetic Bihar, an area of eastern India, collected between 1809 and 1813 by the East India Company surveyor Dr. Francis Buchanan Hamilton. Bagchi compared Hamilton's data with the 1901 Census estimates of the population dependent on industry for the same area. His findings are presented in Table 1. The population dependent on industrial employment requires an estimate of family size, and Bagchi makes two estimates using altenative assumptions. Under Assumption A, each spinner supports only him or herself, and under Assumption B, each spinner also supports one other person. Under both assumptions, non-spinners are assumed to support the survey's modal family size (five). He also removes commercial workers from the 1901 data to make them consistent with the 1809-13 data. Spinners in Gangetic Bihar were almost exclusively women who spun in the afternoons (Dutt 1960: 232-5). Hamilton's estimates show that women earned about Rs. 3.25 annually at spinning, while a male day labourer who worked 200 days would earn about Rs. 8 annually, all of which suggests that Assumption B is more likely to be true. In either case, Bagchi's evidence suggests a substantial decline in the industrial employment share during the 19th century from more than 21 percent to less than 9 percent. When the Bagchi and Thorner evidence is combined, it suggests that most of the de-industrialisation took place in the first half of the century.

While the employment share in "other industrial" occupations fell over the century as well, it is important to note that the largest component of de-industrialisation was the decline of cotton spinning. Table 2 rearranges Bagchi's original numbers, making the contribution of cotton spinning to overall de-industrialisation more transparent. Of the 12.7 percent of the population that depended on cotton weaving and spinning in 1809-1813, more than 80 percent depended on spinning. Since cotton spinning was performed part-time by women at home using extremely simple technology, it may seem implausible to argue that the demise of cotton spinning in the early 19th century destroyed India's platform for modern industrialisation. Yet British economic historians assign the same importance to home-based cotton spinning: 17th and 18th century "proto-industrial" cottage industries are said to have supplied the platform for the factory-based British industrial revolution that followed in the late 18th century (Mokyr 1993: chps. 1-3). Furthermore, employment of women and children was central to the process then too (Mokyr 1993: chp. 1; De Vries 1994).

Finally, in an unpublished study reported by Habib (1985), Amalendu Guha calculated the amount of cotton yarn available for Indian handloom production by subtracting the quantity used in local machine production from total local yarn production and imports. The result documents a huge decline in yarn used for handloom production, from 419 million pounds in 1850, to 240 in 1870 and to 221 in 1900. This indirect evidence suggests that the decline in hand spinning documented for Gangetic Bihar in the early 19th century was widespread, that it was followed by a decline in hand weaving during the mid-century, and that the decline of both hand spinning and weaving was almost complete by 1870. These facts are consistent with Peter Harnetty's summary characterisation of Indian handloom weaving in the 19th century:

> *"At the opening of the century, the handloom weavers had supplied all the textile requirements of the country and had maintained a flourishing export trade, notably to Britain [e.g. re-exports]. This reached its peak in value in 1800 and in volume in 1802, thereafter, imports of Indian piece goods to Britain declined sharply in face of competition from the growing British cotton industry." "From about 1840 ... British imports entered the [local] market in strength." "At the turn of the [20th] century, India was absorbing more than 40 per cent of total British cloth exports to the world" (Harnetty 1991: 472).*

As we have argued, the trouble actually started over the half century before the 1800 peak with Britain's challenge to India's dominant presence in foreign markets.

In 1982, Paul Bairoch used evidence similar to that reviewed above to assess de-industrialisation not only in India, but across the non-European periphery. Table 3 reports Bairoch's survey as it was retold by Colin Simmons (1985). In 1750, China and India together accounted for almost 57 percent of world manufacturing output, while India itself accounted for almost a quarter. By 1800, India's world share had already eroded to less than a fifth, by 1860 to less than a tenth, and by 1880 to less than 3 percent. Bairoch's investigation found that India's share in world manufacturing output declined precipitously in the half century 1750-1800, before factory-led industrialisation took hold in Britain and consistent with our hypothesis the de-industrialisation took place in the 18th century.

Furthermore, India's experience was different than that of China or the rest of the periphery. Between 1750 and 1830 India's world manufacturing output share dropped by 6.9 percentage points from a base of 24.5 percent, much bigger than the fall elsewhere (China lost 3 percentage points, and the rest of the periphery lost 2.6 percentage points). Bairoch's data suggest that during the century before 1830, well before European factories flooded world markets with manufactures, India suffered much more pronounced de-industrialisation than did the rest of the periphery. This fact must be explained by conditions faced by India and not by the rest of the periphery, fully consistent with our agricultural productivity hypothesis.

World output shares can also change due to different rates of output growth across countries. The economic implications of faster growth abroad are much more benign than those of slow growth at home. Anticipating this criticism, Bairoch (1982: Tables 6 and 9) also documented that per capita levels of industrialisation in India fell from an index of 7 in 1750 to 6 in 1830 and 2 in 1880. Since India's export share of total manufacturing output was small in 1750, the loss of its export trade does not show up as dramatic de-industrialisation 1750-1830, but when Europe penetrates local markets after 1830, it certainly does.

In addition, the loss of export trade is hidden by that second event: the declining long run fundamentals are obscured by the short run financial "drain" which increased the demand for Indian textiles, facilitating the real transfer of wealth from India to Britain.

Real Wages and De-industrialisation

Models of de-industrialisation such as that of Paul Krugman and Anthony Venables (1995) suggest that it should be accompanied by a long run decline in real wages. The evidence for 18th and 19th century India is not yet of high quality, but it does document a secular deterioration.

Parthasarathi (1998) argues that real wages in mid-late 18th century South India were comparable to those in the south of England, and thus that the rising living standard gap between the two was a late 18th and early 19th century phenomenon. Robert Allen (2001) uses Mughal manuscript sources to compute the real wage in 1595 Agra, then the capital of the Mughal empire, and compares it to that of 1961, based on a common market basket of consumer goods. Allen's evidence documents a fall in the real wage by about 23 percent over those 366 years, and if Parthasarathi is correct, most of that fall must have taken place in the last 166 years.

Anthropometric evidence on south Indian indentured workers confirms the view that living standards stagnated during the last half of the 19th century (Brannan et al. 1994). But perhaps the most telling evidence of real wage performance, and its timing, comes from Mukerjee (1939) and Broadberry and Gupta (2005), reproduced in Figure 1. Mukerjee reports 1600-1938 real wages in northern India of unskilled and skilled labour (nominal wage rates deflated by grain prices) starting with the same 1595 benchmark used by Allen. Broadberry and Gupta offer grain wages for both north and south India, with the most resolution in the 17th and 18th centuries. According to this evidence, by 1789 real wages had fallen 30-44 percent from their 1600 level. By 1875, real wages are at only 25-50 percent of the 1600 level.

This evidence suggests that the vast majority of the real wage and living standards fall took place before 1850, or even before 1825, not after. Was de-industrialisation responsible for the fall, and were the de-industrialisation forces more powerful before 1850, or even before 1807, than after? The sparse data on employment and output shares suggests de-industrialisation was an important force in the Indian economy during the 19th century. This account can be supplemented and pushed back into the 18th century with (relatively) much richer relative price data, but before doing so we need to model the relationship between relative prices and de-industrialisation.

The Terms of Trade, Relative Prices, and the Own-Wage in Manufactures 1750-1913

We divide the Indian de-industrialisation experience over the century and a half between about 1750 and 1913 into three distinct epochs. Our interpretation of the fundamentals explaining de-industrialisation within each of these epochs implies predictions regarding changes in Indian relative prices.

The first epoch, approximately 1750-1810, was one during which India lost its significant share of world textile markets to Britain. What was an important export sector in India at the beginning of the epoch became an important import-competing sector at the end. While that result can be explained by increasing cost competitiveness favouring Britain, superior factory technology was not yet the main force at work. Instead, we believe that it was reduced agricultural productivity in India that mattered in this epoch. Grain prices rose and thus-in a relatively stable real wage subsistence economy where grain was the key consumption good-pushed up nominal wages economy-wide. Hence, the own wage rose in both tradable sectors, textiles and commodity production, damaging cost competitiveness there. Textiles would thus experience strong de-industrialisation. To the extent that the price of textiles relative to commodities fell, the effect of reduced agricultural productivity would have fallen more heavily on textiles than commodities, a weak de-industrialisation effect.

The second epoch, approximately 1810-1860, was one during which India lost much of its domestic textile market to Britain. This result can be explained by the combined influence of relatively rapid factorybased productivity advance in Britain and by increased world market integration, the latter driven by declining transport costs between the two trading partners, and to a free trade commitment for India on the part of her colonial rulers. The terms of trade moved to favour India and hurt her import competing manufacturing sector. The effects of the economic difficulties of the 18th century were pretty much over, and the induced decline in Indian grain productivity had ceased.

The third epoch, approximately 1860-1913, was one during which the rate of de-industrialisation slowed down and eventually reversed. Late in the epoch, India was "re-industrialising." This result can be explained by the subsidence in both the unbalanced productivity advance favouring European manufacturing and in the world transport revolution. The terms of trade no longer moved in India's favour and thus no longer served to penalize import competing manufacturing.

These predictions are largely confirmed by our new relative price and terms-of-trade evidence, which we plot in Figures 2-6. A full description of how we constructed the data can be found in the Appendix. The analysis which follows will focus on the first two epochs, when de-industrialisation was dramatic. Let us first consider strong de-industrialisation across the first two epochs combined, recalling that strong de-industrialisation is defined as an absolute decline in the industrial workforce, driven in our model by the own wage. Figure 2 documents that between 1765 and 1810 the price of textiles relative to grains fell at a spectacular rate: by 1805-1810, it was only 25 percent of its 1765-1770 level. The decline continued after 1810, but at a much slower rate. Why the spectacular fall in pT/pG in the late 18th century, especially compared with the early 19th century? The answer is that grain prices, while volatile in the short run, soared upwards in the long run. However, this did not serve to reduce real wages (w/pG). Figure 1 shows that grain wages appear to have been largely stable during the last half of the 18th century. Figure 3 presents the grain wage using an alternative series of grain prices and confirms this claim for roughly the same years, between the 1720s and the 1810s. Nominal wages were thus driven up along with grain prices.

While there was great short-run volatility in the grain wage, a Lewis-like assumption about long run real wage stability seems to be reasonable for the first epoch. As a result, the own-wage in Indian manufacturing (Figure 4: w/pT) more than doubled between 1765 and 1810. Since there is no qualitative evidence suggesting significant productivity advance in Indian textiles and other manufacturing production during this epoch, we take this evidence as powerful support for the thesis that reduced agricultural productivity attendant on the dissolution of Mughal hegemony can indeed explain much of India's pre 1810 de-industrialisation and loss of world markets. India lost much of its cost competitiveness as the own-wage in home manufacturing underwent that spectacular rise, and it was the rise in the price of non-tradable grains that pushed the nominal wage up to such high levels. Most of the secular rise in grain prices stopped after around 1810, and the upward pressure on nominal wages began to ease. Thus, conditions in the grain sector stabilised a bit in the second epoch, and the fall in pT dominated de-industrialisation conditions in Indian manufacturing. The relative price pT/pG fell (Figure 2), the own-wage w/pT rose (Figure 4), and de-industrialisation continued-but now driven mainly by exogenous world market forces.

Now let us consider weak de-industrialisation across the first two epochs, recalling that it will be more intense when the own-wage in textiles is growing faster and when the intersectoral terms of trade is shifting most strongly in favour of agricultural commodities. Figure 4 shows w/pT doubling between 1770 and 1810 and more than doubling between 1810 and 1850. Thus, own-wage growth was slightly stronger in the second epoch. Conversely, the terms of trade shift appears to be strongest in the first epoch. Figure 6 documents India's external terms of trade from 1800. It shows two big spikes in the second epoch, the first over the decade of the 1810s and the second over the decade of the 1850s. When the series is smoothed, the measured trend in the terms of trade favouring India (and thus penalising the import competing sector) is very modest. In contrast, during the first epoch the intersectoral terms of trade between textiles and agricultural commodities (Figure 2: pT/pC) underwent a very sharp decline. By 1810 it was only 20 percent of its 1780 level, causing lost agricultural productivity to fall much more heavily on textiles than on agricultural commodities during that period. Indeed, the own wage in agricultural commodities actually fell during this period (Figure 4: w/pC). This pattern suggests that strong de-industrialisation may well have been greater in the first epoch than in the second. In the first epoch, labour left textiles due to labour's demand for nominal higher wages and to a strong shift in the terms of trade favouring agricultural commodity exports and disfavouring textiles, while in the second epoch labour left mainly due to falling world textile prices.

If we take the own-wage in manufacturing as a critical indicator of cost competitiveness, and if England was India's main competitor in world markets, we can compare trends in the own-wage in textiles between the two as an indicator of relative productivity change. We must be cautious here, since a measured increase in the ratio of Indian to English w/pT will understate the role of own-wage inflation to the extent that English productivity growth performance was superior to India even before the great factory boom. Our source for England is Gregory Clark (2004: Table 6 for nominal wages; Table 4 for grain and clothing prices), whose data allow us to construct the price of clothing relative the grain (pT/pG) 1705-1845 and the own-wage in textiles (w/pT). Figure 5a plots an index of the ratio of English pT/pG to Indian pT/pG.

The Indian series uses five-year averages due to the volatility of pG in India, and thus starts in 1770, the end of the first half-decade for which we have data. The price of textiles relative to grains fell in both economies 1765-1845, but it fell five times faster in India due to the much bigger pG boom there. The index of British relative to Indian pT/pG rose from 100 in 1775 to 172 by 1810, and again to 313 by 1845. Grain prices rose almost four times faster in India than England, an event which we argue put greater upward pressure on wage costs in India than England, thus lowering the English own-wage in textiles relative to India.

Indeed, the ratio of w/pT in England relative to India fell from 100 in 1775, to 55 in 1815, and to 23 in 1845, as shown in Figure 5b. More than half of that century fall was completed by 1805, before the great flood of factory-produced textiles hit Indian markets in the second de-industrialisation epoch. But even after 1810, it appears that some part of Indian de-industrialisation was explained by poor productivity performance in grains: after all, pT was pretty much equalised between India and Britain, so the faster decline in India's pT/pG implies a poorer productivity performance in grains there, and perhaps even compared with the rest of the periphery. If we had Indian data for 1705-1765, we think it would extend these trends backwards. After all, the English pT/pG declined only modestly between 1705 and 1765,21 and w/pT hardly changed at all. Our guess is that pT/pG fell sharply in India given that pG about doubled between 1704-1706 and 1764-1766. This added evidence seems to point to reduced agricultural productivity with roots in the decline of the Mughal empire as the central cause of Indian de-industrialisation in the 18th and even in the early 19th century.

Indian Relative Price Trends Compared with the Rest of the Periphery

De-industrialisation appeared everywhere around the 19th century periphery, and globalisation plays a major role in each region's economic history narrative. Here we ask whether 19th century India faced a big or a small deindustrialising global price shock compared with other parts of the periphery. If India's global price shock was small, it follows that domestic supply-side de-industrialisation forces were relatively important in India compared to other parts of the periphery.

Figure 6 shows that India underwent a significant improvement in its terms of trade from 1800 to the mid-1820s, followed by a collapse, and then a significant rise again up to the early 1860s. Over the half century between 1800-1804 and 1855-1859, India's terms of trade rose only 28.6 percent, or less than 0.5 percent per annum. In contrast, the Egyptian terms of trade rose by two and a half times between 1820-1824 and 1855-1859, or 2.7 percent per annum (Figure 7); the Ottoman terms of trade increased by two and a half times between 1815-1819 and 1855-1859, or 2.4 percent per annum (Figure 8); and the Latin American terms of trade increased by 1.7 times between 1820-1824 and 1855-1859, or 1.7 percent per annum (Figure 9).

In short, it appears external price shocks facing India were quite modest compared to the rest of the periphery. Yet, Indian historians discuss de-industrialisation more than do historians of other poor periphery regions. This suggests that domestic supply side conditions played a far more important role in accounting for de-industrialisation in India than elsewhere.

Conclusions

India deindustrialised between 1750 and 1860, and two main epochs, with very different de-industrialisation causes, distinguish that century. The first epoch runs from about 1750 to 1810 and was an indirect result of the dissolution of the Mughal empire. As central authority waned, revenue farming expanded, the rent burden increased, warfare raised the price of agricultural inputs, and regional trade within the sub-continent declined, all serving to drive down the productivity of foodgrain agriculture. Grain prices rose, and given that ordinary workers lived near subsistence, the nominal wage rose as well.

As a consequence, the ownwage in Indian textile manufactures increased, hurting India's competitiveness in the export market. India thus lost ground to Britain in the world textile market during a period when most British production was still carried 22 Terms of trade increases up to the 1860s were also much bigger for Indonesia, Italy and Spain. In addition, after the 1840s their increase was much bigger for Japan and the Mideast (Williamson 2005).

Additionally, the intersectoral terms of trade moved against textiles, encouraging a shift to agricultural commodity production. India's share of world industrial production fell faster than in any other part of the non-European world. During the second epoch, running from roughly 1810 to 1860, productivity advance resulting from the adoption of the factory system drove down the relative price of textiles world-wide, a trend that was magnified in India as a world transport revolution lowered the price of textiles even further everywhere in the periphery.

Thus, while the productivity of Indian agriculture stopped its decline during this period under the relative security of Company rule, and while the rise in grain prices slowed down and then stabilised, the relative price of grain continued to rise. By 1860, India had completed a century-long two-part transition from being a net exporter to a net importer of textiles. A secular rise in the terms of trade stopped, turned around, and started a long run fall that lasted until the late 1930s. A deterioration in the terms of trade meant that the import competing sector (textiles) was no longer being penalised by unfavourable external price shocks. By the late 19th century, India's de-industrialisation was over, and the country began a period of slow re-industrialisation.

The Colonial Exploitation of the Indian Economy

There was a considerable amount of debate generated after Manmohan Singh's speech at Oxford where he spoke about the good governance aspect of the British Empire. Well, Mr. Singh seemed to have ignored the fact that during the British Rule, the Indian economy was totally made subservient to the colonial interests. This has been analysed by R.P.Dutt and many others, here I am presenting the broad classification done by R.P.Dutt about the plunder of the Indian economy carried out by the Britishers.

The Three Phases of Economic Exploitation of the Indian economy under the British rule were first analysed by R.P. Dutt in his work India Today which is considered as one of the best analysis Indian colonial economy. The Three Phases were as follows:

The Mercantilist Phase (1757 to the end of 18th century)

With the victory in the Battle of Plassey began the phase of the Company's trade-cum-plunder of Bengal. Post 1757, East India Company did not remain merely a trading company, henceforth it played it played the role of commercial-cum-military-cum-political body in Bengal.

This phase marked the beginning of the economic plunder of India, it took place in three main forms:

- o Profits from the oppressive land revenue policy
- o Profits from monopolistic trade
- o Exactions made by the Company officials (R.C.Dutt estimates it to be £6 million between 1757-65)

The Company monopolised the raw material needed by the artisans and charged a high price for them. They also dictated the prices of finished products.

The ruin caused by the East India Company Rule can be seen from the fact that during the great Famine of 1770-72 the tax collections rose as nearly 10 million people died in that period.

This phase also marked the beginning of the 'Drain of Wealth' from India to England which continued in various forms through all the three phases till 1947. The focal point of the Drain Theory was that a portion of the national product of India was not available for consumption of her people or for capital formation, but was being drained away to England. The drain of wealth took place through various forms, main among them were: (1) Home Charges: These refer to the expenditure incurred in England by the Secretary of the State on behalf of India. Post 1857 this charge constituted 24% of total revenue of India, (2) Civil and Military charges, (3) Interest on Foreign Capital Investments (especially during the

20th century). Dadabhai Nawroji in 1897 estimated the total drain of wealth from 1883-92 at Rs.30 to 40 crore per annum; Prof. C.N. Vakil estimates the drain of Rs.591 million from 1834 to 1924.

Period of Industrial Capital (developed during the 19th century)

With the advent of Industrial Revolution in England, its expanding textile industries needed raw material and markets for the finished goods. These developments also changed the character of the British colonial exploitation of India; and the mercantilist phase was replaced by the period of industrial capitalism.

India was reduced to a mere status of supplier of raw materials. This period was also marked by total ruin of artisans and massive de-industrialisation. With de-industrialisation, Indian economy tended to become more and more agricultural.

Millions of workers in industrial towns like Dhaka, Murshidabad, Surat etc. were rendered jobless and turned towards agriculture. This led to increase in the number of landless and the subsequent impoverishment of the agricultural sector. The 'stagnation' of agriculture amidst increasing population accounted for recurring famines and increasing poverty in the 19th and first quarter of the 20th century. Further on the commercialisation of agriculture caused by the British policies spelled doom for the cultivators.The ruin of Indian agriculture becomes evident from the fact that from last decade of the 19th century and the middle of the twentieth, when food production in India declined by 7 per cent, that of commercial crops increased by 85 per cent. This period was also marked by recurring and widespread famines. (Kurien C.T., Global Capitalism and India)

Finance Capitalism (from closing decade of 19th century to 1947)

The flow of British capital into India became significant only after 1857, penetrated into diverse economic fields in the latter half of the 19th century but tightened its tentacles over India in the 20th century in the form of finance capital. Finance capitalism now became the most powerful mode of colonial exploitation. The British capital investment took place in two main forms:

- o Loans raised by the Secretary of State in England on behalf of the Indian Government and by semi-public organisations for investment in railways, irrigation etc.
- o Foreign business investment in India.

By 1914, nearly 97% of British investment in India was meant for completion of economic overheads-mainly railways, roads, mining industry and development of financial institutions-all aimed at fuller exploitation of India's resources. The British capitalist retained dominant control over Indian banking and commerce. According to an estimate, in 1913 foreign banks held over 3/4th of total deposits in the Indian Banks. Moreover Indian businessmen were severely discriminated in terms of availing loans from the banks. The British control over the decisive sectors of the economy inhibited indigenous capitalist growth. Thus by the time British left India they left behind a legacy of poverty, devastated agricultural and industrial sector and a stunted growth. The three phases of colonial exploitation through their operation left Indian economy in a state of chronic underdevelopment.

Redesigning Constructive Agro-economic Structure in Transitional Economy

Although agriculture is the backbone of India, but at the same time, the popular belief that India had never been an industrial country is incorrect. Indian Industries also enjoyed a worldwide reputation since ancient time. A wave of industrialisation came into the country's economy in pre and posts independence period, which dismantling the agro economy of India and ultimately disturb the economic balance of the country. Being the largest industry in the country, agriculture is a source of livelihood for over 70% of population in the country, and despite the concerted industrialisation in last four-decades, agriculture occupies a place of pride. Agriculture is most vital sector of economy because:

1. Contribute 32% of the national income *i.e.* 1/3rd of national income only by agricultural sector. (Refer to Table 1)
2. Provide massive employment opportunity to working population
3. Agriculture is much important for industrial development (as it is supplier of raw material to many industries)

4. Playing important role in international trade by exporting, tea, sugar, oil seed, tobacco, spices etc.
5. Agriculture is the main support for India's transport system, since railways and roadways secure bulk of their business from movement of agriculture goods. The failure of agriculture front that has led to failure of economic planning.

Table 1: Sectoral Distribution in GDP (at 1980-81 Price)

Sector	1951-52 to 1955-56	1956-57 to 1960-61	1961-62 to 1965-66	1966-67 to 1970-71	1971-72 to 1975-76	1976-77 to 1980-81	1981-82 to 1985-86	1985-86 to 1989-90
Agriculture	54.91	51.86	46.61	43.76	42.04	38.75	36.48	32.82
Mining	1.15	1.18	1.39	1.45	1.38	1.46	1.69	1.76
Manufacturing	11.86	1.347	15.77	16.17	16.95	18.02	18.85	20.00
Elct., gas & water	0.38	0.53	0.79	1.11	1.33	1.62	1.84	2.14

The significance of agriculture is India arises also from the fact that the development in agriculture is a pre-requisite for the development of the national economy. In other words, general economic development will require agriculture development either to proceed, or to go hand in hand with it, so there is a necessity of redesigning the agro-economic structure in a constructive manner under transitional economy.

Methodology: For Redesigning a constructive agro-economy structure, a study of Indian economy had been conducted under the following heads:

1. Impact of British activities on agro economy and Indian economy (prior to 1950):

   A detailed study had been conducted on the Indian economy during British period and inference will be made about the impact of British activities on the agro economy and Indian economy.

2. Impact of different five year development plan during the 4 decade (1950-51 to 1990-91) of pre transitional economy:

   Data had been collected for first to 7th five year plan regarding the capital outlay for different sectors, specially agriculture, growth rate, etc. and achievement was studied. The cause of success and failure of development plan was studied on the basis of analysis of data.

3. Impact of green revolution on agro-economy of India:

   The four decade period between post independence and pre transition period (1950-51 to 1990-91) is divided into two period *i.e.,* (a) pre green revolution period (1950-65) (b) post green revolution period (1968-91)

   A detailed study was conducted on the impact of green revolution on agro-economy of India by analysing the improvement in food grain production, agricultural technology, vegetable and oil seed production, use of agricultural inputs like fertilizer, pesticides and HYV seeds etc.

4. Impact of decade reforms on agro-economy in transitional economy (1990-91 to 2000):

   In 1991-91, India was suffering from BOP crisis and inflation rate was high. Economic reforms was introduced in 1990-91. A detailed study was conducted on impact of these reforms on agro-economy in transitional economy.

5. Redesigning of agro-economy:

   On the basis of the detailed study of Indian economy including agro-economy in different period a redesigning of agro-economy structure was suggested in constructive manner.

Results:

1. Impact of British activities on agro-economy and Indian economy (prior to 1950):

   The Indian economy in the pre British period consisted of isolated and self-sustaining village on one hand, and town which were the seats of administration, commerce and handicraft on other hand. The British conquest led to the disintegration of the village community partly by the introduction of new land revenue system and partly by the process of commercialisation of agriculture. This commercialisation of Indian agriculture produced very adverse economic consequences on Indian economy. These influence retarded the process of industrialisation of India economy, created "built in depressor" in agriculture and were responsible for the occurrence of famines in India. In 1947, when the British transferred power to India, we inherited a crippled economy with a stagnate agriculture and peasantry steeped in poverty.

2. Impact of different five year development plan during the 4 decade (1950-51 to 1990-91) pre transitional economy:

   In 1947, the planners of India had their own difficulties. India needed industry as well as agriculture for development of Indian economy. At the initiation of first plan (1951-56) India had also to correct the inequlibrium in the economy caused by the second world war and the partition of the country. During first plan the emphasis was given to the agriculture to attain the self-sufficiency in food and agriculture target set in the first plan had been achieved.

In the second plan, the emphasis was given on industrial development. Mahatma Gandhi's fears about the effect of large-scale industrialisation have unfortunately proved correct. The performance of second plan is not satisfactory due to ignorance of agriculture sector.

The experience of first two plans suggested that agriculture should be assigned top priority. The third plan accordingly gave top priority to agriculture, but it also laid adequate emphasis on the development of basic industries also.

The sixth plan was launched at a time when the Indian economy was passing through a difficult period-the severe drought of 1979-80 and high rate of inflation. The sixth plan was successful in achieving the original target growth rate of 5.2%. This rate could be achieved mainly because of good agricultural performance (3.8% growth rate) and rapid rate of growth in the service sector (5.5% growth rate). The industrial sector performed poorly during sixth plan and actual rate of growth in this sector was about half of what was originally targeted.

In the 7th Plan (1985-90) per capita NNP grew on an average, at the rate of 3.5% per annum.

The growth rate of agricultural sector was 5.6% and agriculture achieved the growth rate of 3.0%. During 7th plan the target of industrial production was fulfilled.

There was shortfall in wheat and pulse production and overall target of food production (175 million) could not be achieved due to shortfall in the fulfilment of targets of irrigation and target of 70 million hectares, to be covered under HYV is not achieved.

During 7th plan, slow down of agriculture was the principle cause of slowdown in overall growth. Unless the strategy of development is changed and revitalisation of agriculture is given prime importance, the fulfilment of the plan target will not be achieved. The good impact of these five year planning was observed on the Indian economy.

TABLE 2: GDP Growth, and Rates of Savings In Indian Economy (1951-1990)

Period	*Growth in GDP at factor cost*	*Saving of all sector*
1950-51 to 1955-56	3.61	10.28
1956-57 to 1960-61	4.27	11.73
1961-62 to 1965-66	2.84	13.21
1966-67 to 1970-71	4.66	14.35
1971-72 to 1975-76	3.08	17.27
1976-77 to 1980 81	3.24	21.65
1981-82 to 1985-85	5.06	19.36
1985-86 to 1989-90	5.81	20.37

1. India's macro economic performance has been only moderating good in terms of GDP growth rate. Population has increased by more than 2% annum, the growth in per capita income on an annual average basis has been somewhat less than 2% annum.
2. Savings as a proportion of GDP have risen from 10.4% in 1950-51 to 24.3% in the 1991-92. The following table shows the growth of GDP and savings.

3. The per capita consumption has increased at a very modest rate of 1.4% inspite of increase in population at more than 2% annum..

The following table shows the change in per capita consumption of different food commodities.

Table 3: Per Capita Availability Food Items

Food Items	*1950-51*	*1990-91*
Fish	1.5 Kg	4.9 Kg
Vegetables	10.3 Kg	24.7 Kg
Milk	46.8 Kg	66.5 Kg
Tea	214 Kg	612 Kg
Coffee	61 gm	65 gm
Cereals	33 gm	471 gm
Edible Oil	3.11Kg	6.4 Kg

4. The following table shows the changes of social indicator, which indicate the economic development of the Indian economy during 4 decades of pre-transitional economy.

Table 4: Social Indicator

Social indicator	*1950-51*	*1990-91*
Birth rate	39.9/1000	29.9/1000
Death rate	27.4/1000	9.6/1000
Life expectancy	32 Years	58 Years

Therefore studies of different development plan shows the significant result in improvement of economic and social indicator. There is an increase in per capita income, savings and per capita consumption of different food items. Result also shows in improvement in social indicator like decrease in birth rate, death rate, infant mortality and increase in life expectancy etc. All these are outcome of agricultural progress due to increase in agricultural production and productivity, which resulted in increase in per capita food availability to our vast population. Therefore agro-economy is playing a vital role in improvement of macro-economic and social indicator, which is a prerequisite for health of national economy.

Impact of Green Revolution on Agro-economy of India

As mentioned earlier, the period of 4 decade (1950-51 to 1990-91) divided into; (a) pre-green revolution period (1950-65) and (b) post-green revolution period (1968-91).

The results on studies on impact of green revolution on agro-economy shows that during pre-green revolution period annual growth rate in area under crops was quite impressive (All crop-1.6%, foodgrain-1.4% and non foodgrain-2.5% Refer to Table 4).

The food grain production has increased at an impressive annual growth rate of 3.2%. The output growth rate of non food grain was also impressive (3.5% per year).

This impressive growth in agricultural production was due to area growth rate and partly due to yield growth (Refer to table 6 and 7).

During post green revolution period (1968-91) the annual growth rate in agricultural production was quite low, which is by table 7. During this period, the spectacular growth rate was recorded by wheat (3.2%) and potato (3.0%) per year

Table 5: Growth in Area of Principal Crop Since Independence

Crops	In million hectare			Annual growth rate	
	1949-50	1964-65	1990-91	1949-50 to 1964-65	1967-68 to 1990-91
All food	99	118	128	1.4	0.2
Rice	30	36	43	1.3	0.6
Wheat	10	13	24	2.7	2.0
Coarse cereals	39	44	37	0.9	-1.0
Pulse	20	24	24	1.9	0.3
All non food grain of which	23	33	39	2.5	0.4
Oilseed	10	15	24	2.6	0.3
Sugarcane	1.5	2.6	3.7	2.5	-0.4
Cotton	4.9	8.4	7.4	3.3	1.5
Potato	0.2	0.4	0.9	4.4	3.6
All crop	122	151	167	1.6	0.3

Table 6: Growth in Yield of Principal Crops Since Independence

Crops	In million hectare			Annual growth rate	
	1949-50	1964-65	1990-91	1949-50 to 1964-65	1967-68 to 1990-91
All food	5.5	7.6	13.8	1.4	2.1
Rice	7.1	10.8	17.5	2.1	2.2
Wheat	6.6	9.1	22.7	1.3	3.3
Coarse cereals	4.3	5.1	10.0	1.3	1.3
Pulse	4.0	5.2	5.8	0.2	0.5
All non food grain of which	-	-	-	0.9	1.6
Oilseed	5.2	5.6	7.7	0.1	1.6
Sugarcane	34	47	65	1.0	1.2
Cotton	75	122	224	2.0	2.4
Potato	66	84	-	1.6	3.0
All crop	-	-		1.3	1.9

Table 7: Growth in Production of Principal Crops Since Independence

Crops	In million hectare			Annual growth rate	
	1949-50	1964-65	1990-91	1949-50 to 1964-65	1967-68 to 1990-91
All food	55	89	176	3.2	2.9
Rice	24	39	75	3.5	2.6
Wheat	6	12	55	4.0	5.3
Coarse cereals	17	25	32	2.2	0.4
Pulse	8	-	14	1.4	0.7
All non food grain of which	-	9	-	3.5	2.6
Oilseed	5	122	18	3.3	2.1
Sugarcane	50	6	240	4.3	2.9
Cotton	3	4	10	4.6	1.8
Potato	2	-	15	4.3	6.7
All crop	-		-	3.1	2.6

Impact of Decade Reforms on Agro-economy of India

i) In 1991, the economic crisis reached its peak, because foreign currency reserved had decline to almost 1 billion, inflation soared to annual rate of 17%.

ii) As a result of reforms, the large scale capital outflow was stopped, and capital inflow substantially incresed, so there is improvement in BOP and restoring international confidence in the Indian economy. Economy soon absorbed the shock of the stabilisation measure and bounced back to an average growth rate of 5.7% during the first four year of reforms (1992-96).

iii) Economic reforms helped to restore economic growth to 4% in 1992-93, brought-down the rate of inflation to 7% restored the level of foreign currency reserve to 6.4 billion and stimulated a strong recovery in export towards the end of the financial year.

iv) After recording a decline in 1991-92 agricultural GDP has increased steadily at an average growth rate of 4% per annum during the first four years, despite a slight reversal in 1995-96.

v) In 1992-93, the growth rate from agricultural and allied sector was higher (6.1%) than growth from industry (4.2%). But in 1992-94, the trend was changed and growth from industrial sector was higher (6.8%) than growth agricultural sector (3.0%). In 1995-96, the growth from agricultural and allied sector was 3.0%, while growth, while growth from industrial sector was highest (12.5%). The sharp decline in food grain production by 3.4% was responsible for the slow growth in 1995-96.

vi) Again in 1996-97, the growth of agricultural sector was higher (7.9%) than the industrial sector (6.4%). This high growth rate in agricultural sector was because of steep increase in production of wheat (10%), coarse cereals (10%), pulses (10%), oilseed (12%) and cotton (9%).

Therefore, even though there has been substantial growth in agriculture production, there have been continuous fluctuation in the crop output from year to year. The average growth rate during 1992-97 from agricultural sector is much lower than the industrial sector. Given the structure of Indian economy, the growth in the national income has largely been determined by the hands in the agricultural production. The reason is that agricultural is the largest component of GDP and has overall impact on other sector via input linkage, employment and incomes.

Redesigning of Agro-economy

India is a country with different geographical region under tropical conditions with diversified culture and multi linguistic population with different food habits. Under these conditions, having rich natural resources the agricultural policies to be emphasised in respond to the improvement of agro-economy. This is evident that out of transition agro-economy alone contributed its economy for growth of GDP. Under these circumstances the redesigning will be recommended as an intensive approach.

The intensive approach means a breakthrough of Indian agricultural in the shortest possible time by using minimum requirement in a sustainable manner. Intensive approach divided into two modes.

1. The government policies and departmental exercise.
2. Privatisation and non-governmental approach.

Under the government approach it is to be recommended to provide of proper input at reasonable prices, and price structure of output with appropriate market system. Under the privatisation and non-governmental approach it is recommended the best practices on the farm and off the farm (market and consumer utilisation.)

The designing system will be with sustainable management rather than bureaucratic and diplomacy. It is necessary involvement of educated farmers with self-drive and without selfishness during the framing of the agricultural policies in this intensive approach or intensive agriculture.Although during transition, the importance was not drawn in line of agro-economy but still existed and contributed the growth of national level comparatively equivalent to the other economy like Industrial economy, service economy etc. Therefore if agro-economy graft for proper designing with transitional economy, India would have reached as a highest country in the contribution to the food production. Therefore the solution under these circumstances recommended on intensive agriculture or intensive approach on agriculture. It is a lesson from India showing how agro-economy contributed towards the national economy under transitional period. The same may be applicable for the other developing countries, which are under transition. The failure of the countries like Mexico, Indonesia etc. are due to non picturising the agro-economy on one reason and the other reason is that the agricultural sector is considered equal to the industrial sector wherein with different deficiency of inputs. This results to imbalance the economy under transition of those countries.

Different models of Redesiginig of Agro-economy:

(1) Intensive approach or intensive agriculture approach.

(2) Geographic bifurcated farming system.

(3) Agriculture risk management system.

(4) Micro economy/Rural economy approach.

  (1) Intensive approach already explained as above to be advocated in a country like India with democratic nature and tropical conditions. Other countries considerable and advocated are *e.g.*, Bangladesh, Srilanka, Pakistan, Malawi etc.

  (2) Geographic bifurcated farming system biased with geographic conditions. Other countries considered *e.g.*, Philippines, Costa Rica etc.

  (3) Agricultural risk management: Advocates the risk involving agricultural and allied sectors. Other countries are *e.g.*, Mexico, sub Saharan Zambia, Nigeria etc.

  (4) Micro economy/Rural economy base agriculture consisting with rural employment and rural development. It is best possible for developing nation like Africa, Asia and gulf regions.

Conclusion

Many developing countries are under transition with an emphasis of industrial base, because they are under the impression that industries alone can contribute the growth rate of economy.

But this is not correct by looking to the Indian economy under transition. Indian economy consist with largest rural economy/ micro economy under going through the agricultural sector. Learning this lesson, the different governments, under transition of different nation particularly developing countries should look to agro-economy with major emphasis by redesigning the structure of economy. By using the above models of redesigning the transitional economy can be bent to improve the economy and to balance the economy with agro-economy. Therefore the gap of fiscal balance can be maintained without collapsing the economic structure.

Change in the Work Force in British India, 1881-1921

The period from the late nineteenth century to the early twentieth century witnessed a significant socio-economic transformation in India. With development of railway and irrigation, and export growth, commercialisation of agriculture took place extensively. There would have been a change in life style of those who gained from the commercialisation. Thus demand for goods and services traditionally produced and supplied by village artisans and service castes gradually changed. In the non-farm sector, on the other hand, the so-called labour intensive industrialisation started taking place after the process of de-industrialisation from the late eighteenth century to the mid nineteenth century. Expansion of railway network brought remote areas to economic integration with urban areas. Facing the competition with imported goods and products of urban sectors the traditional jajmani system was gradually undermined.

The purpose of this paper is to examine the census occupation data of British India and to look into changes in occupational structure of work force during the period. It is well known that the census statistics on occupation, female occupation in particular are problematic and scholars such as the Thorners (1962) doubted its reliability. Roy (2005), however, recently suggested to use female occupation data. The paper tries to scrutinising the work force data in British Territories of Madras Presidency and Punjab Provinces at district level from 1881 to 1921. When occupational structure changes, it is assumed that different patterns would be observed under different socio-economic settings. Female work participation, for example, differs markedly between North and South India. It is thus expected that the change could be seen more clearly through a comparison between Madras and Punjab. Regrettably, the 1891 census reported only population (actual workers and dependents altogether) supported by occupation groups in the occupation tables, so that separate figures of workers and dependent were not available. We, therefore, use only four censuses, *i.e.*, 1881, 1901, 1911 and 1921.

The following section briefly introduces the population census instructions and classification schemes of occupations. Section two attempts a reliability test for female worker population ratios. The section also examines problems related to classification of occupations. In the section three we discuss on several aspects of changes in occupational structure of workforce, such as variations in distribution of workers by industry, a decline in worker population ratios of cultivators, and changes in agricultural labourers and workers in hereditary occupations of village artisan and service castes. The last section summarises the paper.

Enumeration of Workers in Population Census

Census of India collected and information on occupations of both males and females since 1881. Since the definition and method of enumeration often changed, it is of importance to review the schedules and instructions briefly.

The census schedule for occupation in 1881 was "Occupation of men; also boys and females who may do work." Since 1901 the schedule was almost same and recorded "principal and subsidiary occupations of actual workers and for dependents, the principal occupation or means of subsistence of actual worker on whom dependent".

The definition of actual worker was "those who actually do work or carry on business whether personally or by means of servants, or who live on house-rent, pension, etc." Thus, the actual workers in the population census in British period include not only persons in gainful employment but also non-workers, like those living on rents or pensions and unproductive workers. For working out figures of workers, therefore, non-workers have to be deducted.

Instructions regarding female workers are as follows;

1881: Only such persons are to be shown in this column as actually do work contributing to the family income. Mere employment in such domestic occupations as spinning will not entitle women to be shown in this column, unless the produce of their labour is regularly brought to market.

1901: Women and children who work at any occupation, of whatever kind not being an amusement or of a purely domestic character, such as cooking, must be entered in this column, whether they earn wages or not.

1911 and 1921: Women and children who work at any occupation which helps to augment the family income must be entered in Column 9 under that occupation and not in Column 11.

The instructions to the superior census staff is as follows;

Only those women and children will be shown as workers who help to augment the family income.

A woman who looks after her house and cooks the food is not a worker but a dependant. But a woman who collects and sells firewood or cow-dung is thereby adding to the family income, and should be shown as a worker. So also a woman who regularly assists her husband in his work, *e.g.*, the wife of a potter who fetches the clay from which he makes his pots, but not one who merely renders a little occasional help.

According to the instructions mentioned above, the definition of workers in 1881 census was much narrower. Thus production for home consumption was outside the boundary of work. In fact, it was reported in 1891 census that "the phrase 'regularly brought to market' (in 1881 census instruction) is said to have excluded a good number of the class to whom it was intended to apply." In this respect the definition in 1901 was wider because it was based on work criterion. Since 1911 income criterion was applied but regular unpaid family helpers were also included in actual workers.

Since 1901 both principal and subsidiary occupations were recorded, and the major time criterion was applied in 1901 whereas the major income criterion was applied in 1911 and 1921 for classification of principal and subsidiary occupations.

Reliability of the Occupation Data

(1) Reliability Test of Female Worker-Population Ratios Changes in the definition of workers and instructions given to enumerators influence on enumeration of workers and make an inter-census comparison difficult. According to Visaria (1995).

An analysis of the changes in the share of non-farm employment in the rural economy must necessary begin with a review of the Worker-Population Ratios (WPRs) because changes in the latter can offset some of the sectoral shifts in the distribution of workers. When the WPRs are not quite comparable, the underlying industrial distribution of workers cannnot be presumed to reflect the reality because the excluded workers are not necessarily distributed at random over different industrial divisions or groups.

Thus the level of WPR could be an index for reliability of work force data. Excluding non-workers from the census occupation data, the WPRs for Madras and Punjab are calculated and are shown in Table-2. The male WPR in Madras was about 62 percent in 1881 and 1901, and declined slowly to 57.3 percent in 1921. In Punjab it was considerably low in 1881, 54.7 percent, and rose to 58.1 percent in 1911 and declined to 54 percent in 1921. There is a marked contrast in the female WPRs between Madras and Punjab. The female WPR in Madras was much higher than that of Punjab. As well known, the difference in female work participation between North and South is due partly to the deep-rooted pardah system which still remains in present-day India. The female WPR in Madras showed a similar trend with that of males, with the peak in 1901. The female WPR in Punjab, on the other hand, was considerably high in 1881 and declined steadily to 7.1 percent in 1921. It is thus noticed that the WPR was higher in earlier censuses than the later years with which the Thorners considered data on female workers as unreliable.

Are the female WPRs in earlier censuses really higher to the extent that inter-census comparison would not be possible? Let us compare these figures with the WPRs in 1961 census which are supposed to be good at enumeration of female workers. The WPRs in Madras in 1881 and 1901 are at almost the same level of Andhra

Pradesh (62.2 percent for male and 41.3 percent for female), but they are much higher than Tamil Nadu (59.7 percent and 31.3 percent), Mysore (58.4 percent and 32.0 percent) and Kerala (47.2 percent and 19.7 percent). The male WPRs in Punjab in 1901 and 1911 are much higher than that of Indian Punjab in 1961 (52.9 percent) while the female WPR in 1881 is higher than 1961 (14.2 percent) by 1.1 percent. However, when taking changes during the six decades in age distribution of population, school attendance, urbanisation and other factors into consideration, it is unlikely that the WPRs of earlier censuses, female WPRs in particular, is abnormally higher.

Let us try an exercise, a reliability test for female WPRs during the period. If a change in the definition and methodology of census operation in a particular year caused a serious over-enumeration or under-enumeration, a year specific upward or downward bias could be observed after controlling the impacts of socio-economic factors on the female work participation. In other words, when the female WPR is regressed to promising explanatory variables and still the year specific bias remains, then we would be able to judge as over-or under-enumeration in the year.

Let us try a regression analysis to explain inter-district and inter-temporal variations of female WPRs. We take two dependent variables, one, the female WPR and the other, the ratio of female WPR to male WPR. The former is directly measuring women's work participation and the latter is measuring the extent of over- or under-enumeration of female workers in relative terms, with the assumption that the enumeration of male workers was comparatively reliable. A crude worker-population ratio varies depending on demographic factors, such as age distribution of population, and socio-economic factors like school attendance, urbanisation, social status of women, and living standard and so on. For explanatory variables, we take population pressure, age distribution of population, proportion of Muslim population, urbanisation, some indicators of agricultural development, such as irrigation ratio, cropping intensity, proportion of area under rice/wheat and commercial crops, and some region dummies. In addition we incorporate year dummy variables to measure a year specific bias. If any coefficient of year dummy is positive (negative) and statistically significant, then it suggests that the WPR of the year is supposedly over-(under-) enumerated either due to errors in enumeration or due to important variables omitted. If the coefficient of year dummy is not statistically significant, it is likely that there was no over-or under-enumeration in the year.

The model for an OLS regression of female WPR (and female WPR/male WPR) is as follows;

Considering data availability, we have to exclude 1881. This is indeed a serious drawback for this exercise. Yet we can judge if female work participation was over-enumerated in 1901. Thus district data pooled for three years are used and regression was run separately for Madras and Punjab.

The results of regression analysis are given in Table-3. The coefficients of determinant for Madras are not high as that of Punjab, though F-values of all models are statistically significant at 1 percent level. As for the direct measuring female WPR in Madras, the coefficients of Muslim population ratio, rice area ratio, non-foodgrain area ratio, and the number of sheep per person are all negative and statistically significant.

The coefficient of Yd01 is positive (0.0037) but not significant statistically, but that of Yd21 is negative (-0.574) and statistically significant. For Punjab the coefficients of proportion of non-labour force, wheat area ratio and the number of ploughs per person are all negative and statistically significant. The coefficient of population pressure is positive and statistically significant at 10 percent level. The signs of coefficients of Yd01 and Yd21 are negative but both are not statistically significant. Regression results for measuring the ratio of female WPR to male WPR are similar to the direct measurement of female WPR.

From the regression analysis mentioned above, it is likely that the variation of female WPR was within the range that could be explained by socio-economic factors and that of 1901 was not over-enumerated. As for the female WPR of Madras in 1921, the coefficients of determinant adjusted are low, suggesting unexplained fluctuations. It is most probable that the negative coefficient of Yd21 is due to omitted variables, rather than due to under-enumeration.

Problems Related to Classification of Occupations

It is very important to differentiate changes which actually took place from the spurious fluctuations in distribution of workers by occupation due to classification errors. If any classification error is detected, adjustment is required accordingly. This is, however, not an easy task. There are supposedly three problems related to classification of occupations, namely (a) how to record the occupation of workers with dual or multi-occupations, (b) frequent change in the system of classification of occupations, and (c) the so called 'general labour' or 'workers otherwise unspecified'.

(a) *Multi-occupations:* It was a common feature of rural India that a person was engaged in several activities. To quote the report of the census of Punjab 1881: We have not here in the Punjab, and least of all in the villages of the Punjab, a differentiation of occupations such as exists in England, where each definite craft or minute branch of labour is confined to a specific class of workmen who follow that craft exclusively. I have shown in discussing the menial and artisan castes how impossible it is to draw any definite lines between the numerous castes whose very basis is the hereditary occupation they follow, and the same vagueness and uncertainty extends to the calling of the individuals composing those castes. They think that the name of the caste to which a menial or artisan belongs is a quite sufficiently accurate and comprehensive definition of his occupation.

It is likely that the concept of occupation in rural India was different from that of common in England. Rather it was a work of a particular caste to perform a set of activities, required for agricultural production and for daily life in a community. A Chamar (leather worker), for example, performed as an agricultural labourer in a busy season in addition to his hereditary leather work.

A Chuhra (sweeper) was expected not only to clean cowshed and make cow-dung but also to participate in agricultural labour. These two occupations, leather work and agricultural labour, or sweeping and agricultural labour, are a set and are inseparable. These are supposedly a Chamar's work and Chuhra's work.

The problem of 'maker and seller' is another example. A Kumhar (potter) was supposed to make earthen pots for Persian wheel and a Tarkhan (carpenter) was supposed to make and repair a plough but their work was not for sale. They received customary dues from farmers, a share of products per well or per plough and other various forms of allowances.

There are two problems with this. One problem is that the classification error might have slipped in. The other is that whole structure of occupation of a person or a caste could not be captured. It is natural that applying Farr's classification system of occupations without any adjustment caused significant confusions while enumerating and classifying the occupation. At enumeration, it is supposed, the name of caste or at most the hereditary occupation of the caste was recorded and accordingly the person's occupation was classified.

Two occupations, principal and subsidiary, were recorded to solve the problem. In 1881 it was only for workers in agriculture that a subsidiary occupation was to be recorded, though it was reported that recording of secondary occupation was insufficient. For workers in non-agricultural occupations, however, only the principal one was to be recorded. An order or sub-order of 'complex occupation' was considered in 1891 census but it was not materialised. Both principal and subsidiary occupations were started being recorded from 1901, with the major time criterion in 1901 and with the major income criterion in 1911 and 1921. It is not an easy task for enumerators to confirm the principal and subsidiary occupations and it is supposed common that the caste name or hereditary caste occupation was simply recorded. Here is a possibility that a classification error comes in.

Agricultural labourers in Madras in 1901 accounted for 18.7 percent and 35.1 percent of total workers for male and female, respectively, while sweepers' share was less than 0.1 percent. In Punjab, on the other hand, agricultural labourers' share was 2.5 percent and 2.1 percent for male and female, respectively, while that of sweepers was as high as 3.4 percent and 11.0 percent respectively. It is not certain if sweepers (and leather workers also) were properly classified according to major time criterion in Punjab.

(b) *Change in the Classification of Occupations:* The English system of classification was adopted in 1881. It was 6 classes, 18 sub-classes, and 78 orders as shown in Table. The number of groups could be adjusted according to local conditions, thus it was 480 in Madras and 334, in Punjab. One of the major problems of 1881 classification system is that grouping was not appropriate for Indian conditions. Thus there was no differentiation between rent receivers and cultivating owners, between farm servants and field labourers, nor further grouping of cotton textile workers, to mention a few. The classification scheme of Bertillon was applied in 1901 with some modifications. This was the most comprehensive classification, with 8 classes, 24 orders, 79 sub-orders and 520 groups (plus some sub-groups), and grouping was adjusted to Indian condition.

The Classification system was considerably changed in 1911 and the number of groups was reduced to 169 from 520 groups and 39 sub-groups in 1901. Thus all occupations were divided into 4 classes, 12 sub-classes, 55 orders and 169 groups. Groups of 'maker and seller' were classified under 'industry'. Unfortunately, spinning and weaving, and farm servants and field labourers were put together, respectively. Again in 1921 some groups were sub-divided and the number of groups was expanded to 191. The group of 'cotton spinning, sizing and weaving' in 1911, for example, was sub-divided into 'cotton spinning' and 'cotton sizing and weaving' in 1921, and the group of 'agricultural labourers' in 1911 was subdivided into 'farm servants' and 'field labourers' in 1921.

When it comes to a comparison at group level between censuses, we have to re-classify groups of other censuses according to the system of 1911 census.

(c) *Size of 'General Labourers' or Unspecified Workers:* There were 477.8 thousand and 698.5 thousand general labourers for males and females, respectively in Madras in 1881. This was a significant number, accounting for 3.5 percent and 4.9 percent of total workers. In Punjab the number of general labourers was comparatively small, 226 thousand and 43.1 thousand, for males and females, respectively. In Madras the number of persons of this category decreased to 315 thousand in 1901 but again increased to one million in 1921. It was reported that this was mainly due to the fact that general and imprecise terms, like 'labour' and 'coolie', were used, though the instruction was repeatedly given for not to use vague terms. There are several opinions on how to handle the general labourers. The Thorners (1962) and Patel (1950) added general labourers to agricultural labourers and Krishnamurthy (1972) distributed them into agricultural, construction, and service labourers. Roy (2005) considered general labourers as a measure of occupational coalescence.

Let us examine correlations between agricultural labourers and general labourers. Since there were often changes in district border it is not possible to calculate actual numbers of increase or decrease for each district.

After adjusting for bifurcation or a creation of new districts, inter-census differentials in the proportion of agricultural labourers and general labourers to total workers are calculated. For example, the proportion of male agricultural labourers in Ganjam district in 1881 was 10.9 percent and it was 16.5 percent in 1901, with the percentage point change being 5.6 percent.

The correlation coefficients between percentage point changes of agricultural labourers and general labourers are shown in Table-4. Since there were district border changes, the coefficient of correlation was not high. Nevertheless it is evident that there was an inverse relationship between changes in the proportion of agricultural labourers and general labourers in Madras. This fact suggests that increase in agricultural labourer and decrease in general labourers were closely inter-related. Regrettably, it is not possible to say that this was due to classification errors or to actual change in employment without further evidence. Interestingly there is no negative correlation between the two variables in Punjab.

This is due partly to a fact that Chamar and Chuhra supplied agricultural labour in Punjab, and they might have returned their caste name or hereditary occupation as their principal occupation. We will return to this topic later when we examine agricultural labour.

Change in the Work Force, 1881-1921

As mentioned above agricultural development took place during the period. Area irrigated increased from 6.3 million acres in 1890-91 to 9.4 million acres in 1920-21 in Madras, and in Punjab, it increased from 7.5 million acres to 13 million acres during the same period. Development of canal colonies in Punjab is well known.

Area under crops increased rapidly and agricultural production increased at 1.8 percent per year in Madras and at 1.9 percent per year in Punjab. Growth of commercial crop production was much faster (annual growth rate was 3.0 and 2.7 percents for Madras and Punjab, respectively) than foodgrain production (1.5 and 2.7 percents), as shown in Figure-1. Development was also seen in the number of cattle and buffalos, sheep and goats, and the number of ploughs and carts. Let us examine what sort of change took place in work participation and in occupational structure under the agricultural development during the period.

Distribution of Workers by Industry

Table-5 indicates the change in distribution of workers by industry in Madras and Punjab from 1881 to 1921. It is convenient to divide the period into two, from 1881 to 1901 and from 1901 to 1920. Note that during the first period the WPRs rose or remained at the higher level, whereas it gradually declined during the second period. The following points are noticed:

1) The share of agricultural sector was higher in Madras while that of non-agricultural sector was much higher in Punjab and this is mainly due to a big difference in the proportion of agricultural labourers between the two Provinces.

2) For males, the proportion of cultivators in total workers rapidly rose from 38.9 percent in 1881 to 49.2 percent in

1901 in Madras, while it slightly increased from 50.0 percent to 51.9 percent in Punjab. After the turn of the century cultivators' share remained stable in Madras and declined slowly in Punjab. The proportion of agricultural labourers increased gradually in Madras and Punjab. The proportion of workers in manufacturing declined gradually in Madras, while it showed a marked fall from 23.3 percent in 1881 to 16.6 percent 1911 in Punjab. The share of non-agriculture (secondary and tertiary sectors) as a whole declined gradually. There was a rapid fall of percentage of general labourers in Madras and Punjab between 1881 and 1901.

3) For females, the share of cultivators increased rapidly, from 24.7 percent in 1881 to 42.5 percent in 1901 in Madras while it decreased from 37.3 percent to 32.8 percent in Punjab. The percentage of agricultural labourers in Madras rose slightly till 1901 and then gradually decline. The proportion of workers in manufacturing fell rapidly during 1881 and 1901 in both Madras and Punjab. The share of workers in non-agriculture as a whole fell in Madras but it rose in Punjab. The percentage of general labourers fell in Madras but it rose in Punjab between 1881 and 1901. It is noticed that the pattern of variation in the distribution of workers during the late nineteenth century was different between Madras and Punjab. In Madras the proportion of male and female workers in manufacturing industry declined and that of cultivators rose. In Punjab, on the other hand the percentage of industrial worker declined but the share of cultivators did not increase. Rather, the share of female cultivators declined.

What happened to female workers in manufacturing industry? When we see a change in female workers in cotton textile industry, it decreased from 457 thousand in 1881 to 236 thousand in 1901 in Madras, while it decreased from 252 thousand to 117 thousand in Punjab, as shown in Table-6. Since the classification scheme changed the strict comparison is not possible but as a majority of female workers were engaged in spinning in Punjab and male workers were mainly in weaving, it is most likely this decrease in female workers was taken place in cotton spinning. With a change in preference for softer and refined cloth and a competition with imports and urban products female workers gave up hand spinning.

Since production activity for home consumption was not regarded as work in the census, those women who were engaged in hand spinning for home consumption were not enumerated as workers. It is, therefore, likely that hand spinning had been common among women of farm households who could afford a charka and they also gave up spinning.

Note that those women were regarded as spinners in 1881 because they could earn wages. By 1901 they gave up spinning and did work as family helper on own farm as before, and they were regarded as cultivators because the work criterion was applied in 1901 census. This is one of the factors behind the large swelling of female cultivators in Madras.

In Punjab, on the other hand, women usually did not work outside their home so that giving up spinning resulted in a decline in work participation. This is one of the reasons for a fall of female WPR from 15.3 percent in 1881 to 10.4 percent in 1901.

Thus 'de-industrialisation' took place during the late nineteenth century, though it is not certain if the term is appropriate in this case. When taking hand spinning for home consumption by women into account, the actual change in occupational structure would have been more drastic than as seen in the census data. Female workers left spinning and returned to cultivation in Madras, and they exited from work participation in Punjab.

Now let us turn to the change in the second period. The pattern of change was rather similar for Madras and Punjab. The proportion of male cultivators remained unchanged or declined gradually, while that of female cultivators declined. The share of industrial worker also declined gradually, though the share of non-agriculture as a whole remained unchanged, except female workers in Punjab. The change in the distribution of workers by industry seems to be rather gradual but significant changes were taking place behind the scene. First, rent receivers increased and second, cultivators' work participation declined, both of which led to a decline in the worker-population ratios as a whole.

Decline in Work Participation among Land Holders and Cultivators

Since a rent receiver is not a worker, we take a proportion of persons whose means of livelihood was rent (rent receivers and their dependents) to total agricultural population (landholders and cultivators and their dependents). The proportion in Madras increased from 4.5 percent in 1901 to 5.5 percent, and further to 12.2% in 1921, as shown in Table-7. Similarly it went up from 3.9 percent to 8.2 percent in Punjab.

The proportion of male tenant cultivators to total workers, on the other hand, increased from 12.0 percent to 17.3 percent in Madras. It swelled from 9.5 percent to 16.8 percent for females. An OLS regression of the variation of percentage of rent receivers defined above on some indicators of agricultural development is tried with the following model;

It is interesting to note that in Madras the model's fitting is not good (F value = 0.85) and none of the coefficients of explanatory variables such as irrigation ratio, share of rice and non-foodgrain crops are not statistically significant. This suggests that the distribution of rent receivers and its variation over time in Madras were not correlated with agricultural development of the district.

Rent receivers migrated to urban areas like Madras and Madura cities. In Punjab, on the other hand, the regression result shows that coefficients of share of wheat and non-foodgrain crops are positive and statistically significant, suggesting the distribution of non-cultivating land owners was correlated with agricultural commercialisation in the district though the coefficient of determinant is not high (0.23), as shown in Table-8.

Next is a decline in WPR of cultivators. The occupation tables of 1901, 1911 and 1921 censuses provide the number of actual workers by sex, dependents and total number of actual workers and dependents which enable us to calculate the worker-population ratios by occupational groups not separately for male and female, but together. Let us call this as a group specific worker population ratio (GSWPR).

Table-9 indicates the GSWPRs for Madras and Punjab. The GSWPR of cultivating household in Madras declined significantly from 51.9 percent in 1901 to 48.1 percent in 1911 and to 45.8% in 1921. It fell from 34.9 percent to 32.1percent in Punjab. There was a slight difference between owner cultivators and tenant cultivators, as seen in the table. Since male workers were in majority and change in their work participation was likely small, it is supposed that female work participation declined largely.

The GSWPR of cultivators' group is regressed on various indicators of agricultural development with the following model.

Agricultural Labourers

In 1881 agricultural labourers in Madras accounted for 17.3 percent and 34.2 percent of total workers for males and females respectively in 1881. Not only the shares, the number of female agricultural labourers was much numerous than males, 2.18 million against 1.66 million.

Thus agricultural labour was one of the most important female occupations in Madras. The number of agricultural labourers increased rapidly during the first period and reached 2.19 million for male and 2.84 million for females. The peak was somewhere between 1901 and 1911, and the number started a decline since then.

Note that there was a fall in general labourers during the first period, and if we put agricultural and general labourers together, the total number of labourers remained unchanged for both males and females during the period. Industrial workers decreased, as mentioned above, and hence de-industrialisation in fact took place during the late nineteenth century. It is, however, not agricultural and general labourers, but cultivators that the number of workers swelled.

Regarding agricultural labourers in Punjab, it is really difficult to measure the variation during the period, as those classified to leather workers and sweepers supplied agricultural labour as well.

It was reported in 1881 census report of Punjab that the water-carriers, leather-workers, and scavengers occupy in the east and centre of the Punjab a very important position in the agricultural community, much of the hardest field-work being performed by them.

We find that the leather-workers, with whom I have included shoe-makers, are most numerous in the Jamna tracts and the hills, where they are recognised field labourers and supply a considerable portion of the agricultural labour employed. In the centre of the province their place is taken by the scavengers who there occupy a precisely similar position.

Chuhra's or Mussali's main work in a village community was supposedly cleaning cowshed of cultivators, and they returned their caste name or the hereditary occupation as their principal occupation. That is why they were classified as sweepers even if they were engaged in agricultural labour. It is, therefore, probable that analysis of secondary occupation of these castes is required, but unfortunately the data is not sufficiently available.

What happened to the mode of agricultural labour? The separate figure is available for farm servants and field labourers in 1901 and 1921. The distribution of agricultural labourers by the mode is given in Table-11. It is clear that the share of female farm servants had a minor share in Madras and Punjab in 1901.

The number of female farm servants in Madras, however, increased by nearly 300 percent and its share rose to 27 percent among female agricultural labourers and their share in total farm servants reached 40 percent by 1921. It is thus likely that women had participated mainly in casual labour during the nineteenth century, as Roy mentioned, but they started participating in farm servants extensively during the early twentieth century.

Village Artisans and Service Castes

Change in non-farm occupation structure in Indian context is regarded as a process in which the jajmani system gradually declined. The jajmani system is a non-market arrangement providing goods and services which are required for agricultural production and for domestic life in one or a group of village communities. The system gradually but steadily declined and has been replaced by market. Yet, the system could be observed in 1970s and 1980s.

The process was brought about partly by a change in demand for goods and services, and partly by a competition with goods manufactured in urban areas. A Kumhar's role as a potter, for example, was eroded by replacement of earthen pots with iron buckets in Persian wheel. Introduction of kerosene lamp reduced the need for a Teli (oil presser). What about service Castes, Dhobi (washer), Nai (barber), Chuhra and Mussalli (sweeper)?

In contrast with artisan castes, it is unlikely that a service provider did face a serious competition from urban area, though a change in life style, safety razor, for example, had affected Nai's work to some extent. Rather it is probable that they wanted to get out of discrimination and severe servitude in a village community, and those eligible left for new opportunity when available.

Table-12 indicates the number of workers, the WPRs, the proportion of workers whose principal occupation was the hereditary occupation for important artisan and service castes in Punjab in 1911 and 1921. It is noticed from the table that there was a considerable variation in the proportion of workers whose principal occupation was the hereditary to the caste, with the range being from 21.3 percent for Mussalli to 87.4 percent for Sunar (goldsmith) in case of males, and from 9.9 percent for Tarkhan (carpenter) to 86.9 percent for Chuhra in case of females.

Lower side were Chamar, Mochi (shoe maker), Machchi (water carrier) and Mussalli, while Sunar, and Nai were higher side. There seems to be a correlation with the cast ranking. It is also noticed that the WPRs of all castes declined, while the proportion of hereditary occupation workers rose. There was a different pattern in division of labour between male and Female. A majority of women of Chuhra were engaged in hereditary occupation, while about a half of male workers left the job. On the other hand both male and female workers of Chamar and Mochchi equally participated in non-hereditary occupations.

These figures indicates that a considerable portion of workers left their hereditary occupation by 1911 but this is somewhat misleading. Cultivation and agricultural labour were included in non-hereditary occupations in the table, but many of these caste workers had been traditionally engaged in agricultural labour, as mentioned above.

Some indispensable castes, like Lohar, Tarkhan and Nai, were granted a patch of agricultural land and hence they returned cultivation as their principal occupation. These were supposedly a part of traditional system. Yet some portion of agricultural labourers were in fact newly emerged due to a decline in their caste occupations. It is not possible to draw a definite line between them.

Let us try an exercise to confirm if workers of a particular caste left from their hereditary occupation due to a change in demand or to a competition. We take Kumhar caste, one of important artisan castes in Punjab for analysis.

Well was one of the most important means of irrigation in Punjab accounting for about 30 percent of total area irrigated. Persian wheels were commonly used for lifting water. Supplying earthen pots for Persian wheel was most important work of Kumhar in addition to pots for water and keeping grains.

The population of Kumhar increased from 467 thousand in 1881 to 583 thousand in 1921 though there was a slight dip in 1911, so that it did not fluctuate abnormally. This indicates that Kumhar was free from the classification error in castes. The male workers in trade in pot was just a few, 276 in 1911 and 536 in 1921, suggesting potters were free from classification error in occupations as well.

With special technique it is expected that an entry from other caste members was rare, so that the workers in pottery exclusively came from Kumhar caste itself. Another consideration is that earthen pots started giving place to iron buckets for Persian wheel during the period.

The dependent variable is the proportion of male 'potters, and earthen pipe and bowl makers' to male population of Kumhar. Explanatory variables were (1) well irrigated area per male of Kumhar, (2) the proportion of Kumhar population to total population and (3) GSWPRs for the group of potters. The first explanatory variable is demand for potters work for irrigation.

The second one is a proxy indicating demand for pots for domestic life, and it is supposed that when Kumhars are numerous then demand for potter's work per potter declines. The last one is to control age composition of Kumhar population. In addition, year dummy (Yd21) is incorporated in the model to see if there was a structural change. Thus the model for an OLS regression of the proportion of male potters in Kumhar male population is as follows;

Conclusion

We scrutinised occupation data of the four census and examined change in work force in Madras and Punjab using district level census data on occupations.

It was found that the census statistics on occupation in 1901, 1911 and 1921 were reliable in a sense that abnormal over-or under-enumeration of female WPR was not detected. The higher WPR in 1881 than 1901 in Punjab could be explained by the fact that women who once classified as industrial workers, spinning for example, exited from work force in the latter year.

The classification scheme of occupation applied to Indian condition without adjustment and frequent change in classification made reclassification even at order or sub-order level rather difficult.

We have to be very careful at inter-census comparison. Taking those occupation groups that is supposed to have been not affected by the change in classification nor by classification errors would be one way. Nevertheless census statistics is a valuable source to study the change in distribution of workers in British Period.

De-industrialisation took place during the late nineteenth century. What we can observe from the census data is that female industrial workers in 1881 were enumerated as cultivators in 1901 in Madras, and they exited from work force in Punjab. Decline in spinning did not lead to swelling of agricultural labourers.

Along with agricultural development, commercialisation in particular, the proportion of rent receivers rose and work participation of cultivators declined, both of which led to a decline in overall WPR.

In Madras the number of agricultural labourers increased but the proportion remained at almost same level during the late nineteenth century. Both the number and share of agricultural labourers declined during the early twentieth century. However, there remain classification problems between agricultural labourers and general labourers in Madras and between agricultural labourers on one hand and leather workers and sweepers on the other in Punjab.

Change in demand for goods and services provided in jajmani system and competition with urban products are supposed to have brought about a decline in artisan caste workers in their hereditary occupation. Regrettably the caste and occupation data of censuses did not provide sufficient information on this process. The regression analysis reveals that there was a structural change between 1911 and 1921 in participation in hereditary occupation among Kumhar workers. This suggests the process in which jajmani system was gradually undermined.

4

Land Tenure System in India: A Historical Perspective

Introduction

The history of mankind is intimately associated with land relationship. The role of the State had been the most controlling factor in augmenting the land resources. In agrarian economy the land is the principal source of government revenue and also the major occupation of the people for subsistence. It holds true even today in modern India. The level of Indian economy is largely decided by the status of land.

Frederic Engels in his classical treaties on 'Origin of Family, Private Property and State', discussed how the land relations activated the social transformation. Individual rights on holding/ inheritance of land is a major event of social history. The kind and, the ruling elite were dependent on income from land and so controlled the entire land holding, either directly or indirectly. Sometimes the land disputes led to war on a local or regional scale.

Institutions framed rules for systematic distribution of lands. Institutional framework had been different on temporal and regional scale. Technology also played a key role in devising modalities for prospective utilisation of land initiating cascading effect for social and economic transformation.

Significance of Land

Land is a fixed asset on the surface of the earth. It can neither be enlarged nor reduced under natural conditions. But the land surface, when subject to human use, may be deteriorated. The deterioration of land may lead to many maladies, including abandonment of its use for prospective agriculture and other functional uses. Being a fixed asset land deserves regulations for optimum utilisation.

The pressure on land is ever increasing. The population explosion in the later half of the twentieth century has caused several constraints for the utilisation of lands. The experts are recommending appropriate policies for scientific use of lands. For framework of such policies we require relevant information on lands, which are usually available from land records and other sources.

Importance of Land Records

Land records are of great importance. Land information from the basis for assignment and settlement of land titles, which are subject to legal scrutiny.

The holding of land is controlled by statutory laws by the state at a given point of time. The access to land is determined by ownership patterns, based not only on statutory laws, but also on customary laws in many cases. India has a long tradition of customary laws in diverse regions of the country.

The land tenure systems were different in different historical periods, as the form of institutions changed in the historical context. The land tenure systems laws in many cases. India has a long tradition of customary laws in diverse regions of the country. The land tenure systems were different in different historical periods, as the form of institutions changed in the historical context. The land tenure systems also differed from region to region. This holds true even today due to prevalent diversity of the country like India.

The importance of land records was recognised even in the past, as it is today. The state largely depended on land revenues for administrative, military and other necessary expenditure. In a democratic polity there have been more stress in evolving a comprehensive system for land management. At various stages of history the level of technology played a significant role in devising the modalities for land records.

History of Land Records

Pre-British India

We have little understanding on land records and tenure system prior to Muslim rule in India. The land belonged to "King" and the property rights of individuals were not specified. Vincent Smith observed, "The native law of India has ordinarily recognised agricultural land as being crown property". (Smith, 1924) The observation by Vincent Smith was also contested. The Arthashastra (Kautilya) has evidence of the cultivator being able to sell and alienate his land But it also states of the right of the king to replace him in his holding if he fails to pay the rent. This is like a double ownership, as prevalent in British India. In many cases the land also belonged to the community or headman of the village.

Muslim 'rule' in India continued from the thirteenth to the eighteenth century. Exception for a few decisions concerning the giving of land as gifts to relatives, generals, or artists, the State's fundamental interest was with assessing, measuring, and collecting the Sovereign's share of the revenue generated from agricultural production. As long as this revenue was collected without much trouble most, though certainly not all, aspects of village life were left to local elites, traditions, and culture. The village had more autonomy in the Mughal period than in the British Raj. The British historian W.H. Moreland defines it as "administrative Philanthropy". (Moreland, 1929).

During the rule of Muslim the king used to collect tax from the land, but the propriety was vested to the peasant, the tiller of land. "The King's right to levy tax was justified by the fact that he gave his subjects protection: there is no suggestion here of the king's right to eject the peasant from his holding; the peasant's right is based on the same basis as the merchant's right to merchandise; as the payment of a tax did not interfere with the proprietary rights of a merchant, similarly the peasant did not lose his right over holding because he paid a tax." (Quereshi, 1956).

This attitude of the Muslim ruler towards the holding by the peasant was natural, as the Muslim legal system recognised that the cultivator was the owner of the land. The ownership of the land by the peasant was such an established principle in Muslim law that hitherto it had never been questioned. The Mughals organised that land revenue system following the footholds of Sher Shah Suri. They found the principal structure of agrarian base well established. The Mughals during the reign of Emperor Akbar, the great Mughal, moderately revised and integrated the system for efficient land revenue collection. They understood that in a dominant agrarian economy the organisation of land administration would be more effective. The Mughals introduced the systems of sharing, appraisement and measurement. Emperor Akbar considered such agrarian reforms as important task for his own reasons. The Mughal empire during his reign was expanding and he had to maintain large number of officers for military and administration. Akbar introduced the Mansabdari system and tied the system, with land revenue collections. He was compelled to initiate, reforms in administration and land revenue system, otherwise the conditions threatened to be more chaotic.

Akbar's mission was fulfilled by his trusted officers like Raja Todarmal and Muzaffar Khan who effected a major change in the system of revenue collection. Raja Todarmal was instrumental in survey. A compendium of land records was prepared through collection of data from the field and entered in a register. It was really a beginning of systematic land records in India for which the British also owe to the Mughals. The dahshala or 10 year revenue system (Census) was the contribution of Raja Todarmal, who along with Diwan Shah Mansur divided the Mughal empire into 12 provinces, each administered by a governor and a Diwan. On the basis of land survey Raja Todarmal prepared the maps showing different holdings and assessed rents, which probably were the first cadastral maps in India. In 1571 he introduced the rational revenue assessment based on intimately surveyed land holdings. It was a revolutionary task in the context of technological level, then prevalent in India. The contribution was no less worthy in the historical context, when at the same period Mercator in 1969 published his world map, using conformal projection in his chart showing 'waxing latitudes'. Mercator was endowed with expanding horizon of scientific knowledge in Europe in the late 16th century, where Raja Todarmal had many hurdles.

The Mughals applied new techniques for land survey. Firstly, they adopted standard units of measurement. A yard, called a Gaz, was introduced consisting of forty one digits. A bigha was measured as equal to an area sixty yards square. The reform was not only confined in adopting a new scale, but in standardising the existing ones. The old practice of measuring length with a rope was replaced with bamboo poles. Because the rope used to shrink when it came in contact with moisture. Instead 'Bamboo rods joined together with iron rings were used which were less affected by moisture'. (Abul-Fazl (Ed.Beveridge), 1939).

The Mughals under the leadership of Raja Todarmal, the revenue and finance minister of Akbar, also instituted the classification of lands for assessment of revenues. The assessment of rent varied for different types of land. Basically the length of the period of cultivation was considered for a land classification. Where a land had been continuously cultivated, it was classified as Polaj land. When it was left uncultivated for a short period to regain fertility it was defined as parauti. When a land was not cultivated for a stretch of three to four years, it was categorised as Chachar. The wastelands, abandoned for cultivation for many years, were called the Banjar.

The land revenue was highest for the Polaj lands, as the yields were usually high from such lands. The parauti land when cultivated was charged the same revenue that of Polaj land. The Mughals encouraged the conversion of wastelands into cultivated lands. The Banjar lands, when brought under cultivation, used to pay nominal taxes in the initial years. The Chachar land was treated similarly like the Banjar land.

The Mughals were keen to expand cultivated area and extended special concessions to the cultivators for bringing new areas under cultivation. The new areas were shown separately in the statements submitted to the higher authorities. The authorities were vigilant to expand the cultivated land, in no case the cultivated land should be permitted for degradation into chachar and Banjar lands. The land policy of Akbar was peasant's friendly. He introduced the quality assessemnt to ensure enhanced land revenue for his expanding empire. But in no case he overburdened the cultivators. The officers were given farman to protect the crops and interest of the peasants. The peasant society in pre-British India had more autonomy and was adored with respect and admiration.

British India

The British domination over Indian land started in the seventeenth century and by the end of that century the British rule extended over large areas with the fall of Mughal empire, defeat of the Marathas and subjugation of local powers. The British inherited the institutional form of agrarian system from the Mughals. The British superimposed a system over the existing pattern in tune with British customs and laws relating land. Broadly three principal types of land revenue system were introduced in British India. The basic characteristic of each system was the attempt to incorporate elements of the preceding agrarian structure. The interaction of colonial policy and existing systems produced widely different local results and hybrid forms. It is interesting to note that the techniques used in land surveying in many parts of India even today remain substantially unchanged since their introduction by Raja Todarmal during the reign of Mughal Emperor Akbar.

Different land revenue systems were introduced in various parts of British India, as the British annexed different parts of India in various periods. Let us have an introduction into three broad land revenue systems introduced by the British. These land revenue systems are (1) Zamindari System, (2) Ryotwari System and (3) Mahalwari System.

Zamindari System

The Zamindari system was introduced in early British period. The Permanent settlement Act was passed in 1793 and initially introduced in Bengal. The system was also found in large parts of Northern India (except Avadh, Agra, Jaipur and Jodhpur), Bihar and Orissa. The system was introduced to ensure the revenue receipt of the British colonial power, where a Zamindar was declared the proprietor of land on condition of fixed revenue payments to the British regime. The peasants were turned into tenant farmers and deprived of the land title including other rights and privileges enjoyed during the Mughal period. The Zamindars collected the rents of land through different intermediate collectors. As a result of such practice there had been creation of multilevel ranks of collector under the Zamindar. The peasantry was subject to deprivation of his share in produce from land and relegated to abject poverty. This revenue system accounted for 57 per cent of cultivated area in the country. The Floud Commission, inquiring the reasons of the Great Bengal Famine in 1943, recommended the abolition of intermediaries on land interest to the British Government.

Ryotwari System

The Ryotwari system was introduced in Madras Presidency in 1792 and in Bombay Presidency in 1817-18. This system recognised the proprietary right of the peasant on land and resembled the revenue system of the Mughal to a great extent. The system covered nearly all the southern states and many western states of India including the erstwhile Central Province (*i.e.* Madhya Pradesh). Even the princely states of Jaipur and Jodhpur had this category of revenue system, as it existed during the Mughal period. However, the pockets of Zamindri prevailed within the Ryotwari regions, particularly in the princely states and the areas governed by the feudal lords. The Ryotwari system covered nearly 38 per cent of the cultivated area in India.

Mahalwari System

The Mahalwari system was introduced between 1840 and 1850. In this system the entire village constituted revenue settlement as collective unit. The peasants paid the revenue share of whole village in proportion according to their individual holdings. The system covered the erstwhile Punjab, parts of Orissa and Madhya Pradesh, and the princely states of Awadh and Agra in Uttar Pradesh. The System was not extensive and included only 5 per cent of the cultivated land in India.

Of the three systems the Ryotwari resembled the Mughal revenue system, wherein the proprietary rights of the cultivators had been recognised. This system is considered to be most convenient and appropriate instrument for social development. However, the British legislation institutionalised the transfer of land and created the base of land-market, which was almost absent in the Mughal period. The legislation enacted during 1850s in Ryotwari and Mahalwari areas enabled money-lenders to recover debts from the mortagaged land holdings. It caused serious impact on transfer of land from the holding of cultivator to non-cultivator.

"As a result, rural society in Ryotwari and Mahalwari areas was polarised into landlords and rich peasants versus tenants and agricultural labourers, and the distribution of land became highly unequal". (The Royal Commission on Agriculture, 1924-25).

Typology of States by Tenure System and Agricultural Growth Rate

Tenure System / State Zamindari (57 Per cent)	Average Annual Growth Rate (Percent)
Uttar Pradesh (Except Awadh & Agra)	1.9
Bihar	1.5
Orissa	2.6
West Bengal	4.4
Rajasthan	1.1
Andhra Pradesh	— —
Ryotwari (38 Per cent)	.
Karnataka	2.7
Gujarat	2.0
Tamil Nadu	1.6
Kerala	0.7
Maharashtra	2.7
Madhya Pradesh (60 Per cent area)	1.6
Andhra Pradesh (except Telangana)	2.7
Assam	0.4
Rajasthan (only Jaipur & Jodhpur)	— —
Mahalwari (5 Per cent)	— —
Punjab	4.5
Haryana	2.4
Madhya Pradesh (40 Per cent)	1.6
Orissa (9 per cent)	— —
Uttar Pradesh (only Awadh & Agra)	— —
All India	2.1

An interesting study has been made on agricultural growth rate relating to types of tenure system prevailing in various states. The study reveals that the former Ryotwari and Mahalwari areas of Southern and Western India have achieved higher rates of agricultural growth than the former Zamindari areas of Northern and Eastern India. However, the exception is the state of West Bengal. West bengal has surpassed all the states in all categories of land tenure system except Punjab. This has been possible in implementing land reforms with the pro-active role of Panchayats. In Punjab higher growth rate has been the outcome of Green Revolution. The following table will show the results.

Comparative Assessment of the British Revenue System with the Mughal System

The British considered that the state had entitlement to a share of the annual produce of each unit of land. Under the Mughal system the State's precise share of the produce varied. The actual claims by the State depended upon local conditions-including the weather conditions (flood or drought), variations in cropping pattern and sources of irrigation. Besides the size of the share, the method of assessment of the gross produce was also left to the Sovereign. Obviously the State needed a large number of officials and functionaries to assess and collect its revenue. The State's method of assessment and revenue collection was to assign a portion of the State revenue to be collected and enjoyed by different ranks of people who were either the employees of the State or its dependents. The British also embraced this aspect of the Mughal System.

The Mughal assessed revenue through estimation and measurement. In the estimation process, the State sent officials who in collaboration with village officials and leaders assessed the cultivator's liability before the product was ripe. The cultivator was to pay this liability in cash after harvest and sale. The measurement procedure applied a schedule of rates prepared on the basis of average yield per unit for each type of crop following a calculation of land size. The average value for different crops was determined on the prevalent price in the area. One third of the calculated price was fixed as revenue for the State. The Mughal, afterwards assessed the land revenue according to the variability of soil fertility, types of crops grown and average prices, prevalent in any locality over a number of years and took measures to collect these data on its own initiative. In modern eyes the Mughal's revenue system appears to be remarkable degree of flexibility towards the specificality of the locale. This practice, however, complicated their revenue collection and burdened their bureaucracy. The British domination in India may be regarded as less ideal and more capitalistic, with an intention for developing the colonial market. They pursued the policy to reap for increasing surplus value unleashed by the logic of empire capital. It was the imperialist design for capital accumulation. The capitalists used to intervene in every pore of the earth's productive surface, transform conceptions of space, time, and culture, thereby assimilation local spaces into the rhythms of global capital. The principles of capitalism also embody commitments to freedom, equity, justice, contract, and individuality. With such dichotomy, the British differed from the Mughal in their design to transform the face of local culture in the process of collecting revenue.

Whatever the long-term effects of the Permanent Settiement, it failed to create the capitalist landowner class of British Model. To the contrary there had been transfer of property from hereditary Zamindars and Rajas to the urban mercantile class. Nor were members of this class able to become agricultural capitalists. The reasons are many, not the least of which is the resistance of the peasants to such appropriation and relegation of their occupational rights. In spite of their struggle, the peasants did lose their customary rights to fixed revenue-rates, and of their rights to common property in wastelands, fisheries, forests, gardens and trees.

Land Tenure Systems

Land Tenure – Meaning

Land tenure refers to the way in which land is held by an individual from the Government. It shows the relationships between the land holder and the State. The absolute ownership of land rests with the Government. Government gives proprietary rights to individuals or communities. Thus, whom we call a land owner, is in that sense is the proprietor of that land and he has to pay land renew for that.

History of Land Tenures in India

In ancient times, the State of India claimed a share of the produce of the land from the cultivator. The laws of Manu mention one sixth of the gross produce at the legitimate share of the King. During the war and other emergencies, it was increased to one fourth.

The institute set up by Timur represented the first systematic attempt in the direction of converting the State's share of the produce into money. Shershah made some improvement. However, it remained incomplete due to his short reign.

The most famous settlement was made under Akbar by his able Finance Minister, Todarmal. While fixing the revenue, scientific and detailed investigation was made to assess the taxable capacity of different soils. Land was carefully measured and divided into four classes representing different grades of fertility. The Government's share was fixed as one-third of the gross produce. Thus, Mughals did not introduce any fundamental changes in the ancient revenue system but put a coherent system in place of customary and unwritten usages of the Hindu administration.

Malik Amber of Ahmednagar made similar improvements in the Deccan. He fixed one-third of the gross value of produce as the revenue. Maratha rulers continued the system. They fixed 'Kamal' or the maximum rates for the best lands. The assessment was not permanent in majority of the cases. However, 'Miras' tenure was subject to the payment of fixed assessment.

In the declining days of Mughal Empire, the control over the revenue officials became weak. The flow of income started declining. So, the system called 'revenue farming' was introduced in Bengal in the reign of Farukhsiyer (1713-19).

Under this system, the revenue farmer paid the Government nine-tenth of the whole collection and kept the rest as his collection charges. However, in the later period, the right of collecting land revenue for a pargana or a district was sold by public auction to the highest bidders. Due to this, the exploitation of the cultivators started. The revenue farmers became more dominant. This revenue farming system which started during the Mughal rule in Bengal was soon extended to other parts of the country.

In Deccan, Nana Fadanis, in the later part of the 18 Century, had introduced a revenue system which was very efficient and equitable. It was universally recognised.

The revenue farming system even came to the Deccan. In Konkan, the Khots who were earlier revenue farmers acquired landlord rights. In United Provinces and in Punjab revenue farmers succeeded in acquiring certain overlord rights.

The disorders in the revenue administration resulted in many complexities of land tenures and rights.

Land Tenures under British Rule

Under British Rule, there were three main types of land tenure systems in India. They were Zamindars, Mahalwari and Rayatwari.

i. *Zamindari:* This system was introduced by Lord Cornwallis in Bengal in 1973. Under this system, the lands of a village or few villages was held by one person or few joint owners who were responsible for payment of land revenue to the Government. There used to be number of intermediaries between the Zamindars and the actual tillers of the soil. The system took were various forms such as Zamindari, Jagirdari, Inamdari, etc. In many cases revenue collectors were raised to the status of land owners. This system was introduced in many parts of the country. In this system, tillers of the soil were exploited by way of exhorbitant rents. There were no incentives for them to improve the land or to use better cultivation practices. There were many other social evils of the system. It is said that the British introduced Zamindari system to achieve two objectives. First, it helped in regular collection of land revenue from a few persons *i.e.* Zamindars. Secondly, it created a class of people who would remain loyal to the British ruler in the country.

ii. *Mahalwari:* Under this system, the village lands were held jointly by the village communities, the members of which were jointly and severally responsible for the payment of land revenue. Land revenue was fixed for the whole village and the village headman (Lumberdar) collected it for which he received 'Panchatra' *i.e.* 5 per cent as commission.

iii. *Rayatwari:* It was introduced by Sir Thomas Munro first in Madras state and then in Bombay State. In this system, there was a direct relationship between Government and the tenant or Rayat *i.e.* individual land holder. Every registered holder was recognised as its proprietor and he could sell or transfer the land. He was assured of permanent tenure as long as he paid the land revenue. The land holder was also allowed to sublet his land. It was a better system as compared to Zamindari or Mahalwari and similar other forms of tenure.

Though we have discussed the above three main systems of land tenure, there was lot of intermixing of characteristics of these systems. It is said that these three systems gravitated towards the tendencies of the Zamindari system. The Mahalwari system in states like Madhya Pradesh and Uttar Pradesh subletting and rock renting became common. It became common even in the Rayatwari areas. There was no proper revenue record. This was the situation which prevailed at the time of independence.

Post-Independence Period

Our leaders had thought about the need for land reforms even prior to independence. For instance, the Agrarian Reforms Committee under Shri J.C.Kumarappa had given the guidelines for the formulation of land reform policies in the independent India. The committee recommended that

i. all intermediary interest should be abolished and land should belong to the tiller;
ii. leasing of land should be prohibited except in case of widows, minors and other disabled persons.
iii. All the tenants who had been cultivating land for a period of 6 years should be granted occupancy rights
iv. The tenants should have the right to purchase the holdings at reasonable price to be determined by the land tribunal;
v. The agrarian economy should provide an opportunity for the development of the farmers.

Abolition of Zamindari and Intermediaries Acts; India's First Five year plan has clearly mentioned the land policy and the specific land reform measures to be undertaken. Most of the states passed the legislation for abolition of zamindari and similar exploitative land tenure systems. The first act in this respect was passed in Madras in 1948. The other states followed it. Now land tenure systems like Zamindari, Mahalwari, Jagir, Inam, etc. are abolished in all the states in the country.

It has been said that in implementation of land reforms, this first and the important step of abolition of zaminari was completed peacefully. As a result of abolition of Zamindari and intermediaries, about 26 lakh intermediaries and 20 lakh tenants got proprietory rights of lands *i.e.* they became the land owners. This has resulted in improving their economic and social conditions. The land revenue income of the states also increased.

Tenancy Reforms

Tenancy refers to the relation between the land holder (owner) and the actual tiller of the soil. Many of the land owners did not cultivate their lands personally but gave it to some tiller and took rent for that. They were absentee landlords. The tenancy prevailed in all forms of land tenure systems including Rayatwari system. The main reason was the increase in the population of landless labourers. In 1951, of the total families dependent on agriculture, as many as 23.6 per cent families belonged to the tenant class. The National Sample Survey (8th round) indicated that the lands leased out varied from 11 per cent to 26 per cent of the total, in different states. The tenants were exploited by the land owners by way of heavy rents (50 per cent or even 2/3rd of the produce). There was no protection of tenure (evictions on minor pretexts). Thus, there were no incentives for tenants to make land improvements or to increase production. This necessitated enacting the legislation for tenancy reforms. Tenancy Acts were passed in most of the States, they provided for

i. regulation of rents
ii. security of tenure, and
iii. confirment of ownership on tenants.

Bombay State promptly enacted the legislation as early as in 1950. As regards the regulation of rents, different states fixed different rates. For instance, in Bombay (Maharashtra), Gujarat and Rajasthan, one-sixth of the grass produce has been fixed as the maximum rent; while in Punjab rent fixed is one-third of the produce. It was found that there were large scale evictions of tenants on the plea of resumption for personal cultivation.

As reported in the draft fourth five year plan, as a result of tenancy legislation in India, 3 million tenants or share croppers became the land owners. Uttar Pradesh was in the forefront in this respect. The next state in order is Maharashtra where 13.56 lakh tenants got the ownership rights of about 32 lakh hectares of land by September, 1992.

Protection of tenants and regulation of rent is the first step in the tenancy reforms. The ultimate object of the reform is "land to the tiller". The Tenancy Acts have been moved in that direction.

It could be said that the land reform measures adopted by the States soon after independence, provided a sound basis for agricultural developments that took place in the country in the later period.

Indian Prelude to British Cadastral and Revenue Maps

Raja Todarmal was the minister for revenue in the court of Akbar. Building upon the foundations laid by Sher Shah, Todarmal introduced a system of land reforms, the essence of which was an assessment of the land revenue according to the extent of cultivation, the nature of the soil and the quality of the crops. He set up a scheme of laborious measurement, analysis of possibilities and calculation of prospects. The actual demand was adjusted to meet seasonal price and cultivated area variation. Though at times it broke down and was deployed unevenly within the Mughal Empire, it is the underlying basis of the later day revenue systems. The British became the pupils of the Mughal School, being impressed by the range and thoroughness of the system. In spite of false starts and harsh application in the early days, the British could build up a rural administration not only stable but generally equable and equitable.

The Mughal revenue administration demanded precise measurement of productive cultivated land. A number of units came into force. The llahi gaz, a measure of length and standard gauge was used throughout the Mughal Hindustan in long, middling and short forms, each divided into 24 equal parts and each was called a tussuj, equal to 8, 7 or 6 barley-corns. The gaz is equal to two spans of 16 gerths each. There were however variations of the length of the gaz even with Mughal India. The bigha is a land measure of 60×60 gaz. A larger unit was the Kos or Karoh, each consisting of 50 llahi gaz or 400 poles, each of length 12.5 gaz. Thus the kos is a length of 5000 gaz. Abul Fazal states that there were significant variations in the length of the kos in different parts of Mughal India.

Raja Todarmal was not however the first to generate a revenue system available in all parts of the empire. Much before him, others have had their notable contributions in this regard in different parts of the country. Kautilya's Arthashastra in the Maurya period was one of the earliest to recognize the relevance of land revenue collection from productive farmlands, in villages with settled population of farmers. The Sukra neeti talks of recognition of revenue estimation from cultivated land according to the fact the land is watered by tanks and lakes, by rivers, by wells and sluices apart from dry farming rainfed areas and the nature and number of crops raised in each parcel.

An area of significant development of land information for revenue levies is the Tamil Nadu agricultural plains. Though Tamil Nadu has been occupied at least since the Neolithic age, early settlements of a shifting character were confirmed to the Kurinji or the hills, gradually down-migrating over centuries to the pastoral foothills or mullai by early Christian era. The further occupation of the river plains and the agriculturally fertile deltas led to sedentary population living amidst riverine farm country. Peasant technology led to use of irrigation through different methods and raising of more than one seasonal crop, apart from tree crops. By mid-10th century, with the advent of the later Cholas, specially Raja productive cultivated land constituted a major source of land revenue for the upkeep of the Chola mandalam. Farm villages came to be precisely defined. As per Chola stone inscriptions and numerous copper plates, a village came to be defined as comprising wet lands, dry lands, ur (cultivators), village site, houses, houses house gardens, manram (meeting place), wastelands for grazing cattle, tanks, cow pens, hedges, forest land, barren lands, brackish lands, streams, channels, rivers, Arabic land near rivers, pits of water, trees. (Subbarayalu) Villages were further grouped as brahmadeyas (Brahmin villages), Vellala villages (farmer villages), taniyur, devadana villages (gifted to Brahmins, temples and those who have rendered recognised state service. Hundreds of descriptions are noted in inscriptions and copper plates of temple donations (of land or land income), endorsed by the state that give precise locations and measures of lands donated, together with their boundary limits. Though verbal, these descriptions of individual plots of land give indication of an early system of cadastral plans.

The land measurement units used in Tamil Nadu however differ from those prevalent in the northern plains. The smallest unit used is a viral (finger). 12 virals (9") make a chaan and 24 virals (18") make a muzham (cubit). A muzhakol (cubit pole) is 9 or 12 ft long and is used as a measuring rod. The smallest land plot is a 12 ft. square called a Kuzhi. Hundred Kuzhis make a Kaani and five Kaanis is a veil, somewhat similar to the northern bigha. Land as small in extent as 1/52.4288 millions of a veli was measured in the productive Cauvery valley in the Chola period (equal to 1/500000th of a square foot, (Burton Stein). While the basic cultivated field plot was a veli, and a village was defined as stated in the above para and comprised many farm plots, that were as far as possible rectangular of square in shape, except where natural features like water channels formed the bounding limits. The basic agrarian unit was nadu comprising many villages. With land reclamation in the newer delta fringes, new nadus came into existence, though of lower fertility than the core Chola heartland. The Chola system of land management went on a decline post-fourteenth century, (Heitzman) but the basic framework and structure remained intact to become the basis of the later British cadastral and revenue surveys.

In the well-watered Travancore and Malabar, a compact village was not the agricultural unit. The tarawad of the Namboodri and Nair constituted the land unit, with lzhavas and Tiyars as the main farm labour. The hills and slopes terrain with a network of backwaters and lagoons lent to a hierarchy of land rights of the janmis that were multilayered. The land was held on lesser forms of tenure, and sharecropping was quite common. Land was devoted not only to rice farming but also a variety of tree crops. The traditional system did not undergo any major change with the coming of the Islam, nor did it get disturbed by the arrival of the Portuguese and the Dutch. However, a gradual break-up of the larger tarawads did materialize. Temple lands and garden lands were given patta by the Travancore maharaja since mid eighteenth century. Actual survey by traverses or baseline and offset system did not materialize till independence. A somewhat similar land ownership system evolved in the Lakshadweep with the government pandaram. Lands not being held in private property, but it is the trees that were owned. The middle class Vellala identification of the Tamil country finds its reflection in the Okkaliga and Lingayat land ownership in larger plots in the semi-dry Mysore Maidan.

A major step taken by Shivaji in western Maharashtra for land administration was to have a survey of the lands and then to assess the rents and dues payable by the cultivators. While the land ownership in Deccan was in large land holdings, in Konkan they were in much smaller tillable plots on slopes and valley sides. Land surveys were carried out at different times and basically followed the system of Malik Ambar in Mughal Deccan. The main features of this system were the classification of land according to fertility, ascertainment of their produce, fixing the government share. Collection of rents in kind or money and abolition of intermediate collecting agents. Three fifths of the share of the crop produce was left to the farmer. Using the tagai and istawa principles new lands were brought under the plough and the farmer was subsidised with seeds and cattle. Land revenue varied from year to year dependant on assessment by village officers like Karnams and tatatis, the local Kuilkarnis and Patels managing the village administration. However, there are large variations dependant on jagirdars. Salsette (Suburban Bombay) for example had nine different tenure systems within an area of 16 sq. miles. When the British took over similar such principles and methods were developed locally in different parts of Central and Northern India, and these with remarkable internal variations are too traced here. In Portuguese Goa, there evolved a communido system unique to itself.

When the British set themselves the task of ground level detailed large and medium scale surveys, they took to precise direct measurement of distance and directions between each night's camp, that took the form of route surveys in traverses, often using Gunther's chain and tape and taking measures along sides and diagonals. This technique of establishing a framework for observation formed the basis of different scales of mapping in a map graticule. Rennell, Dalirymple, Robert Kelly, Buchanan and others did pioneering work in this regard. These surveys were carried by trained local surveyors and collectors and the data gathered were sent to Calcutta. Bombay and Madras. Since the surveyors were appointed by the London office and the cartographers at central office had little control on data sent to them led to great disparities in survey standards, and a chaos. The company management though aware of the chaos did not know how to materialize and the three surveyor generals moved in different directions. Many manuscript maps went missing and field officers often did not get maps.

Using indigenous methods for land measurement and assessment of revenues, based upon a decision of the Company and the Surveyor General at Calcutta to accept the assessment in eastern India as permanent settlement for all time, and there was a need to assess new wastelands newly reclaimed in Sunderbans and 24 paraganas. The local zamindari system facilitated to an extent permanent settlement. In Madras Presidency, Since even the jagirs were not so large zamins, and the land holders were mainly of a ryotwari system, a different guideline was established for the Madras revenue surveys, and these were later introduced to Bombay Presidency in 1772 with little change. This settlement done by the extraordinary work of great surveyors like Thomas Munro, Read, Col. Mackenzie and Dickinson became basis for a temporary settlement, with opportunities for constant reviews at intervals. The data base was highly comprehensive, going into the plot size, soil and its taram, slope, water access, crops seasonally, ownership, etc. The Madras Adangal even today is the standard adopted gradually all over the country. The Satbara of Bombay Presidency is of a very similar order. The baffing problem of land survey was the subject of futile experiments in Bengal, but in Madras reached a viable practical solution, dependent on standard supervision. With insufficient resources, the British mapping of India proceeded in a crisis-driven, anarchic manner.

In the early decades of the 19th century, under the regulation of William Lambton and later George Everest, the primary and secondary triangulation networks began taking shape with minimal linear measures and precise angular measures to cover the whole country with a network of triangles, interconnected. The priority given by the Company Directors and the Indian Surveyor-Generals no doubt provided a pivotal role in unification and helped in creating an image of imperial space, unique and precise in the world. This system imposed from above did not contribute in any manner to the build up of a coordinates revenue and cadastral survey system in the country at the grass root level, and then building it up. The twain shall never meet, in the decades to follow proceeding on different planes and the Survey of India gradually lost sight of one of its primary tasks leaving it in the hands of talatis, revenue inspectors and Collectors. The cartographic anarchy was complete and Surveyor Generals combined into one group, who unfortunately never realised the importance of ground level surveys.

Now, there is a growing realisation and desire to link the triangulation network not only with the topographical map grid, but also bring the cadastral plans into its fold. Having flown high in the regime of map projections, photogrammetry aerial surveys and photos, and the latest in satellite imagery maps of high power of spatial resolution. Survey of India is struggling to come to terms with grass root level linkages. Problems are many: the grid used, the projection for plane table level survey plan the search for control points to merge the two and others. On the front of the cadastral plans, shrinkage due to age of the old handmade paper it is drawn on, subsequent plot level changes and what is worse changes in the physical landscapes by way of erosion or accretion. The job is gigantic and full of challenges!

Having made a brief and spotty review of the cadastral and revenue surveys that had come to stay in different parts of the country, it is time to turn to cadastral plans of villages and towns and revenue maps of villages. It is not very easy to visualize when the first Indian cadastral and revenue survey maps came into being. It can at best be a broad conjecture. Since Pallava and Chola days inscriptions and copper plates of donations reveal a widespread network of agricultural villages, careful demarcations of village fields and land rights and their precise delineations with boundary fixtures by measurements correct to virals. This necessarily leads to believe that cadastral plans and maps of adjoining fields in relation to natural features like rivers, wells, canals and tanks had come into vogue. In all probability, none of them have come down the centuries to us, possibly because they were in palm leaf manuscripts. Yet this land of the farmers of many cent are not bereft of some, rare, pieces of evidences, and if some concerted work is initiated more such map plans may get revealed.

The adjoining map is one such of a field area (not the full village) on the south bands of the Pennar river close to Tirukoilur in Nadu, that shows the gifted devadana lands to the Shiva and Vishnu temples as placed in the natural environment as per inscriptions. The square and rectangular plots of farmlands were of the Chola period imprinted in the later day British cadastral surveys and plans. A map drawn Frank Perlin's collection is again a part of the village field plan belonging to Fasli 1193 (AD1784) on paper in Chitnis Modi script presented to and accepted as a piece of evidence in a civil litigation for land rights between two farmers.

The place is south of and close to Pune in Maharashtra, and is known as Vadhana. The plan also provides measurement. The map is reproduced and rendered in English.

Belonging to a relatively to a relatively late period, somewhat similar to Mughal land reform methods, this Maratha map, of the Peshwa period reflects the land reform effected by Chhatrapati Shivaji. A cadastral map in a part of native western Nepal, that is dated AD 1830 with distinct boundaries and their revenue estimates is also shown. Just before the British introduced their cadastral survey and map in Maratha land by the beginning of the 18th century, revenue and village locations in the hills within a forest belt of the Sahyadri was a difficult task but the Maratha cartography had an answer in their graphic mapping of valley heads, as shown in Map. Cadastral plots even within urban areas found map expression in local language, as can be seen from Map of Jaiphalwadi, in the heart of the city, which today is a multistoreyed built up area, though strangely bearing the same name. The microland form facets that find a place in elaborate details in extraordinary, well conceived cadastral survey details, as contained in Adangal is well expressed in the map of Vanamadevi in coastal Tamil Nadu that I had myself surveyed in 1951. A similar map of a village in Bihar dated 1832. Drawing his data base from Abul Fazl's Ain-I-Akbari, the eminent historian, Irfan Habib mapped on the present day map format, the revenue villages of Akbar's subas as defined by Raja Todarmal. The maps are economic as well as political, and the Mughal Atlas is an authentic land record of Akbar's times. Jean Baptiste Joseph Gentil, the military advisor of the Nawab of Oudh, with the aid of three Indian artists compiled a large Mughal Atlas in 43 tblios of the entire Mughal empire, suhbawise, together with a listing of sarkars and parganas, again the data base being provided by the Ain-I-Akbari, rather than by direct surveys of the revenue villages. Two of the Indian artists who helped Gentil were Niwasi Lal and Mohan Singh, both Hindus. The Atlas was completed around AD 1770. The map beside is an illustration of one such subha. The map are drawn employing indigenous cartographic methods, though they carry scribe-work in French. A unique feature of the Atlas is the wealth of marginal illustrations of life style, people, flora and fauna, war ammunitions and even traditions. The Atlas, held in Paris archives, is a treasure house of the Mughal Period.

Marathas in 18th century excelled in the preparation of area maps of revenue villages for the aid of native rulers. They became quite handy in the first half of the nineteenth century, when the British revenue surveys carried out their work in Konkan and Western Desh. There are many such maps, a few of which are taken for illustration in this paper. The Bavda jagir (Map) in Kolhapur area is in colour, and distinguishes between khalsa and inam (grant) villages and the map is in devnagri script. A revenue map of Vijaydurg is in two scripts; the text is in devnagri but the unique marginal legend in Modi. The legend gives details of the colour code and groups of villages according to revenue control (Map) such as Amal Bavdekar. Two similar maps of South Konkan also exist, one of which depicts forest areas in decorative tree symbols. Interestingly, there are no revenue villages in the forested areas. An interesting map of Bardol state near Solapur in India pargana is an inam group of 30 villages (Map). The map is striking in that distances are estimated through a series of evenly spaced concentric circles around the main place, Bardol, at distances of one Kos each. A revenue village map of North Kanara (Map), used by Cohn Mackenzie during the Anglo-Mysore war of 1799 was prepared by the Marathas in the second half of eighteenth century in Modi script. An interesting feature of this is the extensive depiction of hills, ghats, forests differentiated as per density, variety of vegetable cover. This map delimits revenue villages and names them.

The brief analysis adequately demonstrates that pre-British India had its own systems of cadastral and revenue mapping. What has come to light is but a small fraction. Indian cartographers and revenue officials have much to delve in the past and unearth our own heritage of revenue of revenue measures and systems.

Economic and Social Developments under the Mughals

It was the normal policy of the Timurid rulers, both in their original Central Asian homelands and in India, to encourage trade. As in much else, Sher Shah Suri during his brief reign (1538–1545) set a pattern that was followed by the later Mughals, especially Akbar, when he encouraged trade by linking together various parts of the country through an efficient system of roads and abolishing many inland tolls and duties. The Mughals maintained this general policy, but their rule was distinguished by the importance which foreign trade attained by the end of the sixteenth century. This was partly the result of the discovery of the new sea-route to India; but even so, progress would have been limited if conditions within the country had not been favourable.

Trade and Industry

Both Akbar and Jahangir interested themselves in the foreign seaborne trade, and Akbar himself took part in commercial activities for a time. The Mughals welcomed the foreign trader, provided ample protection and security for his transactions, and levied a very low custom duty (usually no more than 2½ percent ad valorem). Furthermore, the expansion of local handicrafts and industry resulted in a reservoir of exportable goods. Indian exports consisted mainly of manufactured articles, with cotton cloth in great demand in Europe and elsewhere. Indigo, saltpeter, spices, opium, sugar, woollen and silk cloth of various kinds, yarn, asafoetida, salt, beads, borax, turmeric, lac, sealing wax, and drugs of various kinds, were also exported. The principal imports were bullion, horses, and a certain quantity of luxury goods for the upper classes, like raw silk, coral, amber, precious stones, superior textiles (silk, velvet, brocade, broadcloth), perfumes, drugs, china goods, and European wines. By and large, however, in return for their goods Indian merchants insisted on payment in gold or silver. Naturally this was not popular in England and the rest of Europe, and writers on economic affairs in the seventeenth century frequently complained, as did Sir Thomas Roe, that "Europe bleedeth to enrich Asia." The demand for articles supplied by India was so great, however, and her requirements of European goods so limited, that Europe was obliged to trade on India's own terms until the eighteenth century, when special measures were taken in England and elsewhere to discourage the demand for Indian goods.

The manufacture of cotton goods had assumed such extensive proportions that in addition to satisfying her own needs, India sent cloth to almost half the world: the east coast of Africa, Arabia, Egypt, Southeast Asia, as well as Europe. The textile industry, well established in Akbar's day, continued to flourish under his successors, and soon the operations of Dutch and English traders brought India into direct touch with Western markets. This resulted in great demand for Indian cotton goods from Europe, which naturally increased production at home. Even the silk industry—especially in Bengal—was in flourishing condition. Bernier wrote: "There is in Bengal such a quantity of cotton and silk, that the kingdom may be called the common storehouse for these two kinds of merchandise, not of Hindustan or the Empire of the Great Mughal only, but of all the neighbouring kingdoms, and even of Europe."

Apart from silk and cotton textiles, other industries were shawl and carpet weaving, woollen goods, pottery, leather goods, and articles made of wood. Owing to its proximity to sources of suitable timbers, Chittagong specialised in shipbuilding, and at one time supplied ships to distant Istanbul. The commercial side of the industry was in the hands of middlemen, but the Mughal government, like the earlier sultans, made its own contribution. The emperor controlled a large number of royal workshops, busily turning out articles for his own use, for his household, for the court, and for the imperial army. Akbar took a special interest in the development of indigenous industry. He was directly responsible for the expansion of silk weaving at Lahore, Agra, Fatehpur-Sikri, and in Gujarat. He opened a large number of factories at important centres, importing master weavers from Persia, Kashmir, and Turkistan. Akbar frequently visited the workshops near the palace to watch the artisans at work, which encouraged the craftsmen and raised their status. It is said that he took such an interest in the industry that to foster demand he "ordered people of certain ranks to wear particular kinds of locally woven coverings ... an order which resulted in the establishment of a large number of shawl manufactories in Lahore; and inducements were offered to foreign carpet-weavers to settle in Agra, Fathepur Sikri, and Lahore, and manufacture carpets to compete with those imported from Persia." In the course of time, the foreign traders established close contracts with important markets in India, and new articles which were more in demand in Western Europe began to be produced in increasing quantities. Among the foreign inventions that excited Akbar's interest was an organ, "one of the wonders of creation," that had been brought from Europe.

Urban Life

All foreign travellers speak of the wealth and prosperity of Mughal cities and large towns. Monserrate stated that Lahore in 1581 was "not second to any city in Europe or Asia." Finch, who travelled in the early days of Jahangir, found both Agra and Lahore to be much larger than London, and his testimony is supported by others. Other cities like Surat ("A city of good quantity, with many fair merchants and houses therein"), Ahemadabad, Allahabad, Benares, and Patna similarly excited the admiration of visitors. The new port towns of Bombay, Calcutta, Madras, and Karachi developed under British rule, but they had their predecessors in Satgaon, Surat, Cambay, Lari Bunder, and other ports.

The efficient system of city government under the Mughals encouraged trade. The pivot of urban administration was the kotwal, the city governor. In addition to his executive and judicial powers, it was his duty to prevent and detect crime, to perform many of the functions now assigned to the municipal boards, to regulate prices, and in general, to be responsible for the peace and prosperity of the city. The efficient discharge of these duties depended on the personality of the individual city governor, but the Mughals tried to ensure high standards by making the kotwal personally responsible for the property and the security of the citizens. Akbar had decreed (probably following Sher Shah Suri's example of fixing the responsibility on village chiefs for highway robberies in their territory) that the kotwal was to either recover stolen goods or be held responsible for their loss. That this was not only a pious hope is borne out by the testimony of several foreign travellers who state that the kotwal was personally liable to make good the value of any stolen property which he was unable to recover. The kotwals often found pretexts to evade the ultimate responsibility, but in general they took elaborate measures to prevent thefts.

Most of this flourishing commerce was in the hands of the traditional Hindu merchant classes, whose business acumen was proverbial. Their caste guilds added to the skills in trade and commerce that they had learned through the centuries. Not only were their disputes settled by their panchayats, but they would frequently impose pressure on the government by organised action. Foreign visitors record that the governors and kotwals were very sensitive to this, and in spite of hardships inseparable from a despotic system of administration, the business communities had their own means of obtaining redress. Bernier, writing during Aurangzeb's time, declared that the Hindus possessed "almost exclusively the trade and wealth of the country." If Muslims enjoyed advantages in higher administrative posts and in the army, Hindu merchants maintained the monopoly in trade and finance that they had during the sultanate. A Dutch traveller in the early seventeenth century was struck by the fact that few Muslims engaged in handicraft industries, and that even when a Muslim merchant did have a large business, he employed Hindu bookkeepers and agents. Banking was almost exclusively in Hindu hands. In the years of the decline of the Mughals, a rich Hindu banker would finance his favourite rival claimant for the throne. The role of Jagat Seth of Murshidabad in the history of Bengal is well known. Even the "war of succession" out of which Aurangzeb emerged victorious was financed by a loan of five and a half lakhs of rupees from the Jain bankers of Ahemadabad. Here one sees a contrast with British rule, when the British not only monopolised the higher civil service posts but also controlled most of the major industries as well as the great banks and trading agencies.

Rural Conditions

Conditions in the rural areas during the Mughal period were much the same as at present, with one important difference—the Muslim rulers had scarcely disturbed the old organisation of the villages. The panchayats continued to settle most disputes, with the state impinging very little on village life, except for the collection of land revenue, and even this was very often done on a village basis rather than through individuals, with the age-old arrangements being preserved. The incidence of land revenue was substantially higher under the Mughals and in Hindu states like Vijayanagar than in British India, but the administration was more flexible, both in theory and in practice, in its assessment and collection. Apart from the remission of land revenue when crops failed, there was reduction in government demand even when bumper crops caused prices to fall. For example, between 1585 and 1590 very large sums had to be written off because a series of exceptionally good harvests had resulted in a surplus, and peasants could not sell their crops. The state also advanced loans to the cultivators, and occasionally provided seed as well as implements for digging wells. Loans advanced to the cultivators for seeds, implements, bullocks, or digging of wells were called *taqavi*—an expression which has continued in modern land revenue administration.

Health and Medical Facilities

A feature noticed by many foreign travellers was the good health of the local inhabitants. Fryer, writing of the mortality among the English at Bombay and the adjacent parts, says that "the country people lived to a good old age, supposed to be the reward of their temperance." Bernier also speaks of "general habits of sobriety among the people," though this did not apply to a few cases among the upper classes or the royal family. The European travellers found "less vigour among the people than in the colder climates, but greater enjoyment of health." From their accounts, even the climate would appear to have been healthy.

"Gout, stone complaints in the kidneys, catarrh ... are nearly unknown; and persons who arrive in the country afflicted with any of these disorders soon experience a complete cure." The Mughal emphasis on physical fitness and encouragement of out-of-door manly games also raised the general standard of health. The ideal was that everyone was to be trained to be a soldier, a good rider, a keen shikari, and able to distinguish himself in games. Ovington found that the English at Surat were "much less vigorous and athletic in their bodies than Indians." It is possible that the drinking habits of the Europeans made them an easy prey to ill-health in the tropics.

Public hospitals had been provided in Muslim India, at least since the days of Firuz Tughluq (1351–1388), and though it would be ridiculous to compare them with the arrangements introduced by the British, the system seems to have been extended during the Mughal period. Jahangir states in his autobiography that on his accession to the throne he ordered the establishment, at government expense, of hospitals in large cities. That this order was actually made effective is shown by the records of salaries paid by the government and of grants for the distribution of medicine.

The supply of local physicians was not plentiful; and judged by the demand for European doctors, particularly surgeons, they were apparently not equal to all demands. The general health of the inhabitants suggests, however, that the medical services were not completely inadequate, and the local physicians were able to deal with normal problems. As early as 1616 they knew the important characteristics of the bubonic plague and suggested suitable preventive measures.

According to an account in *Iqbal Nama*, which was written in Jahangir's reign: "When the disease was about to break out, a mouse would rush out of its hole, as if mad, and striking itself against the door and the walls of the house, would expire. If immediately after this signal the occupants left the house and went away to the jungle, their lives were safe. If otherwise, the inhabitants of the village would be spirited away by the hands of death." As modern scholars have pointed out, this observation includes two facts about the plague whose significance has been corroborated by modern science: the association of the death of rodents with the disease, and the necessity of evacuating the infected quarter.

A crude form of vaccination against smallpox seems to have been employed by Eastern doctors, for it was vaguely realised that the introduction of a mild form of cowpox prevented the virulent form of smallpox. An article in the Asiatic Register of London for 1804 contained a translation of a memorandum by Nawab Mirza Mehdi Ali Khan describing from personal observations the method adopted by a Hindu medical practitioner of Benares. A thread drenched in "the matter of a pustule on the cow" was placed on the arms of a child to cause an easy erruption, thus avoiding a virulent attack of smallpox.

In ancient times, the use of medicines had been well developed among the Hindus, but dissection was considered to be irreligious. The Muslims, who did not have this restriction, performed a number of operations. As Elphinstone pointed out: "Their surgery is as remarkable as their medicine especially when we recollect their ignorance of anatomy. They cut for the stone, couched for the cataract, and extracted the feotus from the womb, and in their early works enunciate no less than one hundred and twenty-seven surgical works." According to Manucci, Muslim surgeons could provide artificial limbs.

Social Customs

The marriage customs of Hindus and Muslims had many similarities. Early marriages were much in vogue amongst the Hindus, with seven considered the proper age for a girl to be married. To leave a daughter unmarried beyond twelve years of age was to risk the displeasure of one's caste. The Muslims also betrothed their children between the ages of six and eight, but the marriage was generally not solemnised before they had attained the age of puberty.

Among the wealthier classes polygamy and divorce are said to have been very common. The custom of secluding women, known as purdah, was very strictly observed. Marriage negotiations were undertaken by the professional broker or the friends of either party. The marriage ceremonies were more or less the same as they are at present, and the character of the average Indian or Pakistani home and the socio-ethical ideas which influence it have not undergone any fundamental change. The son's duty to his parents and the wife's duty to her husband were viewed almost as religious obligations.

"Superstitions played a prominent part in the daily life of the people. Charms were used not merely to ensnare a restive husband but also to secure such other ends as the birth of a son or cure of a disease. The fear of the evil eye was ever present ... and the young child was considered particularly susceptible. ... People believed in all sorts of omens." Astrologers were very much in demand, even at the Mughal court.

The Muslim aristocrats lived in great houses decorated with rich hangings and carpets. Their clothing was made of finest cotton or silk, decorated with gold; and they carried beautiful scimitars. There was a considerable element of ostentatious display involved in this, however, for their domestic arrangements did not match the outward splendour of their dress and equipment. Manucci, a keen observer, refers to Pathans who came to court "well-clad and well-armed, caracolling on fine horses richly caparisoned and followed by several servants," but when they reached home, divested themselves of "all this finery, and tying a scanty cloth around their loins and wrapping a rag around their head, they take their seat on a mat, and live on ... rice and lentils or badly cooked cow's flesh of low quality, which is very abundant in the Mogul country and very cheap."

The courtly manners and the elaborate etiquette of the Muslim upper classes impressed foreign visitors. In social gatherings they spoke "in a very low voice with much order, moderation, gravity, and sweetness. ... Betel and betelnut were presented to the visitors and they were escorted with much civility at the time of departure. Rigid forms were observed at meals. ... Dice was their favourite indoor game.

Polo or chaugan—for which there was a special playground at Dacca—elephant-fights, hunting, excursions and picnics, were also very popular." The grandees rode in palkis, preceded by uniformed mounted servants. Many "drove in fine two-wheeled carts, carved with gilt and gold, covered in silk, and drawn by two little bulls which could race with the fastest horses."

The Position of the Hindus

The Hindu upper classes undoubtedly shared in the material culture of the Mughals, for, as already noted, they had a virtual monopoly of trade and finance. Furthermore, they had long held many high posts in the government. The contrast between the position of Hindus under the Mughals and of Indians in general under the British was often made by Indian historians during the period of the nationalist movement. Thus a Hindu historian writing in 1940 could argue that "under Shah Jahan Hindus occupied a higher status in the government than that occupied by the Indians today."

The vitality of the Hindus was shown in more than their ability to maintain footholds within administrative and commercial life. Widespread religious movements, having, as we have seen, their roots partly in the vivifying contacts of Hinduism with Islam, had produced a religious enthusiasm among the masses that was transforming the older Brahmanical religion.

Although Muslim historians ignore this religious revival among the Hindus, there is enough evidence to indicate its importance during Mughal rule. The new regional literature of Bengal and Maharashtra, which owed much to the new movement, is a clear mirror of what was taking place in Hindu society. In Bengal, there was not only the rise of a new literature, but numerous temples were built during the late seventeenth century. The significance of this phenomenon becomes clear if it is remembered that practically throughout the second half of the seventeenth century, Aurangzeb was on the throne. His alleged ceaseless campaign of temple destruction obviously could have been neither thoroughgoing nor universal.

The developments in intellectual life were even more marked. The rise of Navadipa as a great centre of Sanskritic learning, and the vogue of navyanyaya (new logic) belong to this period.

In relation to Islam, Hinduism exhibited a new vigour, greater self-confidence, and even a spirit of defiance. Hinduism is not generally thought of as a missionary religion, and it is often assumed that during Muslim rule conversions were only from Hinduism to Islam. This is, however, not true. Hinduism by now was very much on the offensive and was absorbing a number of

Muslims. When Shah Jahan returned from Kashmir, in the sixth year of his reign, he discovered that Hindus of Bhadauri and Bhimbar were forcibly marrying Muslim girls and converting them to the Hindu faith. At death these women were cremated according to the Hindu rites. Jahangir had tried to stop this practice but with no success, and Shah Jahan also issued orders declaring such marriages unlawful. Four thousand such conversions are said to have been discovered.

Many cases were also found in Gujarat and in parts of the Punjab. Partly to deal with such cases, and partly to conform to his early notions of an orthodox Muslim king, Shah Jahan established a special department to deal with conversions. After the tenth year of his reign, he seems to have ceased trying to prevent the proselytising activities of the Hindus. There are several later cases of the conversion of Muslims, not recorded by the court historians. A number of Muslims—including at least two Muslim nobles, Mirza Salih and Mirza Haider—were converted to Hinduism by the vairagis, the wandering ascetics of the Chaitanya movement, which had become a powerful religious force in Bengal. There were also cases of conversions from Islam to Sikhism. When Guru Hargovind took up his residence at Kiratpur in the Punjab some time before 1645, he is said to have succeeded in converting a large number of Muslims. It was reported that not a Muslim was left between the hills near Kiratpur and the frontiers of Tibet and Khotan. His predecessor, Guru Arjan, had proselytised so actively that he incurred Jahangir's anger, and, as Jahangir mentions in his autobiography, the Hindu shrines of Kangra and Mathura attracted a number of Muslim pilgrims.

The Hindu position was so strong that in some places Aurangzeb's order for the collection of jizya was defied. On January 29, 1693, the officials in Malwa sent a soldier to collect jizya from a zamindar called Devi Singh. When he reached the place, Devi Singh's men fell upon him, pulled his beard and hair, and sent him back empty-handed. The emperor thereupon ordered a reduction in the jagir of Devi Singh. Earlier, another official had fared much worse. He himself proceeded to the jagir to collect the tax, but was killed by the Hindu mansabdar. Orders to destroy newly built temples met with similar opposition. A Muslim officer who was sent in 1671 to destroy temples at the ancient pilgrimage city of

Ujjain was killed in a riot that broke out as he tried to carry out his orders.

Muslim historians, in order to show the extreme orthodoxy of Aurangzeb, have recorded many reports of temple destruction. On a closer scrutiny, however, there seem to be good grounds for believing that all the reports were not correct, and that quite often no action was taken on imperial orders. We read, for example, about the destruction of a certain temple at Somnath during the reign of Shah Jahan and again under Aurangzeb. It is likely that in this and in many similar cases, the temple was not destroyed on the first order. According to accounts by English merchants, Aurangzeb's officers would leave the temples standing on payment of large sums of money by the priests. However, new temples whose construction had not been authorised were often closed. If the situation is closely examined, it appears that the complaint of Sheikh Ahmad that under Muslim rule as it existed in India, Islam was in need of greater protection than other religions does not appear to have been completely unfounded. Aurangzeb tried, of course, to reverse this trend, and some other rulers also had occasional spells of Islamic zeal, either from political or religious causes. But by and large, it is perhaps fair to say that during Muslim rule, Islam suffered from handicaps which almost outweighed the advantages it enjoyed as the religion of the ruling dynasty. This paradox becomes understandable if the basic Muslim political theory is kept in mind, under which the non-Muslim communities, so long as they paid certain taxes, were left to manage their own affairs. This local and communal autonomy severely circumscribed the sovereignty of the Muslim state, and in most matters the caste guilds and the village panchayats exercised real sovereignty, which they naturally utilised to safeguard their creed and way of life. It was this power which enabled them to evade, or even defy, unwelcome orders from the capital. A curious light on the situation is thrown by the penalties and economic losses which a Hindu had to suffer on the adoption of Islam. Practically until the end of Muslim rule, a Hindu who became a Muslim automatically lost all claim to ancestral property.

This extraordinary position was a natural result of the application of Hindu law, which, according to the Muslim legal system, governed Hindu society even under Muslim government, and under which apostacy resulted in disinheritance. Shah Jahan, who began as an orthodox Muslim, tried to redress the balance by issuing orders that "family pressure should not prevent a Hindu from being admitted to Islam," and laid down that a convert should not be disinherited.

Whether these orders could overcome the subtle but solid pressure of the joint family system and the power of the caste panchayats must remain a matter of speculation. The question, however, of handicaps or advantages of one community against another is not of fundamental significance.

The important fact is that during normal times conditions of tolerance prevailed. This was of special interest to European visitors, almost all of whom commented on the concessions enjoyed by non-Muslims under Muslim rule.

The Jesuits were critical of this policy of tolerance, declaring the destruction of Hindu temples by Muslims "a praiseworthy action," but noting their "carelessness" in allowing public performance of Hindu sacrifices and religious practices. When Akbar granted the followers of the Raushaniya sect the freedom to follow their religion, Monserrate sadly commented that "He cared little that in allowing everyone to follow his own religion he was in reality violating all religions."

Even in Aurangzeb's reign a cow could not be slaughtered in important places like Surat, and attempts made by some English merchants to obtain beef led to riots. According to one account: "In Surat the Hindus paid a fixed sum to the Mohammadans in return for sparing the cows.

In 1608 a riot was caused at Surat by a drunken sailor Tom Tucker who killed a calf. Similar occurrences at Karwar and Honavar led to outbreaks, in one of which the whole factory was murdered." But nothing brings out the Mughal administration's respect for the susceptibilities of the Hindus as well as the experience of the Portuguese missionary traveller, Manrique. "In a village where he stopped for the night, one of his followers, a Musalman, killed two peacocks, birds sacred in the eyes of Hindus, and did his best to conceal the traces of his deed by burying their feathers. The sacrilege was, however, detected, the whole party arrested, and the offender sentenced to have a hand amputated, though this punishment was eventually commuted to a whipping by the local official, who explained that the emperor had taken an oath that he and his successors would let the Hindus live under their own laws and customs and tolerate no breach of them."

Although the Mughals interfered little with Hindu customs, there was one ancient practice which they sought to stop. This was sati, or the custom of widows, particularly those of the higher classes, burning themselves on their husbands' funeral pyres.

Akbar had issued general orders prohibiting sati, and in one noteworthy case, personally intervened to save a Rajput princess from immolating herself on the bier of her husband. Similar efforts continued to be made in the succeeding reigns. According to the European traveller Pelsaert, governors did their best to dissuade widows from immolating themselves, but by Jahangir's orders were not allowed to withhold their sanction if the woman persisted. Tavernier, writing in the reign of Shah Jahan, observed that widows with children were not allowed in any circumstances to burn, and that in other cases governors did not readily give permission, but could be bribed to do so.

Aurangzeb was most forthright in his efforts to stop sati. According to Manucci, on his return from Kashmir in December, 1663, he "issued an order that in all lands under Mughal control, never again should the officials allow a woman to be burnt." Manucci adds that "This order endures to this day." This order, though not mentioned in the formal histories, is recorded in the official guidebooks of the reign. Although the possibility of an evasion of government orders through payment of bribes existed, later European travellers record that sati was not much practised by the end of Aurangzeb's reign. As Ovington says in his Voyage to Surat: "Since the Mahometans became Masters of the Indies, this execrable custom is much abated, and almost laid aside, by the orders which nabobs receive for suppressing and extinguishing it in all their provinces. And now it is very rare, except it be some Rajah's wives, that the Indian women burn at all."

Any generalisation about Indian history is dangerous, but the impression one gains from looking at social conditions during the Mughal period is of a society moving towards an integration of its manifold political regions, social systems, and cultural inheritances. The greatness of the Mughals consisted in part at least in the fact that the influence of their court and government permeated society, giving it a new measure of harmony. The common people suffered from poverty, disease, and the oppression of the powerful; court life was marked by intrigue and cruelty as well as by refinement of taste and elegant manners.

Yet the rulers and their officials had moral standards which gave coherence to the administration and which they shared to some extent with most of their subjects. Undeniably, there were ugly scars on the face of Mughal society, but the sixteenth and seventeenth centuries had a quality of life that lent them a peculiar charm. The clearest reflection of this is seen in the creative arts of the period.

5

Land Reform in India

Issues and Challenges

As the basis of all economic activity, land can either serve as an essential asset for the country to achieve economic growth and social equity, or it could be used as a tool in the hands of a few to hijack a country's economic independence and subvert its social processes.

During the two centuries of British colonisation, India had experienced the latter reality.

During colonialism, India's traditional land ownership and land use patterns were changed to ease acquisition of land at low prices by British entrepreneurs for mines, plantations etc. The introduction of the institution of private property de-legitimised community ownership systems of tribal societies. Moreover, with the introduction of the land tax under the Permanent Settlement Act 1793, the British popularised the zamindari system at the cost of the jajmani relationship that the landless shared with the land owning class. By no means a just system, the latter at least ensured the material security of those without land.

Owing to these developments, at independence, India inherited a semi-feudal agrarian system. The ownership and control of land was highly concentrated in a few landlords and intermediaries whose main intention was to extract maximum rent, either in cash or kind, from tenants. Under this arrangement, the sharecropper or the tenant farmer had little economic motivation to develop farmland for increased production. Naturally, a cultivator who did not have security of tenure, and was required to pay a high proportion of output in rents, was less likely to invest in land improvements, or use high yielding varieties or other expensive inputs likely to yield higher returns. At the same time, neither was the landlord particularly concerned about improving the economic condition of the cultivators. As a result, agricultural productivity suffered and oppression of tenants resulted in a progressive deterioration of their plight.

In the years immediately following India's independence, a conscious process of nation building looked upon problems of land with a pressing urgency. In fact, the national objective of poverty abolition envisaged simultaneous progress on two fronts, high productivity and equitable distribution. Accordingly, reforms of the land were visualised as an important pillar for a strong and prosperous country.

The first few five-year plans allocated substantial budgetary amounts for the implementation of land reforms. A degree of success was even registered in certain regions and states, and especially in areas like the abolition of intermediaries, protection to tenants, rationalisation of different tenure systems and the imposition of ceiling on land holdings. Fifty-four years down the line, however, a number of problems are still far from satisfactorily resolved.

Most studies indicate that inequalities have increased, rather than decreased. The number of landless labour has gone up and the top ten percent monopolises more land now than in 1951. Meanwhile, the issue of land reforms has over the years, either unconsciously faded from public mind or deliberately been glossed over. Vested interests of the landed elite and their powerful nexus with the political-bureaucratic system have blocked meaningful land reforms and /or their earnest implementation.

The oppressed have either been co-opted with some benefits, or further subjugated as the new focus on LPG has altered government priorities and public perceptions.

As a result, we are today at a juncture where land, mostly for the urban, educated elite, and who also happens to be the powerful decision-maker, has become more a matter for housing, investment and infrastructure building. In the bargain, the existence of land as a basis of livelihood-for subsistence, survival, social justice and human dignity has largely been lost.

Objectives

It is against this background that the specific objectives of the Project in India have been articulated as:

- To raise popular and elite awareness on issues related to land, particularly in the present context of the LPG thrust of the government since the 1990s.
- To monitor specific projects and programmes being aided by international financial institutions in some states of India in order to assess their true impact on the rural community directly affected.
- To monitor and scrutinise national and transnational economic trends that have a specific bearing on issues related to land and agriculture.
- To explore the efficacy of the current developmental model that perceives land only as a factor of production, and not as a means of survival, equity and dignity.
- To examine possible strategies for facilitating reconciliation between the claims of the market over land and land reforms to ensure social change based on justice and equity.
- To document historical strategies of land reforms and place them in the socio-economic-political context in which they were effective or not and accordingly cull out lessons for the future.
- To recommend alternative policies and approaches to contemporary land challenges.
- To provide research and analytical support to the existing land movements, and facilitate better networking among them.
- To awaken the weakening social consciousness of an increasingly consumerist society by drawing linkages between the economic policies of globalisation at the macro level and its impact on human livelihoods at the micro level.

IFIs and Issues Related to Land in India

The task of the articulation of objectives is several times easier compared to the challenges that lie ahead in realising these goals. Any reform is as difficult an economic exercise as a political undertaking since it involves a realignment of economic and political power. The groups that are likely to be the losers naturally resist reallocation of power, property and status. Obviously, the landholding class is unlikely to willingly vote itself out of possession. Neither should it be expected that it would be uniformly inflamed by altruistic passions to voluntarily undertake the exercise. Hence, one cannot underestimate the complexity of the task at hand. Loopholes in legislation have facilitated the evasion of some of the provisions, for instance in ceiling reforms, by those who wanted to maintain the status quo. At the same time, tardy implementation at the bureaucratic level and a political hijacking of the land reforms agenda have traditionally posed impediments in the path of effective land reforms. Even in states that have attempted reforms, the process has often halted mid-way with the co-option of the beneficiaries by the status quoits to resist any further reforms.

For instance, with the abolition of intermediary interests, the erstwhile superior tenants belonging mostly to the upper and middle classes have acquired a higher social status. Rise in agricultural productivity, rising land values and higher incomes from cultivation have added to their economic strength. These classes have since become opposed to any erosion in their newly acquired financial or social status.

Hence, problems related to land such as concentration, tenancy rights, access to the landless etc. still continue to challenge India. The criticality of the issue, in fact, may be gauged from the fact that notwithstanding the decline in the share of agriculture to the GDP, nearly 58% of India's population is still dependant on agriculture for livelihood.

More than half of this percentage (nearly 63%), however, owns small holdings of less than 1 hectare while the large parcels of 10 hectares of land or more are in the hands of less than 2%. The absolute landless and the near landless (those owning up to .2 ha of land) account for as much as 43% of the total peasant households.

This reality, however, had come to worry the governments little during the late 1970s and 80s. It was only in the 1990s, with the initiation of the economic restructuring process that the issue of land reforms resurfaced, albeit in a different garb and with a different objective and motivation. If the government-led land reforms had been imbued with a degree, though the extent is debatable, of desire for attaining equity, social justice and dignity, the new land reforms agenda is market-driven, as everything else in this phase of economic globalisation, and has at its heart certain other kinds of objectives. Being promoted and guided by various IFIs, contemporary emphasis on land reforms reflects and seeks to fulfil the macroeconomic objectives of these multilateral economic institutions.

While the return of land reforms to the government's list of priorities is a welcome development, the manner in which it is being undertaken, its objectives, and consequently the impact on people, especially those that are already marginalised and are being further deprived of a stake in the system, raises a number of questions and prompts one to look for alternatives. The Project, therefore, shall devote its energies to identifying and monitoring the implementation of certain specific IFI sponsored programmes in particular states with a view to examining their short-term and long-term impact on the lives and livelihoods of local residents. This shall enable an informed critique of the IFI-led land reforms programmes and serve as a lesson for peoples else where in India and in other regions of the globe as well.

Market-Led Land Reforms—The Current Emphasis on Land Administration, Titling and Registration

In their analysis of India's land reforms programme, most IFIs have highlighted that one of the basic problem that the rural poor face is access to land and security of tenure. Consequently, they advocate redemption of this situation through structural reforms of property rights to create land markets as part of a broader strategy of fostering economic growth and reducing rural poverty.

A large emphasis has, therefore, been placed on the need to establish the basic legal and institutional framework that would improve secure property rights as a means to protect environmental and cultural resources, to facilitate productivity-enhancing exchanges of land in rental and sales markets, to link land to financial markets, to use land as a sustainable source of revenue for local governments, and to improve land access by the poor and traditionally disenfranchised. (Emphasis added).

The package the IFIs offer includes comprehensive reforms of land tenure, including titling, cadastral surveys and settlement operations, land registries, improvements in land revenue systems, land legislation, land administration, land sale-purchase transactions, and removal of restrictions on land leasing.

In fact, it may be recalled that even in 1975, a Land Reforms Policy Paper brought out by the WB had described land registration and titling as the main instruments for increasing individual's tenure security, the main facilitators for the establishment of flourishing land markets and the major tools to enable the use of land as collateral for credit. However, the emphasis on these issues then was much less. But today, these ingredients constitute the mainstay of IFI-led land reforms across the world.

Through this approach, land reforms are envisaged in two phases:

Phase One-Dismantling Distortionary Policies.

- This would involve the removal of all restrictions on the sale and purchase of land, including those related to minimum and maximum size, and revision of procedures for sale of public lands.
- It would envisage the complete elimination of rent controls so as to increase investments and efficiency in agriculture.
- Zoning would also be eliminated, except in the case of safeguarding certain environmental concerns. Restrictions on land use, if necessary in specific areas, would be achieved through instruments other than government legislation, such as creation of a market for development rights.

Phase Two-Institutional and Legal Reforms

- Constraints in the operations of the land markets to be removed through reforms that aim that reducing costs of land adjudication, issuing of correct titles, and easy availability of crucial market information to interested parties.

- Creation of land laws that remove uncertainty facilitates easy and transparent access to the land administration system, establish dispute settlement institutions and institutionalize property rights.

As is evident, the bottom line of all these measures is the facilitation of land markets wherein land is available for sale-purchase from less to more productive users. It is believed that with proper title deeds being available for property, it would become easier and less risky to buy and sell land. As a private commodity, the owner will have a stake in putting the land to best use, which in WB terminology implies use that can generate maximum profits.

The manner in which this exercise would generate access to land for the rural poor is through the provision of credit to them for purchase of land, making available to them technical assistance to enable them to plough the land in keeping with the needs of commercial farming, and providing them with marketing support. Of course, everything would come for a price with the farmer being gradually pushed into a process of indebtedness. Credit would be easily available to have access to land and other expensive agricultural inputs such as seeds, fertilizers, pesticides, irrigation, market mechanisms etc. The market forces at every step would encourage the farmer to take easily available loans, but vagaries of nature as much as those of the market could easily bring him to ruin. Bankrupt, he may be forced to sell the land and either move out of the land market completely, leaving the fields for the richer and more able farmers/corporations, or get into the process once again to try his luck.

It is in this context that the market-driven land reforms that are being encouraged by the IFIs need to be looked into. None can deny the need for reform in land administration agencies, for updating of land records through surveys and settlement of rights, computerisation of land records etc. In fact, one can recall that in the first two decades of government land reforms after independence, the reformers demanded these measures. At that time, however, the issues were largely ignored or neglected owing to lack of institutional support such as trained staff, equipment, capital etc. The IFIs have rightly discovered this lacuna and are now offering the financial help and technical expertise in carrying out the exercise. However, the purpose for which these reforms are being undertaken in the present context raises several issues since the motives may not measure up to those of social justice and dignity for the individual:

1. The IFIs proclaim increasing access to land for the rural poor by offering credit.

   However, how does this help if they simultaneously encourage macroeconomic and trade policies that negate the benefits of such an exercise? Policies such as trade liberalisation, cutbacks in price supports and subsidies for food producers, privatisation of credit, commercialisation of agriculture, excessive export promotion and promotion of research in expensive technologies such as genetic engineering etc. undercut the economic viability of the smaller and poorer farmers. The onslaught of these policies adversely affects the small farmers leading to high failure rates, mass sell-offs, increased landlessness, land concentration, even intensified land degradation, and rural-urban migration. What then is the efficacy of such land reforms?

2. The emergence of land markets and the consequent commodification of land raises several issues for the status of the common property resources because by codifying social and property relations that were hitherto implicit, land titling could reduce the asset-endowment of vulnerable groups with inadequate access to political power. Therefore, their privatisation would spell severe consequences for those who have survived on it for generations but have no legal documents to show for the same. Does this not lead to situations, where common lands may be acquired by powerful individuals/ corporations in violation of long-established rights of indigenous communities?

3. What impact would the process of titling and land registration have on the status of women and indigenous

people who often tend to be left out of these processes?. The market-driven economy emphasises short-term profit motives with little regard for the people or environment. Rather, the primacy of commercial interests in a market society encourages the view that stretches of densely vegetated forests or other open lands that may have an intangible ecological value but are not being utilised to carry out activities that can fetch tangible foreign exchange are non-optimally used resources.' With such perceptions becoming prevalent, would not the environment, too, become victim to a thoughtless extraction of maximum profits with little consideration for the actual ecological value of land? For instance, the conversion of non-agricultural land to agricultural, or vice versa, may not be the most judicious use of the land but may be resorted to for the sake of maximising profits.

5. The benefits of secure titles to land may be nullified by market distortions caused when land is used as a commodity for investment and speculation. This then inflates land value, making access to land even more difficult. Therefore, how can land speculation, an inevitable accompaniment of land market development, help in providing secure tenure for all—the major World Bank motivation for market-led land reforms?

6. While data is not yet available, most observers feel that the net result of the predominance of land markets in regions where they have become operative has been a deterioration in the access of the poor to land as they are forced/tempted to sell off land they own, or lose it by defaulting on credit. None can argue against the need for straightening land records and the provision of secure land titles and registration, the motivation for the exercise must delve deeper than the mere creation of land markets for private profit. The Project proposes to undertake a study of this issue and its actual impact on the rural poor by studying the implementation of the activity in the state of Maharashtra. It also proposes to study alternative schemes in this regard, such as the one undertaken by the Maharashtra government in Pune. The simultaneous

analysis of two different methods of undertaking regularisation of land records would reveal lessons for others. It shall also weigh the benefits costs of these measures against those of land redistribution as a means of poverty alleviation and for promotion of ecological sustainability.

The Heights and Economic well-being of North Indians under British Rule

In 1965 Morris David Morris, by questioning the view that British rule had led to the impoverishment of the Indian people, reopened the debate about the course of Indian economic welfare in the nineteenth century. Aspects of the question continue to concern scholars.

The debate about the British impact on the Indian economy has a number of elements. These include the effect of British competition on handicraft production (Bagchi 1976), the significance of the "Home charges" paid by the Indian government for expenditures related to the government of India in Britain (Charlesworth 1982: 51-55), and most importantly for this paper, the experience of cultivators and labourers in an agricultural society changing through commercialisation and railway expansion. Morris (1965) argued that political order led to greater stability of cultivation, increased irrigation reduced the extent of marginal land, and given a low rate of population growth, the extension of cultivation meant rising output per capita. His point that the expansion of domestic and foreign markets, along with improvements in transportation, encouraged regional specialisation and, therefore, increased output was taken up by McAlpin (1983), who concluded that in western India the raw cotton producers benefited from access to world markets, and that the cultivators, rather than having to store some grain as famine insurance, were able to sell more of their crop.

The outcome was that benefits became available for cultivators, agricultural labourers, and artisans, and that, with the assistance of new government relief systems, famine occurred less often.

The contrary view was put initially, and forcefully, by Bipan Chandra (1968) and Tapan Raychaudhuri (1968). Apart from questioning the extent of the Pax Britannica in the period up to the mutiny of 1857, they also argued that inhibitions such as heavy taxation, the tenurial system, and the expansion of moneylending prevented the cultivator (let alone the labourer) from securing a share of any surplus. They also argued that commercial nonfood crops were only a small proportion of total production, and that income distribution in this sector was biased in favour of the nonproducing classes. More recently, Bayly (1983: 468) and Washbrook (1988: 80) have explained the expansion of cultivation from those born in the 1830s as the result of the movement into agriculture of those retrenched from the occupations that had surrounded the old regional regimes and those who had lived by pastoral and forest pursuits. One critic of McAlpin points out that while the growth of railways and of markets, both foreign and domestic, had taken place since the 1860s, there were substantiaial famines in the 1870s and 1890s (S. Guha 1986: 238). Others argue that no evidence is adduced that labourers benefited from the higher prices in the markets and that access to world markets for cash crops like cotton opened the way for wider price variation than previously and made the region dependent on grain imports (Bates 1985: 869; Appadurai 1984: 487-88). Commercialisation of agriculture in North India focused on different crops from those in western India (sugar, wheat, indigo, and opium rather than cotton) and may have been less significant in the agricultural economy, but the question of whether the process benefited the labourers and their families remains open. Did the growth of markets and increase in trade improve their condition or not?

The normal methods of settling such arguments by analysing trends in economic conditions displayed by carefully collected figures of gross national product and per capita income are not possible in the Indian case. Alan Heston (1983: 379) and his predecessors have constructed tables for India as a whole that suggest that per capita income grew by about 0.5% per year between 1860 and 1920-that is, by at least 5%. But Irfan Habib (1985:368-74) is critical of Heston's calculations and argues that the evidence suggests that per capita income remained stable in the period 1875-1900. S. Guha (1992:1-48), in a wide-ranging analysis of the patchy evidence available on agricultural productivity, concludes that between 1825 and 1891 it was unlikely the area under cultivation did more than keep up with population growth, and that productivity probably fell except on irrigated land. For the first half of the twentieth century Guha follows Blyn (1966), arguing that there was an initial growth in per capita food production during the first twenty years, followed by a quarter century in which population increased faster than agricultural production.

For North India between the Punjab and Bengal, there are also institutional studies of agrarian conditions such as those by Whitcombe (1972), Metcalf (1979), Chaudhuri (1983), Stokes (1983), Bayly (1983), and Reeves (1991), but there are no equivalents of Baker (1984) for South India or S. Guha (1985) for the Bombay Deccan, who explicitly chart the general economic trends for the nineteenth century. This paper, encouraged by the view of Heston (1983: 409) that there is a case for using measures based on nutrition and health to flesh out or correct economic and institutional data, discusses trends in height-as a proxy for childhood nutrition and health-among men and women from North India during the nineteenth and twentieth centuries.

Height and History

Biologists have shown that although the explanation for the observed distribution of heights of a population at any point in time is partly genetic and partly environmental, changes in the distribution over time are mainly due to environmental factors, such as changes in the nutritional status of mothers and their children and changes in the incidence of disease (as childhood morbidity can stunt growth). It is also well recognised that improvements in nutrition and the declining incidence of disease during the past century have brought about a secular increase in average height and the earlier maturation of children (so that their final height is reached earlier) in many populations (Eveleth and Tanner 1990).

Anthropologists have also used information on height and other anthropometric data to study the differences between social groups in a given population, and the differences between various peoples. One focus of their studies is on how the distribution of the heights of a people may reflect their morphological and physiological adaptation to environmental conditions such as climate, altitude, and so on (Basu 1990: t10-11, 209-10). During the past decade or two, a number of economic historians have investigated the potential of data on height to illuminate trends in economic well-being over the past three centuries in a number of countries. They have used time-series data to trace the secular and cyclical patterns of average heights, and they have used cross-section data to show the variation in average height by region and social class (Fogel 1986; Komlos 1989; Floud et al. 1990; Nicholas and Steckel 1991). Up to the present, his research effort has been restricted to Europeans and the free and slave inhabitants of North America and the Caribbean.

In India, anthropologists have attempted to use anthropometric evidence to investigate the differences between India's various social groups: castes, religions, and tribes. The pioneers in this endeavour were Risley (1891, 1903) and Crooke (1896) for North Indians, and Thurston (1909) for South Indians. Most of their findings were incorporated in the census of 1901, as was B. S. Guha's (1935) survey in the census of 1931. Important surveys were also made in the United Provinces in 1941 (relating to 2,836 individuals from 22 social groups) and in Bengal in 1945 (relating to 3,240 individuals from 41 social groups); the raw data of these two surveys were inculcate in published survey reports (Mahalanobis et al. 1949; Majumdar and Rao 1958). The summary statistics of most of these various studies have been brought together in Gupta and Dutta (1966) and discussed by Basu (1990) and Sen (1971), among others.

Whereas these studies were restricted to relatively small samples of usually less than 100 adult males belonging to any one social group in particular localities, the first (and up to the present, the only) random sample of the entire Indian population was conducted by the Indian Council of Medical Research between 1956 and 1965. This survey covered both male and female children up to the age of 21 (ICMR 1972).

Although many anthropologists have speculated whether there has been secular change in Indian heights, only one scholar has made a reasonably systematic attempt to throw light on this issue. Drawing on earlier published studies, Ganguly (1979) compared the average height of 60 social groups at two points in time during the past century and concluded that there has been a secular decrease in heights. The decline, however, was not uniform all over the country but was more pronounced for North Indians than for South Indians. Caution should be used in generalising on the basis of Ganguly's sample: the sample is not random, it is based on a relatively small number of individuals measured, and it is restricted to males, Clearly, more research is needed to make stronger inferences about possible secular changes in Indian heights.

This paper is part of a wider research project that attempts to help fill this gap in the literature. It expands the body of evidence available to evaluate Indian heights by drawing upon the previously untapped emigrant passes of Indian indentured workers who were measured at Calcutta, Madras, and Bombay as they departed for Mauritius, Natal, the Caribbean, and Fiji. Hundreds of thousands of Indian workers were measured between 1842 and 1916, and these measurements were recorded on emigrant passes. Most of the original documents are extant, deposited in the national or provincial archives of Mauritius, Fiji, Trinidad, Jamaica, and Natal.

The present research project aims to computerize this entire body of evidence so that trends in the average height of Indians born from the first decade to the final decade of the nineteenth century can be traced and compared to more recent surveys conducted during the twentieth century. In the first stage of the project, the data relating to Indian workers departing from Calcutta and Madras to Fiji between 1879 and 1916 are analysed. The data for North Indians departing from Calcutta and South Indians departing from Madras are kept separate-mainly because there are important differences in the caste structure among North and South Indians-and are analysed in separate papers. This paper evaluates the data on North Indians, while companion papers address the South Indians (Brennan et al 1992a,1992b).

For the purposes of this paper, North India refers to the present-day states of Uttar Pradesh (UP) and Bihar. The two major ecologies of North India are located in the Gangetic plain. In the districts of western UP the average annual rainfall runs from 50 inches near the foothills to 25 inches in the southwest, supporting an agriculture based on wheat, millets, and pulses on rainfed land, with sugarcane and rice on irrigated land. In eastern UP and Bihar, rainfall is more abundant, especially near the northern foothills, so that rice is the staple crop and sugarcane can grow without irrigation; other crops include wheat, millets, and pulses. Most of the emigrants to Fiji came from this region. The fundamental agrarian structure in nineteenth-century UP comprised a fourfold division between landlords, who each held large numbers of villages; moliks, or landholders, who lived in and controlled the estates in which they had substantial shares; kisons, or cultivating peasants, who might be petty zamindars but in most cases cultivated land they held as tenants; and, mozdurs, or cultivators of smallholdings, sharecroppers, and agricultural labourers (Reeves 1991:25-27). Agricultural labourers were often linked by patron-client (jojmoni) relationships to the moliks for whom they worked: in southern Bihar this took an extreme form between maliks and their bonded labourers (homios), most of whom were low-caste Bhuinyas.

The Agrarian Reforms since Independence

During the last years of the colonial era, numerous congresses and commissions called for agrarian reforms and worked out appropriate suggestions. If, prior to independence, the demand for agrarian reforms was part of the strategy of the leading parties to gain power, independence fostered not only a favourable climate for such measures, but helped the new governments to legitimize their power. Not only the motivation, but the measures, too, were very similar in India and in Pakistan. However, each time, they were enforced more rapidly and strictly in India, whereas Pakistan showed more regard for the landowning strata.

Agrarian Reform Measures

It is not easy to obtain a general idea of the agrarian reform measures in India since, according to the federal constitution, every state enacted laws; specific laws were made far each of the sub measures; and some of these laws were repeatedly changed and supplemented. This is why the Indian legislation on agrarian reforms comprises far more than 100 laws. Just as an Pakistan, however, these measures can be divided into three groups: those concerning the abolition of 'intermediaries' (the numerous people who occupy a position between the government and the cultivators, *e.g.*, the "jagirdars," the "zamindars;" etc.; the improvement of tenancy; and the stipulation of the maximum ceilings of landed property allowed.

Abolition of the 'Intermediaries'

In 1951, as the first agrarian reform measure, the intermediaries, the numerous revenue collectors who often did not have a definite function, lost their rights. Considerable problems cropped up because of the large number of very different cases. This measure did not aim at abolishing the ownership of large amounts of land, but only of specific rights. Among those who were affected were numerous small zamindars who earned low incomes from a few acres of land. Often, this was their only source of income, and they had come legally into possession of it, either through purchase or inheritance. Illegal methods my also have played a role when the titles were acquired, but some jagirs were conferred in return for important services. For all the above as well as constitutional reasons, the government took over these rights in return for quite high compensations whose rates increased inversely to the amount of income earned from the land. The compensation was paid in instalments without binding conditions for its use and burdened the government in India with Rs. 6.3 billion and in Pakistan with Rs. 360 million.

An exceptional situation arose in the former jagirs which had often been very badly administered. Not only was the government forced to make considerable investments in health services, schools, etc. to bring these regions or the same level as the rest of the country, but it had to take over the jagirdars' staff as well as pay their pensions. An additional burden resulted from the fact that many jagirdar families were not in a position to make a new start in life. After having spent the sum they had received as compensation, they became destitute, and it became necessary to draw up special rehabilitation programmes.

Since the measures aimed at abolishing specific legal conditions, land which belonged to the same people under other legal conditions was not affected by this measure. Nor was land expropriated that was self-cultivated. To provide them with a basis for existence, those who until then had not cultivated any land themselves, were granted the right to dismiss tenants of land up to three times the size of an average family farm before expropriation was enforced. The term "self cultivation" was not clearly defined and gave rise to many manipulations. The zamindars began to let hired labourers cultivate land they had leased to tenants until then and even persuaded illiterate tenants to give up their rights. This abuse took on such proportions that special laws had to be passed to cancel the voluntary waives made during the last years. In spite of this, the number of protected tenants decreased considerably.

Despite all these problems, by the mid fifties, the intermediaries had been abolished in the two countries. The farmers in these regions more than 20 million in India alone had come into direct contact with the government whose tax revenues increased considerably. However, the above described higher burdens largely counterbalanced this increase. For the farmers, this meant freedom from the arbitrariness of the zamindars and of the numerous "abwabs," but the tax burden remained the same with the only difference being that the government was now the recipient. At any rate, the legal status of the "occupancy tenants" was now clearer. However, only those who were well off could avail themselves of the possibility of purchasing land rights since most of the actual tenants lacked the necessary funds to that end. The larger cultivators could thus enlarge their farms and became the new lessors in the village. These measures did not affect in any way the large number of subtenants who had leased land from occupancy tenants.

Tenancy Reforms

However successful the first step of the agrarian reform turned out to be in achieving its objective of eliminating functionless revenue collectors, the efforts to improve the situation of the majority of the tenants proved to be ineffectual. The objective of the tenancy reform laws was to establish and strengthen the tenants' rights. To that end, a minimum leasing period of 5 to 10 years was introduced, and eviction was only allowed on the basis of specific reasons. Sub-leasing was forbidden and, in the case of eviction, the tenant was to be paid compensation for his investments. Finally, the tenant was granted the right to purchase the land he cultivated. Sub-tenants who had cultivated a plot of land for already more than 12 years gained the status of occupancy tenants and were, thus, protected against eviction. The laws foresaw a restriction of the rent to one third to one sixth of the gross harvest, and payment of the land tax was shifted to the landlord.

These measures proved to be an extremely serious encroachment on the lessors' rights. This is why it became indispensable to offer them an alternative in way of compensation. Before the laws were enforced, they were granted the right to give notice in case they wanted to cultivate the land themselves. Since the term "self cultivation" was not clearly defined and was finally understood as "supervision of cultivation," this meant a set back for the tenants.

Many of them were dismissed and re-employed as agricultural labourers or sharecroppers. It was possible to re-employ them as sharecroppers because the many types of sharecropping were not defined as tenancy in the laws. Thus, a large number of tenants lost their rights as a result of the laws passed to improve their condition.

The other measures did not prove to be very successful either. The poor administration which, moreover, was more on the side of the landlords on account of its origin, simply could not cope with the tasks of the tenancy reform. Here, it was not only a question of a non-recurring control of the lease contracts, but of the permanent enforcement of the regulations as well. It proved to be particularly disadvantageous that the law had not given any aid to the administration by means of tenants' associations which would have had to be founded and which could have examined specific cases at the local level. Besides, the legal measures were sometimes very unrealistic. If the usual rent has, for a long time, amounted to more than 50% of the gross yields, the prospects of imposing, by law, rents of 16% to 33% are negligible. The other measures are also unfavourable to the conditions on the tenancy market. If there is a great demand and a limited supply, some of the potential tenants will always be prepared to make to the landlords concessions which infringe the law.

Altogether, it can be ascertained that tenancy laws in the two countries have not meant much success for the tenants. The majority of the sharecroppers was not included in the measures at all and, of the occupancy tenants, many lost their status, and only a few gained anything at all.

Consequences of the Agrarian Reforms

If one takes stock of the 15 years of agrarian reforms in India and Pakistan, the difference between the objectives of the reforms at the time of independence and the actual results is particularly striking. In simple terms, one say that the reforms were directed against the feudal landlords and against the poor tenants and agricultural labourers, whereas they benefited the rural middle class, especially the upper middle class. The top of the traditional upper class, especially the revenue collectors who had no definite function, were eliminated as well as the largest landowners, especially in India. But large scale landed property was not abolished, only restricted, and land concentration was thus somewhat reduced. These measures were especially directed against the landlords who did not cultivate their own land or at least manage its cultivation, but restricted themselves to collecting rent. This old feudal upper class was decisively weakened and today no longer plays an important role in these countries. But the lower class, among whom great expectations were aroused but not fulfilled, is the actual loser in the agrarian reform process. The landless and the sharecroppers were not affected at all by the reform measures and benefited from land allotments only in specific cases.

A large number of the previously protected tenants were deprived of their rights owing to the transition to self cultivation and quite a number of them new cultivate the same land, but under less favourable conditions. They now have only short term lease contracts, and these sometimes still comprise supplementary agreements. They are not beneficiaries, but the losers in the agrarian reform process.

Those who actually benefited from the agrarian reforms belonged to the rural middle class, *i.e.*, small landlords and larger owner cultivators. The emphasis on the promotion of owner cultivation in the laws and the way in which this term was defined resulted in a concentration of land in the hands of this middle group. Former landlords, who cultivated the rest of their land after part of it had been expropriated, were forced downwards into this middle group. From below, economically sound cultivators who had the means to buy the titles to the land they cultivated rose into the group. They all increased the number of economically viable medium sised farms. This middle stratum consisting of small landlords and large cultivators became, after the old feudal landlords had been eliminated, the main stratum in these countries and held not only a large number of the parliamentary seats, but exercised great influence due to their being related to high officials and members of the military. Many members of this stratum deal intensively with the cultivation of their land, partly because they want to balance out their losses resulting from losing land by cultivating their land more intensively, partly as a reaction to the more advantageous prices for agricultural products that arose in the course of time. But their more commercial attitude towards agriculture is of considerable importance. Their aim was not to skim off high rents, but to achieve profits through appropriate methods of cultivation, and this was further encouraged by the government's agrarian policy.

This change of attitude again had an unfavourable effect on the lower stratum. The replacement of feudal landlords by commercial farmers led to a transition from traditional to contractual labour relations. Thus the tenants and agricultural labourers were further deprived of the minimal securities which the former reciprocal relations with, and concern of, the landlords represented and were thrown into the struggle for life without any protection so that, in view of the prevailing market conditions, they could only be losers. By bringing about such a change, the agrarian reforms established the basis for further changes. They became more drastic in the case of the Green Revolution and showed their actual implications.

The Green Revolution and Land Tenure

One of the objectives of those concerned with agrarian reforms was to increase production. In the countries where food shortages are chronic-India and Pakistan-as well, agrarian reforms have been justified by the necessity to increase the production of basic foodstuffs. Since the measures were mostly restricted to a redistribution of control over land but brought about little change in the traditional cultivation, little production increases ensued from the reforms. The lack of measures to change cultivation caused the two countries to depend largely on cereal imports with the ensuing economic and political consequences.

In the second half of the sixties, technological changes took place in agriculture which exercised a strong influence on the production level. The yield increases resulting from the Green Revolution were so obvious that, within just a few years, the new technology had taken over in all of the regions where it was possible to apply it. It was remarkable that these large yield increases bad been achieved without institutional changes in the agrarian sector. This soon led to the assumption that it was possible to develop agriculture without institutional reforms and that one could do without complicated agrarian reforms. However, this soon proved to be an erroneous conclusion. A more comprehensive analysis of the process shows that numerous bottlenecks arose due to the prevailing agrarian structure and that the implications of the Green Revolution actually made a change in the agrarian structure even more necessary.

The Process of the Green Revolution

The increased production in agriculture as a result of the utilisation of new varieties with a high yield potential in conjunction with more water, fertilizers, and pesticides is called the Green Revolution. The new varieties are not of themselves high yielding, but rather, genetically, they are a yield potential which can only develop if sufficient water and plant nutrients are available. If these are lacking, the yields are sometimes lower than those of local varieties. As is often the case as far as high bred varieties are concerned, they are susceptible to diseases and require careful plant protection measures, Besides, on account of their low resistance and rapid degeneration, the varieties must be replaced by newly bred varieties after only a few years.

When the new seeds are grown with sufficient water, fertilizers, and pesticides, the increases in the yields are astonishingly high. Many a farmer has, from one year to the next, harvested three times as large a wheat yield from the same area using the new seeds. This obvious increase in the yield caused the new varieties to be rapidly adopted. During the first years, the shortage of seed, and not a lack of readiness to utilize it, constituted a bottleneck when the new varieties were introduced. All the same, one should be conscious of the narrow limits of this technological change that is misleadingly called a "revolution." It is not a general breakthrough in agricultural production. The changes apply primarily to the cultivation of wheat and rice, whereas the other cereals are hardly affected. Thus, cereals from the arid regions as well as cotton, pulses, and oil plants are more or less excluded.

As far as rice is concerned, the problems are far more difficult. The new rice varieties require not only that irrigation be available, but also make great demands on the quality of irrigation. The varieties suffer damage from too much as well as too little water. Thus, while controlled irrigation is necessary, frequently an irrigation system is used that consists of rain water overflooding the upper terraces and flowing down to the lower terraces so that the amount of water cannot be controlled. In such cases, it is a definite necessity to improve the irrigation systems before the new varieties can be successfully cultivated.

Since irrigation is an indispensable factor for this new technology, regions which depend on rainfall are implicitly excluded from partaking in these changes. But in India and in Pakistan, only about one third of the arable land is irrigated. This results in tremendous regional differences. The Green Revolution is restricted to irrigated regions and, therefore, to regions which have always produced better yields and thus belonged to the wealthier states. The regional differences became, therefore, even more pronounced.

Similar differences in participation are found according to farm size. Better information, a greater capacity to take risks, and readiness to adopt innovations explain why the large farms adopted the innovation at an early stage, In addition, they had the advantage of obtaining high subsidies during the first years and better prices for seed production. Small farms followed later with some hesitance. In some cases, tenants were forbidden to use the new seed. The more delayed adoption by the small farms can also be explained partly by the initially poor baking quality when the technology which existed in the villages was used and by its poorer taste. Even after the initial phase, the large farms were more advantaged than the small ones. There is no doubt that the new technology can be split up. Seed, fertilizers, water and pesticides can be used on small as well as on large areas. They are therefore neutral as far as farm size is concerned. However, this is no longer true in the case of tractors and pumps. In trying to improve the new opportunities by utilising machines, the large farms had, therefore, advantages. However, the different farm inputs are still more important. In this aspect, the large farms have decisive advantages. They are better informed, have better transport facilities, and more credit, and, when capital goods are scarce, they are frequently more likely to be supplied on a preferential basis. The new technology utilises to a greater extent purchased inputs, *i.e.*, that are not produced on the farm. Thus, the interdependence with the market, capital expenditure, and thus risk are increased, especially for inexperienced farmers. Formerly, crop failures could be overcome by tightening ones belt', but this no longer helps if one has considerable debts to be paid to the farm input suppliers.

But precisely the risk ensuing from climatic fluctuations cannot be eliminated. Soon, there were crop failures because the farmers had not learned how to react promptly to infestation with disease. For those who were in a better economic position, the integration in the market economy and simultaneous implementation of the technological innovation meant new possibilities of action. For the economically weak, the path leading to market integration often led to new dependences.

Likewise, under the aspect of the overall economy, the Green Revolution has not brought advantages alone. It is true that the yield increases in the two countries improved the supply of foodstuffs for a few years. This was more lasting in India because the necessary research stations were built to produce the constantly required new varieties. Today, Pakistan is still or again dependent on cereal imports.

Moreover, the intensified utilisation of purchased inputs has not made production less expensive and has led to considerable price increases. The utilisation of inputs previously unknown to the farmers can easily damage the environment. Quite often, pesticides and herbicides are applied in a wrong concentration. But increased irrigation also has consequences. The ground water level is raised and the risk of salinisation is increased. Many regions have irrigation but insufficient drainage. In some regions, the water reserves also decrease. The overwhelming production increases also distracted from several alternatives. In countries where 20-30% of the harvest is lost, it would surely be less expensive to reduce the losses than to increase production at high costs, especially when increasing oil prices bring about a considerable rise in the cost of inputs.

It must also be mentioned that the Green Revolution meant increased production at drastically rising social costs. The society subsidises seeds, finances research stations, invests in fertilizer factories and irrigation systems, builds roads, and organises farm systems. Since part of the higher yields can be attributed to these expenses incurred by the society, and not to the efforts of the individual farmers, some of the profits should be skimmed off and go to the government for further economic development. But this is not taking place due to the prevailing power structure.

The Green Revolution is therefore a mixed blessing. It brought about decisive advances in agricultural production, but also serious economic and social problems. It is important to realize that these problems are not actually the consequences of the new technologies per se. They are the result of the prevailing economic and social conditions which only become more evident. Therefore, it cannot be a matter of putting a stop to new technology but, at the most, to keep it within bounds. It is important to take measures to solve the prevailing problems, especially the deficiencies in the agrarian structure so that new technologies no longer lead to negative consequences. The problem of the man-land relations following the Green Revolution becomes even more crucial. As will be shown in the following, the prospects in that respect have sooner diminished. This becomes especially evident if the implications of the agrarian changes for various strata of the rural population are more thoroughly examined.

Improving Land Access for India's Rural Poor

India contains the largest numbers of both rural poor and landless households on the planet. And, the two are related. Landlessness is the best indicator of rural poverty in India, better than either caste or illiteracy. Indian leaders have been well aware of the connection and the country has taken substantial policy and legislative steps to address the problem since independence. Perhaps no country has matched the volume of land reform legislation produced by India since its independence in 1947. India's experience is yet another reminder, however, that adopting well-intended laws, by itself, does not guarantee good results. From the perspective of most rural poor, India's land reform laws have not had the desired effect; and some legislative provisions have resulted in perverse and unintended consequences. Today, India's poorest households still struggle for access to rural land and land tenure security.

The story of land reform in India need not end here, however. With relatively modest revisions, some of India's existing policies and laws can further their original intent of increasing the poor's access to rural land and providing for secure land tenure. Other areas require more drastic measures. Old land reform approaches, such as blind adherence to land ceiling legislation and tenancy reform, need reconsideration. Narrowly conceived and ineffective programmes that ignore local realities must be terminated. The time has arrived for policymakers to take inventory of its land reform experience, distill lessons learned, and more innovatively use land laws, policies, and programmes to broaden land access and strengthen land rights for the poorest and least empowered of India's poor. The "land route" is not the only route out of poverty, but in a country where landlessness is the best predictor of poverty, it is a route that cannot be ignored.

Land reform in India over the past 50 years was founded on legislatively driven efforts to provide the rural poor with access to agricultural land. Since Independence, most of the legislative energy to increase land access was funneled into three areas: the abolition of intermediaries, tenancy reform, and enactment of ceilings on land holdings. This paper is a summary review of those efforts and it attempts to distill some broad lessons that might inform possible policy paths ahead. The perspective is that of an outsider-a non-Indian land lawyer with comparative experience on land policy and law reform in many other countries who has also spent considerable time conducting field research on the topic in India. The paper reviews India's efforts to provide the poor with access to rural land through the enactment of laws and policies to extinguish intermediary interests (section II), regulate tenancy relationships (section III), set ceilings on land holdings (section IV), allocate government wasteland (section V), and allocate house sites to the poor (section VI). For each, the paper examines the extent to which those laws have been successful in increasing land access, and makes an initial effort to distill lessons learned for moving ahead.

Abolition of Intermediaries

The first wave of land reform legislation after India's independence concentrated on the abolition of intermediary land right holders between the tillers and the government. While these efforts are largely of historical significance, a summary review is warranted because the efforts provided a foundation for subsequent land reform initiatives and because they provide some broad lessons still applicable today.

At the time of Independence in 1947, Indian agricultural land was administered under three broad types of land tenure systems: the zamindari system, ryotwari system, and mahalwari system. The zamindari system was the most widespread, covering 57 percent of cultivated land in British India. Under this system, the British regime had declared feudal lords (zamindars, jagirdars, talukdars, etc.) and other persons previously designated as land tax collectors to be proprietors of the land. Although such persons (all of whom became generally referred to as zamindars) had not previously owned much or any of the land given to them, the British administrators dubbed them owners with permanent rights and contracted with them for the payment of land revenue (tax). The empowerment of zamindars transformed the tillers of the land into tenants whose fortunes were dependent upon the wishes and whims of the zamindars.

The zamindar's estates ranged in size from a few acres to tens of thousands of acres. Over time, the larger zamindars freed themselves from the burden of managing their estates and collecting rents from cultivators by leasing out the rent-collecting rights. In some areas, several layers-in some areas as many as 50—of intermediary rights separated the zamindar from the actual cultivator, with the zamindars seated at the top level, at the feet of the state. At all levels, intermediaries gleaned their principal income from the monetary difference between the amount of rent they collected from the layer below and the rent they were obligated to provide to the layer above. The zamindari system of receiving rent through levels of legally recognised tenure holders was generally more developed in northern India than in south or central India. This system prevailed in Bengal, Uttar Pradesh, Bihar, Rajasthan, Bengal, and Orissa, and parts of Assam, Andhra Pradesh, and Madhya Pradesh.

The second broad type of land tenure system was the ryotwari system, which covered about 38 percent of cultivated land in British India. The ryotwari system prevailed in much of southern India including present-day Maharashtra, Karnataka, Tamil Nadu, as well as most of Andhra Pradesh and Madhya Pradesh and parts of Assam, Bihar, and Rajasthan. The ryotwari system recognised individual cultivators (ryots or raiyats) as proprietors of their land with generally recognised rights to sell, lease, mortgage, and otherwise transfer their land. The system did not legally recognize any kind of intermediary interest between the cultivator and the state; the proprietors paid land revenue directly to the colonial administration. Nonetheless, informal intermediaries of the zamindari type emerged even in areas where the ryotwari (and mahalwari) systems had strongholds. While some raiyats were owner-cultivators, many rented out part or all of their land to tenants, mostly sharecroppers.

Only approximately five percent of British India's cultivated land was administered under the third type of land tenure scheme, the mahalwari system. Under this system, land revenue was assigned to and paid by entire village units (mahals). Peasant farmers contributed shares of the total amount of land revenue owned by the village in proportion to their holdings. The mahalwari system existed in most of present-day Punjab and Haryana, as well as parts of Madhya Pradesh, Orissa, and Uttar Pradesh.

The existence of intermediary interests, particularly within the zamindari system, led to highly inefficient and inequitable results. British authorities had assumed that by giving the zamindars and other tax-collecting authorities proprietary rights and fixed tax amounts, efficient collaboration between landlords and tenants would surely follow. The authorities assumed that the zamindars would provide managerial expertise, technical knowledge, and capital, and the tenants would supply their labour—a complementary relationship that would increase agricultural production and productivity. Such symmetry of contribution was never achieved on a large scale. Instead, "the sole concern of the parasitic groups of intermediaries was to extort the largest possible share of the produce of the land without making any contribution whatsoever to agricultural production."

Initially, the colonial administration gave the zamindars free rein to manage their tenants as they pleased. As the British authorities began to recognize that many zamindars were mistreating tenants through practices such as rack-renting and summary evictions, they introduced various limited pieces of legislation, starting with the Bengal Tenancy Act of 1885, that gave some protection to certain categories of tenants. These efforts were inadequate to curtail the abuses. In particular, the laws offered little or no protection to tenants under zamindar's self-managed or home farms and those under the ryotwari system.

The abuses of the zamindari system attracted attention during the struggle for independence, and in the period immediately following Independence, as the country's new leaders turned their attention toward land reform, they gave particular attention to the abolition of intermediary interests in land. The effectiveness of their efforts reflected the extent of discontent with the intermediary system. The injustices practised by zamindars, coupled with their support of the British colonial administration, fuelled the political will to undermine or eliminate intermediary rights to land.

The Indian Constitution, which grants states exclusive authority to enact land tenure legislation, provided a starting point. Soon after assuming power, several state governments initiated action to extinguish intermediary interests. By the end of the 1950s, almost all states had enacted legislation aimed at abolishing intermediary interests upon the payment of compensation.

Results were mixed. On one hand, the legislation transformed some 20 to 25 million "superior" tenants into landowners or "government tenants" holding land directly under the government, placed large areas of privately owned forests and wasteland under state ownership, and altered the rural power structures. On the other hand, the laws to abolish intermediary interests fell well short of their potential because of the protracted nature of the legislative process, the shortcomings in the legislative content, the complex and time consuming procedures for implementation, and the role of the judiciary in frustrating the intent and implementation of the laws. The positive results and the shortcomings of the laws as a whole are discussed below.

Positive Results

The laws to abolish intermediary interests brought an estimated 20 to 25 million erstwhile tenants into a direct relationship with the State, with many if not most of the beneficiaries in Uttar Pradesh and West Bengal. The economic benefits realised by beneficiaries were somewhat limited for at least three reasons. First, many of the tenants who were brought into direct relationship with the state had already received some tenure security and rent regulation from tenancy laws enacted prior to independence. Second, most of the state laws required the former tenants to make payments to the government for acquiring ownership rights (to offset the compensation paid by the government to the intermediaries). Third, most of the state laws obliged the beneficiaries to pay annual land revenue (tax) at an amount equal to what they had been paying the intermediary.

The legislation significantly reduced forced labour, agrestic serfdom, and other forms of oppression prevalent in many parts of the country, and forced the zamindars to share power with the beneficiaries, their erstwhile "superior" tenants, most of whom belonged to the upper and middle castes. These beneficiaries gained increased social status and, more gradually, increased political power.

In addition to the social and political gains of beneficiaries, the abolition of intermediaries brought large areas of cultivable wasteland, forests, and abadi land (house plots and other land in villages) under state ownership. States subsequently distributed a considerable amount of this land to poor beneficiaries.

The legislation to abolish intermediaries also reduced the multiplicity of legal land tenures that previously existed and thus simplified and clarified land tenure law in most Indian states.

Uttar Pradesh, for example, had some 40 types of legally recognised tenure types before the adoption of legislation to abolish intermediaries reduced the number of tenure types to three. Especially in a country with substantial illiteracy in rural areas, complexity of land tenure law tends to disfavour the poor; the more educated and well-off are more capable of understanding, using, and taking advantage of the law-to the disadvantage of those less capable, usually the poorest.

Shortcomings

The legislative shortcomings resulted in harmful consequences and missed opportunities. Most significantly, the laws created the impetus for zamindars to evict substantial numbers of tenants forcibly. Employing legal and illegal methods, the zamindars were particularly successful at evicting "non-superior" tenants (including tenants-at-will, under-tenants, and sharecroppers), many of whom had farmed the land from which they were evicted for generations.

Substantial loopholes and flaws in the law allowed zamindars to accomplish much of these evictions through largely legal means. In every state, legislation permitted ex-intermediaries to retain their home-farms or "personally cultivated" land; only a handful of states placed a limit on the size of such home-farm land retained. The legislation loosely defined "personal cultivation" to include cultivation through sharecroppers, servants, and wage labourers. Most state laws even allowed the intermediary to evict tenants from land he had not been "personally cultivating" but now wished to "personally cultivate," and the legislation allowed the ex-intermediaries to select the land they wanted to retain. Only West Bengal and Jammu & Kashmir simultaneously adopted land ceiling limits to restrict the total amount of land ex-intermediaries could own. The lengthy processes of adopting and implementing the laws, coupled with administrative indifference and judicial delays, frequently allowed zamindars to use other illegal and extra-legal methods to evade the law including: (1) fictitious partition of properties; (2) influence of the village officials for manipulative changes in land records; and (3) registration of tenants as farm servants or wage labourers.

The states generally compensated the ex-intermediaries more than adequately for the rights they did lose, at a substantial burden to the state exchequer. According to the National Planning Commission Report, the compensation paid to the lowest slab of ex-intermediaries reached as high as 15 to 30 times of their annual net income. Frustratingly, most did not repay the favour: the ex-intermediaries were generally disinclined to invest their compensation in industry or other worthwhile economic activities.

Finally, while state laws often granted tenants the right to purchase lands from willing landlords at set rates, these provisions had serious shortcomings that precluded any significant change in landownership patterns. Prices fixed for land were high, particularly given the limited nature of the landlord's rights, and instalment payments spaced within too limited a period of time. The end result: an opportunity for tenants to become owners slipped by. In sum, the legislation abolishing intermediary rights gets mixed reviews. Most informed observers praise the beneficial impacts; the legislation reduced (and in cases entirely extinguished) the feudal nature of agrarian relationships in many parts of India. Observers also note that despite the deficiencies of the legislation, the states implemented this phase of India's land reforms more successfully than the land ceiling and tenancy reforms that were to follow. However, flawed legal provisions and less-than-effective Gunnar Myrdal's assessment, in contrast, emphasises the end of the reign of powerful intermediaries as semi-feudal chiefs, while acknowledging that inferior tenants drew essentially no benefits from the reform. Finally, Wolf Ladejinsky observes:

> *Despite opposition and administrative and technical problems, the zamindari tenures were virtually abolished. Not all have been benefited equally and not all 20 million cultivators affected have received permanent, heritable, and transferable rights. Nevertheless the effort was a great step forward for reconstruction of Indian agriculture.*

Lessons from Abolition of Intermediaries

The legislation abolishing intermediaries is largely of historical significance and has limited relevance for current land policy reform dialogue. These reforms were introduced decades ago and whatever implementation that is to happen has largely happened. Devoting policy attention to these laws would be wasted effort; such policy attention is much more warranted on other topics such as tenancy reform. However, the design and implementation experience of these laws does provide a few general lessons that may be applicable in revising other types of land legislation:

- Provide adequate compensation to existing holders of land rights when extinguishing their rights. One important reason why abolition of intermediary laws were more fully implemented than land ceiling laws is that the former provided more compensation than the latter, which decreased resistance from those whose land rights were to be taken.
- Simplify land tenure types and land legislation generally. When land legislation is exceedingly complex and when land tenures recognised by laws are numerous, poor (and especially illiterate) people suffer. Such complexity can and often is
- Land law and policy reform can lead to beneficial social change that is at least as important as the direct economic benefits. Intermediary abolition legislation is a case in point. In considering land policy reform alternatives and their likely impacts, policy makers should consider the social and political impacts as well as the potential economic impacts.

Tenancy Reform

The abolition of most intermediary tenures brought the whole of India under a uniform tenurial system (albeit with some local variation) within the first decade after Independence. The efforts to abolish intermediary interests did not, however, extinguish tenancy. Provisions in the abolition of intermediary laws intending to secure the right of tenants of ex-intermediaries were largely ineffective and, in some cases, counter-effective. Renting out of land was widespread in ryotwari and mahalwari areas even where no intermediaries existed. In zamindari areas, even the lowest level of legally recognised land right holders relied on sub-leasing land.

By the end of the 1950s, tenancy was ubiquitous and circumstances had converged to create a perfect storm that favoured already powerful landlords at the expense of their tenants. Most tenancies were oral and terminable at will. Laws provided no (or virtually no) protection or even legal recognition of the most vulnerable tenants, including sharecroppers and tenants-at-will on ex-intermediaries' home farms. The relationships were ripe for legislative intervention.

National Policy Framework on Agricultural Tenancy

In the 1960s and 1970s, every Indian state passed tenancy reform legislation. As with their earlier efforts to abolish intermediaries, equity and efficiency concerns supplied the fuel for the tenancy reform. However, unlike the legislation to abolish intermediaries, policy guidelines from the central government strongly directed state tenancy legislation. As discussed below, the additional direction brought little additional success. Assessed against objectives, the results of tenancy reform laws were, with some exceptions, weak or even counterproductive. While the laws allowed tenants to acquire ownership or

The national policy on tenancy reform evolved gradually over decades and is embodied in various policy documents issued by the National Planning Commission. The First Five-Year Plan (1951-1956), contained the first authoritative exposition of national tenancy reform policy and included four important guidelines. First, rent should not exceed one-fifth to one-fourth of the gross produce. Second, landowners should be allowed to evict tenants-at-will and bring under "personal cultivation" land up to a ceiling amount determined by each state. Third, tenants on the non-resumed land of "large landowners" should be given permanent and heritable rights to such land. Finally, tenants on the non-resumed land of "small and medium landowners" should be given 5-10 year rights.

The Second and Third Five-Year Plans essentially reiterated and tried to fine-tune the policy guidelines established in the First Plan. By the end of the Third Plan, virtually all states had adopted tenancy reform legislation that broadly followed the policy guidelines. In all the laws, "personal cultivation" was loosely defined to include cultivation of land without using the landowner's own labour or, in most cases, even their personal supervision. Landlords took full advantage of resuming previously tenanted land for "personal cultivation" up to the generous ceiling amounts.

Many also engaged in actual or fictitious transfer in order to evade the resumption ceilings. The laws also permitted the voluntary surrender of tenancies, leading to numerous cases of tenancy surrenders under duress, but on paper shown as voluntary. Many laws left sharecroppers out of their purview altogether. Even in states that recognised sharecroppers as tenants, such sharecroppers faced an extremely difficult task of proving the existence of their tenancy. Most tenancies were oral and not entered into the land records maintained by the village-level functionaries of the state revenue departments.

The Fourth Five-Year Plan (1969-1974) noted that even after years of tenancy reforms, the objectives of the tenancy reform policies and laws had not been achieved. Since these efforts to mend tenancy had failed, the Fourth Plan called for ending tenancy. The Plan recommended that the states amend tenancy reform legislation to make all existing tenants owners of the land they had been cultivating upon payment of compensation and future tenancies should be prohibited (except for special cases such as widows, disabled persons, and active members of the armed forces). Numerous states did amend their legislation.

The problem of proving existing tenancies, however, continued. The primary consequence of the new policy and corresponding legislation was to push tenancies further underground. The Fifth through Ninth Five-Year Plans largely reiterated the earlier policies, while noting the shortcomings in the laws and their inadequate implementation.

Further, the Plan states that the prohibition on tenancy "has not really ended the practice" but instead "has resulted in agricultural practices that are not conducive to increased production," which "in turn, depresses employment opportunities for the landless agricultural labourers." This most recent authoritative national policy statement on tenancy reform concludes that a fresh look at tenancy laws is warranted and that "one option could be to completely free tenancy laws of restrictive conditions."

Key Legislative Provisions in State Tenancy Reform Laws

As previously mentioned, all Indian states adopted legislation concerning agricultural tenancies in the 1960s or 1970s. Most of those laws were amended from time to time, partially in response to policy guidance from the national government articulated in the Five Year Plans. The key aspects of these laws relate to:

- Defining tenant
- Landlord's right to resume tenanted land for personal cultivation
- Conferment of ownership rights on tenants
- Voluntary surrender of tenant's rights by the tenant
- Prohibition of future tenancies
- Rent levels for those tenancies that are allowed
- Length of term for those tenancies that are allowed
- Tenants' rights of pre-emptive purchase
- Public recording of tenancies

The aims and provisions of the tenancy laws are most properly analysed by making a distinction between their affect on existing tenancies (at the time the law was adopted) and their affect on tenancies that might be created in the future.

The initial inquiry is: what provisions addressed tenancy relationships that were existing at the time the laws were adopted and what was the impact of those provisions on those relationships? A separate inquiry should follow: what provisions are aimed at tenancy relationships that might be created in the future, after the law's adoption?

In general, when considering the ten key aspects listed above, the second through fourth aspects related most to tenancies that existed at the time of (or before) the law's adoption, and the fifth through ninth aspects relate mostly to tenancies that are to be created in the future.

Defining Tenant

All state laws treated persons who cultivated the land of others upon the payment of a fixed rent (whether in cash or in kind) as tenants. At least initially, some states excluded sharecroppers from the definition of tenant and thus denied them legislative protections. In West Bengal, for example, the 1955 Land Reforms Act did not extend protection to sharecroppers until it was amended in 1970.

Landlord's Right to Resume Personal Cultivation of Tenanted Land

The single largest legal loophole in the tenancy reform laws was probably the generous rights of resumption for "personal cultivation" granted landowners. Landowners took full advantage of the unfettered rights of resumption in most state laws, resulting in tenant evictions. Two states distinguished themselves by limiting resumption rights. Upon the abolition of intermediaries in Uttar Pradesh and West Bengal, tenancy laws in those states prohibited landowners from resuming any tenanted land outside of their home-farms; the laws granted existing tenants on the non-home-farm lands permanent and heritable rights on that tenanted land.

In all other states, tenancy reform laws permitted landowners to resume tenanted land for personal cultivation. As earlier mentioned, these states loosely defined "personal cultivation" to include cultivation through servants or labourers.

No tenancy law mandated direct landowner supervision of the labour or residence in or near the village in which the land was located (although some laws adopted a residential requirement for at least one family member). Only the state laws of Manipur and Tripura (later) required the input of at least some personal labour in cultivating resumed land. In short, the "personal cultivation" provision presented no barrier to resumption; even absentee landowners easily satisfied the requirement.

In some states (Gujarat, Jammu & Kashmir, Kerala, Madhya Pradesh, Maharashtra, Karnataka, Orissa, and Rajasthan), the laws permitted landowners to exercise their right of resumption only within a specified time period after the legislation had been adopted.

In these states, this time period has now passed. Other states allow a continuing right of resumption on at least some land (Assam, Bihar, Haryana, Punjab, Tamil Nadu, and West Bengal).

The amount of land that can be resumed for personal cultivation varied from state to state. All states placed some ceiling on the amount of land that could be resumed. In some states, this ceiling for resuming personal cultivation of tenanted land was the same as the ceiling for the total amount of land that could be owned (see discussion on landownership ceilings in Section I (C)). In other states, it was lower. Because the landowner could select the tenanted land to be resumed for personal cultivation, he could (and often did) at least threaten-if not evict-his tenants, fostering insecurity among all tenants.

The law in several states provides that a minimum area of land must be left with the tenant after the landlord exercised his right of resumption for personal cultivation. In Kerala, Orissa, Gujarat, Himachal Pradesh, Maharashtra, Karnataka and Tamil Nadu, the law states that half of the tenanted land must be left with the tenant. In Bihar, half the area tenanted or five acres, whichever is less, must remain with the tenant if the landlord owns land in excess of the ceiling area. Landowners in West Bengal must leave one hectare or all the tenanted area, whichever is less, with the tenant. In Assam, Punjab and Haryana, landowners must leave a specified minimum area of land with the tenants until the government allots other land to them.

Conferment of Ownership Rights on Tenants

Most state laws confer ownership on existing tenants who remained on non-resumable tenanted land. Exceptions include:

- Tenancy laws of Tamil Nadu and the Andhra area of Andhra Pradesh include no provisions for conferring rights of ownership on tenants;
- In Bihar, Punjab, and Haryana, tenants of landlords who own land below the ceiling limit (virtually all) are not entitled to ownership rights on the tenanted lands;
- In Rajasthan, tenants whose tenancy contracts started after 1961 are not entitled to ownership; and
- In Uttar Pradesh and West Bengal, sharecroppers are not entitled to receive ownership rights.

All other state laws include provisions to confer ownership rights to tenants on non-resumable land. The approaches vary. Some states deem eligible tenants to be owners, their ownership becoming final on payment of the price established by the government (which is typically paid to the government rather than directly to the landlord). Other states assumed ownership of eligible tenanted land by paying compensation to the landlord, and subsequently transferring rights to tenants based on their application and payment, which may or may not equal the amount paid to the landlord.

Voluntary Surrender by Tenants

"Voluntary" surrenders of tenancy rights by tenants have frustrated the objectives of tenancy reform. Many landlords have repossessed even their non-resumable land by "persuading" their tenant(s) to give up their tenancy rights "voluntarily." Once such coercive tactics became widely recognised (and probably after most forced surrenders), the National Planning Commission recommended that states amend their legislation to protect against coercion by requiring that revenue department officials verify tenant surrenders, prohibiting landowners from taking possession of land in excess of the resumption limits even if voluntarily surrendered, and (later) assuming state ownership of voluntarily surrendered land.

Most states responded to the central policy recommendations by amending their laws. All state laws now provide for revenue department authorities to verify that surrenders are bona fide, except for Haryana, Punjab, Rajasthan, Tamil Nadu, and Uttar Pradesh. Some state laws (including Gujarat, Himachal Pradesh, Karnataka, Kerala, and Tripura) call for the government-rather than the landlord-to take ownership of land voluntarily surrendered by the tenant.

Prohibition of Agricultural Tenancies

Whether states would permit the creation of future tenancies was perhaps the most controversial aspect of tenancy laws. Heated debates resulted in provisions that fall into four broad categories.

- Complete prohibition. The laws in two states (Kerala and Jammu & Kashmir) place a virtual or absolute prohibition on the creation of agricultural tenancies.
- General prohibition/limited leasing. The laws in eight states—Andhra Pradesh (Telengana area), Karnataka, Madhya Pradesh, West Bengal, Bihar, Himachal Pradesh, Uttar Pradesh, and Orissa—are characterised by a general prohibition on future tenancies combined with an

allowance of leasing by certain defined categories of landowners and/or under certain other conditions. In some cases, the legal effect of such general prohibitions is fairly limited because the exceptions are very broad. For example, in the Telangana area of Andhra Pradesh, landowners who own less than three times a "family holding" may lease out land. This includes at least 95 percent of all landowners in Andhra Pradesh. In other states, the exceptions are much more narrowly defined. For example, Karnataka's legislation only allows soldiers and sailors to lease out their land. Most other states that have a general prohibition combined with defined exceptions fall between these two extremes; although they tend to be more similar to Karnataka, only allowing additional exceptions for minors, widows, unmarried women, female divorcees, physically disabled, imprisoned, and/or students. Madhya Pradesh and West Bengal are unique. Madhya Pradesh's exceptions to its general prohibition on leasing include a provision allowing any landowner to lease out their land for at least one year during a consecutive three-year period. West Bengal does not allow fixed-rent tenancies, but does allow sharecropping (although, because the law gives permanent rights to such sharecroppers, it creates a powerful chilling effect on the creation of future sharecropping relationships).

- Permissible leasing with ownership potential. Five states permit leasing, but with a stipulation that the tenant acquires a right of ownership or a right to purchase ownership after some specified period. These states include Assam, Gujarat, Haryana, Maharashtra, and Punjab. The time period ranges from one year in Gujarat and Maharashtra to six years in Haryana and Punjab.
- No prohibitions on leasing. Three states place virtually no prohibitions on leasing. These include the Andhra area of Andhra Pradesh, Rajasthan, and Tamil Nadu. Even in these states, however, provisions on maximum rent, minimum length of term, and tenants' rights to purchase land can have the effect of preventing landowners from renting out their land or pushing tenancies "underground."

Regulation of Rent

Nearly all state laws include provisions designed to limit the amount of rent payable by those tenants who are legally permitted. These maximum rent levels are stated in terms of a multiple of land revenue (tax) or an amount equivalent to a portion of the gross produce. The maximum rent levels are typically well below prevailing market rents and have proven difficult if not impossible to enforce in nearly all states where they exist. Perhaps most importantly, since most agricultural tenants in India remain concealed and thus with little or no tenure security, any effort by them to enforce legal "maximum rent" provisions is likely to result in eviction.

Length of Term

Certain states have prescribed minimum periods for allowable tenancies. Andhra Pradesh's prescribes a five-year minimum for the Telengana area and a six-year minimum (renewable) for the Andhra area. Punjab establishes a three-year minimum.

Right of Pre-emptive Purchase

A right of pre-emptive purchase means that before a landlord chooses to sell the tenanted land to a third party, he must give the tenant the opportunity to purchase the land. The laws in at least five states (Andhra area of Andhra Pradesh, Haryana, Maharashtra, Punjab, and West Bengal) give tenants a continuing right of pre-emptive purchase.

Land Records

Accurate and current records of existing tenancies is a pre-requisite for the effective implementation of tenancy reform policies. Numerous state laws (including Gujarat, Haryana, Himachal Pradesh, Jammu & Kashmir, Madhya Pradesh, Maharashtra, Punjab, Rajasthan, Uttar Pradesh, and West Bengal) call for including the names of tenants in land revenue records. Except West Bengal, no state has effectively implemented such a provision. In other states, the names of tenants are seldom recorded, and in many cases the omission is a result of tenant insistence in the face of possible eviction. Even where tenants attempt to record their names, the revenue department functionaries often act in collusion with the landowners and refuse to make such entries.

Extent and Impact of Tenancy Reform Law Implementation

The state tenancy reform laws contain prominent defects and sizeable loopholes that have limited their potential reach. Half-conceived, often lackluster implementation methods led to even wider gaps between the declared objectives of the tenancy reform policy and law and their actual achievements in the field.

According to Government of India statistics, by the end of 2002, 12.4 million tenants on 15.6 million acres of land had benefited by either having ownership rights conferred upon them or otherwise having their rights protected. (See Table 1 below.) This comprises approximately 12 percent of all agricultural households and about 4.5 percent of India's cultivated land. Eighty-one percent of these reported tenancy reform beneficiaries are concentrated in five states—Assam, Gujarat, Kerala, Maharashtra, and West Bengal.

Another 17 percent of the reported tenancy reform beneficiaries are in four additional states—Himachal Pradesh, Jammu & Kashmir, Karnataka, and Tamil Nadu. Significantly, government statistics indicate that tenancy reforms did not confer ownership rights on—or protect the rights of—any tenants in Bihar, Madhya Pradesh, Rajasthan, or Uttar Pradesh.

TABLE 1: Number of Tenants Conferred Ownership Rights (or Rights Protected) and Area Accrued to them (As of 31 Dec. 2002)

Sl. No	State	No. Tenants (in Thousands)	Area Accrued (Thousands of Acres)
1.	Andhra Pradesh	107	595
2.	Arunachal Pradesh	Tenancy not reported	
3.	Assam	2,908	3,175
4.	Bihar[1]	NR	NR
5.	Gujarat	1,276	2,592
6.	Goa	NR	NR
7.	Haryana	Tenancy not reported	
8.	Himachal Pradesh	401	NR
9.	Jammu and Kashmir	610	NR
10.	Karnataka	605	2,632

Contd...

Sl. No	State	No. Tenants (in Thousands)	Area Accrued (Thousands of Acres)
11.	Kerala	2,842	1,450
12.	Madhya Pradesh[2]	Tenancy not reported	
13.	Maharashtra	1,492	4,290
14.	Manipur	NR	NR
15.	Meghalaya	Nil	Nil
16.	Mizoram	Nil	Nil
17.	Nagaland	NR	NR
18.	Orissa	165	98
19.	Punjab	NR	NR
20.	Rajasthan	18	NR
21.	Sikkim	NR	NR
22.	Tamil Nadu	498	695
23.	Tripura	14	39
24.	Uttar Pradesh[3]	NR	NR
25.	West Bengal	1,460	1,100
Union Territories			
26.	A.N. Islands	Nil	Nil
27.	Chandigarh	NR	NR
28.	D&N Haveli	26	64
29.	Delhi	NR	NR
30.	Daman and Diu	NR	NR
31.	Lakshadweep	Neg	Neg
32.	Pondicherry	Neg	Neg
All India:		12,422	15,630

NR Not reported.

1. Including Jharkhand
2. Including Chhattisgarh
3. Including Uttaranchal

Source: Government of India, Ministry of Rural Development Annual Report 2002-2003.

Making allowances for the fact that NSS data do not reflect fully the extent of concealed tenancies, the total estimated amount of tenanted area does not exceed 17 percent. Thus, tenants operated at least 50 percent of the operated area at the time of Independence and not more than 17 percent now, meaning that tenant families have been deprived of approximately 33 percent of the operated area.

Not all of those tenants who lost access to land did so as a direct result of the tenancy reform legislation. Arguably, however, such legislation, coupled with the laws to abolish intermediaries, was the major cause.

In addition to causing active dispossession of tenants through evictions, tenancy laws have, in some cases, led to passive dispossession because they prevent poor farmers from accessing land through tenancy. How many rural households are denied access to land through tenancy because of the ongoing legal restrictions should be carefully explored through rigorous field research. Less systematic field research has certainly found a multitude if inhibiting impacts.

- The legislative restrictions and provisions that aim to provide ownership or other premium rights to tenants in reality cause some land holders to lease out less land than they otherwise would, resulting in decreased land access for poor (and other) households who desire to rent-in.
- In some cases, the restrictions have encouraged the under-utilisation of land by landowners who are unwilling or unable to cultivate their land but fear losing their land if they rent it out.

Tenancy Reform Recommendations

Tenancy reform is a topic that deserves high priority in India's land policy reform agenda. Throughout much of the 20th Century, tenancy in India (as in many parts of the developing world) was cast in the role of an exploitative institution and charged with negatively impacting socially optimal equity and productivity outcomes. Ascribing tenancy as exploitative in pre-and immediately post-independence was understandable. In an agrarian setting characterised by strict social and economic hierarchy and where overwhelming numbers of rural poor lacked access to land and any other economic opportunity, tenants had little bargaining power and many landlords exploited their positions of social and economic privilege.

Since the enactment of the legislation, a broader consensus in the economic literature has emerged that concludes land rental markets in general-and sharecropping relationships in particular-can play a substantial role in increasing land access for the poor. Rental markets can supply a critical rung on the "agricultural ladder" toward land ownership, particularly as growing economic opportunity (especially non-agricultural) and socio-political advancements begin to remove feudal-like vestiges and improve the bargaining position of poor tenants. Both land sales and land rental markets are capable of enhancing transfers of land from land-rich to land-poor households. Of the two, theory and empirical evidence indicate that the rental market supplies the more

Land ownership remains desirable and conveys greater benefits (particularly concerning credit access, tenure security, and wealth), but access to land via land rental is often a local, first-best alternative to land ownership when the pre-conditions for the efficient and equitable functioning of land sale markets are absent.

Land tenancy markets can also reduce the vulnerability of poor households by offering a more stable livelihood source than frequently volatile and imperfect labour markets. As opportunities in the non-farm economy increase, tenancy markets can facilitate a broader choice of livelihood opportunities such as migration, specialisation, and investment. Households better suited to pursue non-farm livelihoods will be benefited if they are able to rent out their land for others to cultivate. Looking to other countries, China's experience indicates that in a growing economy, the role of land tenancy will expand and increase incomes for all. Other research teaches that rental markets have more potential for providing access to the poor in settings where agriculture is not capital-intensive.

In India today, land rental markets play an important but probably under-utilised role in providing land access for the poor. As a consequence of tenancy restrictions and protections, landowners who rent-out must select tenants they trust not to reveal the relationship or assert their rights. Thus, it is generally considered that, all things being equal, larger farmers (who qualify for tenancy protections or because they belong to the same socio-economic class as the landowner) present lesser risks as tenants. If true, then liberalising the tenancy markets could provide proportionally greater access to the poor.

The author of this report, although quite sympathetic with the pro-poor agenda objectives of those who promote continued or even stronger tenancy regulation/restriction, has seen more and more evidence and become increasingly convinced that much of the current tenancy legislation in India operates to restrict livelihood opportunities for the poor.

For example, in a recent survey of 400 rural households in Karnataka, the authors found:

- 91 percent of respondents answering definitively state that the existing tenancy restrictions harm landowners.
- 94 percent of respondents answering definitively state that existing tenancy restrictions harm the landless.

In the course of ongoing rapid rural appraisal research in various states, the author generally finds that:

- Knowledge of the specific tenancy reform provisions in law is low, but most rural households recognize that landowners risk losing some (often substantial) rights to their land when they rent it out. Thus, when land is rented, it is given to people who can be trusted not to assert rights and, for an extra measure of protection, those tenants are typically rotated, often every year.
- Although tenancy reform laws are rarely implemented, they often play a major role in landowner decisions about renting out land and lead to less active rental markets than would otherwise be expected and to some sub-optimal utilisation of land.
- Land-poor households almost always wish that more land was available for rental. They do not fear exploitive landlord practices near as much as they fear not being able to access land to improve their livelihoods.

A recent, more systematic economic study provides strong empirical support that tenancy restrictions in India result in decreased land access by both the landless and more efficient producers. The study's findings suggest that lifting such tenancy restrictions would lead to increased land access and income for many poor and landless families and increase agricultural productivity.

Recommendations on Legislative Change

In general, Indian states should consider amending tenancy legislation to better meet (and, in some cases balance) equity and efficiency objectives. The basic aim should be two-fold. First, consolidate the benefits of past tenancy reform by converting "protected," "registered," or "occupancy" tenants into owners. Second, liberalise ongoing tenancy prohibitions and excessive tenant "protections."

The specific content of these amendments will differ from state to state and should be informed by the results of rigorous field research. In general, however, we recommend the following guidelines for policy and legislative changes:

- In settings where past tenancy reform beneficiaries are not full owners, states should consider converting them into owners. This will require legislative changes that will differ from state to state. In West Bengal for example the state with the largest number of tenancy reform beneficiaries (bargadars)—the law could be improved by giving bargadars a unilateral right to become owners by "buying out" the landlord for a government-determined sum, by providing for a streamlined voluntary transaction process, and/or by activating the financing mechanism for bargadar purchases of barga land that is already contemplated by the Land Reform Act.
- In settings where tenancy is allowed, but subject to maximum rent levels and/or a minimum lease term, states should consider amending the legislation to remove the maximum rents and minimum length terms. If that is not politically feasible, the states should revise the maximum rent levels and/or minimum lease terms to reflect more accurately what is reasonable and enforceable. The Central Government's recommended policy for limiting rents to 20-25 percent of the produce (and "slightly more" if the inputs are provided by the owner) is well below prevailing

market rents throughout India and therefore difficult or impossible to enforce. One reason that West Bengal succeeded in implementing tenancy reform is because its legislation provided that the landlord shall receive 50 percent of the produce (when the landlord provided inputs). The reasonableness of the percentage assigned landlords made implementation feasible, while still improving the position of the tenants (bargadars).

Agricultural Landownership Ceilings

All Indian states have adopted legislation that places ceilings on the amount of agricultural land a person or family can own, with the objective of redistributing land in excess of the ceiling to poor, landless, or marginal farmers. The ceiling laws were enacted and enforced in two phases: (1) the period from 1960 to 1972, when no specific policy guidelines were present; and (2) the period since 1972, after the adoption of national policy guidelines. The end result is that approximately 5.4 million of acres of land have been redistributed to 5.6 million beneficiary households (see Table 2, below). West Bengal accounts for 20 percent of that redistributed land and 47 percent of the ceiling-surplus beneficiaries.

The policy of imposing landownership ceilings evolved slowly after Independence, and, in general, enjoyed less consensus than land tenancy reforms. In a draft outline of the First Five-Year Plan in 1951, the National Planning Commission identified the preponderance of small, "uneconomic" holdings as the greatest handicap to increasing agricultural production and rejected the idea of imposing ceilings on large holdings outright.

The legislative measures adopted in this first round were full of loopholes that large landowners used to circumvent the laws' objectives. Several of these state laws were also successfully challenged in the courts.

By the end of 1970, these ceiling laws had resulted in the vesting of approximately 2.4 million acres of land. Of this land, about 50 percent had been distributed to the rural poor, although not necessarily to the landless as no clear eligibility requirements had been prescribed in many of the laws.

Table 2: State-wise Distribution of Ceiling Surplus Land (As of 31st March, 2002)

(Area in thousands of acres)

S. No.	States/Uts	Area Declared surplus	Area Taken possession benef.	Area Distributed to indiv.	Total No. of benef. (,000s)
1	2	3	4	5	6
1	Andhra Pradesh	799.66	641.66	582.32	540.34
2	Assam	613.40	575.38	545.87	445.85
3	Bihar	415.45	390.75	306.96	379.53
4	Gujarat	227.40	160.80	139.85	32.31
5	Haryana	107.49	103.02	102.12	29.23
6	Himachal Pradesh	316.56	304.90	6.17	6.26
7	Jammu & Kashmir	455.58	450.00	450.00	450.00
8	Karnataka	268.48	161.83	123.20	33.61
9	Kerala	141.43	96.85	68.75	166.81
10	Madhya Pradesh	298.76	260.32	186.94	74.71
11	Maharashtra	740.00	670.45	642.84	140.85
12	Manipur	1.83	1.69	1.68	1.26
13	Orissa	179.18	167.25	156.95	139.60
14	Punjab	223.12	105.83	104.23	28.57
15	Rajasthan	611.10	569.21	461.85	81.81
16	Tamil Nadu	200.92	191.63	181.30	143.68
17	Tripura	2.00	1.94	1.60	1.42
18	Uttar Pradesh	374.13	341.46	258.70	294.06
19	West Bengal	1,383.85	1,294.74	1,064.04	2,651.62
20	D&N Haveli	9.41	9.31	6.85	3.35
21	Delhi	1.13	0.39	0.39	0.65
22	Pondicherry	2.33	1.21	1.07	1.46
TOTAL		**7,376.18**	**6,504.62**	**5,398.68**	**5,652.99**

Source: Government of India, Ministry of Rural Development

The perceived ineffectiveness of the ceiling laws during the first phase led to an establishment of a Central Land Reforms Committee and several high-level policy meetings on land reforms. The Central Land Reforms Committee convened a Chief Minister's Conference in July, 1972 at the height of Indira Gandhi's political power. At this conference, the Prime Minister was able to push through a set of National Guidelines for future state laws on land ceilings.

Following the formulation of these National Guidelines, all states introduced legislative changes in response. While the new or newly amended laws on land ceiling followed a common pattern, variations existed on several key aspects. Some of those aspects are summarised below including: (1) the unit to which the ceiling applies; (2) the ceiling area; (3) exemptions from ceiling; (4) retrospective application; (5) compensation; and (6) defining and prioritising beneficiaries.

Unit for Application of Ceiling

The unit of application in every state is a family of up to five members. "Family" is generally defined in relationship to the head of household and includes the head of household, his spouse, and their minor sons and unmarried daughters. Variations occur concerning adult sons (married or unmarried) and married daughters. Most laws allow an increased ceiling area for each additional family member (beyond five) up to a certain maximum number. Only in two states (West Bengal and Tripura) does the ceiling area decrease for a family of less than five members.

Ceiling Area

There is little commonality concerning the definition of the ceiling area limit. Most state laws express the ceiling limit in terms of a standard acre (or hectare) and a standard holding. The definition of a standard acre (or hectare) and standard holding differs from state to state and even within a state depending on the classification (whether irrigated or not and type of soil). In some states, the ceiling area applies only to owned land. In other states, it applies to the sum of owned and rented-in land. All states reduced their ceiling laws after the 1972 policy. The ceilings now range from nine standard acres in parts of Jammu & Kashmir to 54 standard acres for certain circumstances in Gujarat, Haryana, Karnataka, Madhya Pradesh, Punjab, Rajasthan, and Tamil Nadu.

Exemptions from Ceiling

Most state laws reduced the number of exemptions in the

early 1970s. The common exempted categories now include: (1) land held by any level of government; (2) land held by educational institutions; (3) land held by industrial or commercial undertakings; and (4) plantations of coffee, cocoa, or tea. Most state laws also include some additional minor exceptions.

Retroactive Application

Many large landowners conducted malafide or benami transactions or land use changes in anticipation of the ceiling laws in order to evade the ceilings. The methods included: converting agricultural land into non-agricultural land; partitioning land among friends, relatives, or even servants; initiating fictitious divorces in order to divide land among spouses; and adopting in order to increase the ceiling limit. The National Guidelines urged states to ban malafide transactions or partitions retrospectively. Some of the state laws impose a blanket ban on such transactions, rendering them null and void. In other states, transferrers have to prove before a competent authority that the transfers were not malafide.

Effect of Irrigation Projects: Re-determination of Ceiling Area

One of the controversial subjects discussed at the Chief Ministers' Conference in July 1992 was the impact of irrigation schemes on the ceiling imposed. Many supported higher ceilings for land irrigated by private schemes in order to encourage private investment and initiative. The final recommendations gave a slight advantage to owners of privately irrigated land. The Chief Ministers also recommended that land should not be reclassified for purposes of imposing a new ceiling as a result of any private irrigation project completed after August 15, 1972. The guidelines did not address how future government irrigation projects should impact ceilings.

The state ceiling laws address subsequent irrigation projects in a variety of ways. Some states require reassessment of the ceiling if the nature of the land changes because of any irrigation project, whether state or private. In Andhra Pradesh, any future alteration in the classification of land requires reapplication of the ceiling law. More specifically, under the Madhya Pradesh Ceiling on Agricultural Holdings Act, 1960, the nature of a landholding changes in the future as a result of irrigation, the land holder must notify the Tahsildar within 90 days of the change in the nature of the land, and the provisions of the Ceiling Act shall be applied again at that time. The Act only notes examples of dry land becoming irrigated, but the language of the provision is broad enough to allow for reapplication of the ceiling in the event previously irrigated land becomes dry. The Act does allow for additional compensation to landowners for improvements to surplus land; the Act does not make a deduction (or exempt land) where the land is improved due to state-sponsored projects. Similarly, in Maharashtra, the state retains the power to vary the ceiling area for a number of reasons, including a change in "the situation of the land" and its productive capacity. In other states, the requirement for re-evaluation of the ceiling only applies when state projects provide irrigation. The Uttar Pradesh Imposition of Ceiling on Land Holdings Act, 1960, provides that if any unirrigated land becomes irrigated as a result of any state project, then the ceiling area shall be redetermined. In West Bengal, the standard for measurement of land for purposes of application of the ceiling is one hectare in an irrigated area. "Irrigated area" is defined to include land that is irrigated after the date for ceiling determinations as a result of a state irrigation project. Under both laws, the landowner is eligible for compensation for any surplus land created as a result of the state irrigation project.

Compensation

The state laws vary in the amount of compensation paid to landowners whose ceiling-surplus land is taken by the state. Some states use the assessed land revenue while others use the land classification to determine the compensation amount. In all state laws, however, the compensation amount is negligible when compared with the market value of the land. As discussed above, the constitutionality of the compensation amount cannot be questioned in a court of law after the 1971 amendments to the Indian Constitution.

Distributing Ceiling-Surplus Land to Beneficiaries

In all states, the landowner with land in excess of the ceiling is allowed to choose what land is to be taken. In terms of distributing that land, the National Guidelines stipulate that priority should be given to landless agricultural workers, particularly those belonging to Scheduled Castes and Scheduled Tribes. Most states have generally followed this advice.

Some states include the priority of distribution within the law itself, while other states include this stipulation in the statutory rules or regulations. In some states, first priority is given in distribution of ceiling land to the tenants dispossessed in that area (due either to the vesting of ceiling-surplus land or to resumption by landowners for personal cultivation subject to certain limits). In other states, no such priority is given for dispossessed tenants. Some states provided for distributing the ceiling-surplus land free-of-charge to beneficiaries (including West Bengal, Bihar, Orissa, and Uttar Pradesh). Other states require the beneficiaries to pay an "amount" in suitable installments, which in some cases is equal to the amount paid by the state government to the losing landowner.

State laws also vary in the type of rights received by the beneficiaries. Many states (including West Bengal) permanently prohibit transfers by beneficiaries. Other states, such as Karnataka, prohibit the beneficiaries from transferring their land for a period of years (ranging from 10 to 20 years).

Still other states allow such transfers only with the permission of the local revenue authority. Some states have provisions for setting some ceiling-surplus land apart for public purposes (including Andhra Pradesh, Bihar, Jammu & Kashmir, Karnataka, Kerala, Maharashtra, Madhya Pradesh, and Uttar Pradesh). Other states do not provide for reservation for public purposes unless the land is unfit for cultivation or was used for grasing before vesting.

Extent and Impact of Land Ceiling Laws

Excluding these three states, Appu concludes that "the imposition of ceilings has not led to any worthwhile redistribution of agricultural land in the rest of the country." Defects in the law are a partial cause for the failure of most such laws to achieve their objectives, but the more relevant factor is the absence of political will at both the central and, apart from a few exceptions during limited time periods, state levels. That lack of political will continues today, despite occasional political rhetoric to the contrary.

Land Ceiling Recommendations

Given (1) the lack of political will, (2) the limited success of past efforts (even when the political climate for redistribution was friendlier), and, particularly, (3) the existence of more practical tools for providing meaningful land rights to the poorest, India should not view ceiling laws as a fundamental component of future land reform efforts.

On the other hand, without solid empirical evidence to the contrary, neither should Indian states race to increase or remove existing land ceilings. While in most states the ceilings have not led to a significant government redistribution of land, those ceilings may be serving a useful role in preventing a further excessive concentration of land and in States might consider focusing their efforts in this area on the following:

- Remove the obstacles preventing the distribution of the nearly 20 lakh acres (India-wide) that have been declared surplus but not yet distributed to individual beneficiaries. Because lengthy litigation is a principal obstacle, Indian states could focus more legal aid resources or establish special tribunals to resolve long-standing cases.
- Allocate the remaining land for distribution in smaller plots in order to benefit greater numbers of landless. States should consider allocating the remaining unallocated land as either house-and-garden plots or small field plots (one acre or less) so that the benefits can be enjoyed by a larger number of families. The role that small plots can play in enhancing the rural livelihoods is visible in the fields of West Bengal. As part of its land reform efforts, West Bengal redistributed 1.04 million acres of ceiling-surplus land to 2.54 million land-poor households. In recent years, the state has been allocating ceiling-surplus lands in very small plots, averaging less than one-third of an acre. In a small field study covering two districts, RDI interviewed 34 erstwhile landless land reform beneficiaries who had received plots averaging 0.16 acres (ranging from 0.07 to 0.38 acres). The majority of the households farmed their plots intensively and reported significant increases in food intake, income, and social status—a mix of human,

financial, and social assets that they attributed to the small field plots. Other more comprehensive studies are consistent with RDI's findings: West Bengal's land reform beneficiaries have realised important benefits from plots of land much smaller than an acre. Some question the potential impact of distributing small plots, noting that the income earned from the plot is not itself sufficient to raise the beneficiary households above the poverty line. From a livelihoods perspective, however, this is not a relevant standard. A sustainable livelihoods approach recognises that people draw on a range of capital assets to further their livelihood objectives and acknowledges that in many cases, a diversity of assets provides the best buffer against the vulnerability factors that threaten the rural poor. Even after receiving small plots, the beneficiary households typically pursue other income-generating strategies such as working as agricultural labourers. Receiving land through the land reform has not, in most cases, changed the primary "occupation" of most beneficiaries. The land has, however, provided those households with a significant opportunity to supplement their nutrition and income, in addition to increasing their status and credit worthiness.

- Amend legislation so that land ceiling beneficiaries are not permanently prohibited from selling their land. International experience indicates that permanent prohibitions on sale are unnecessarily restrictive and not a good practice. States with permanent prohibitions should consider revising the law to provide for time-bound restrictions of perhaps 10-15 years.

If any Indian states do plan to continue using land ceilings as tool to redistribute land, the following legislative changes should be considered:

- Increase the amount of compensation provided to landowners who lose ceiling-surplus land. While constitutional case law makes clear that higher compensation is not legally required, it is recommended. Compensation need not be market value, but should be something meaningful, not bordering on confiscation as is the case in many state laws.

- Use individuals rather than families as the unit to which the ceiling applies. West Bengal's experience indicates that this ensures greater equity and eliminates an easy loophole by which larger families split into additional families in order to retain more land.
- Limit the amount of ceiling-surplus land that a beneficiary family can receive to one acre. Given the large numbers of rural, landless households, it is more important to increase the number of beneficiary families than to provide each beneficiary family an "ideal" amount of land.

If any states are seriously considering increasing or removing land ceilings, they should first undertake rigorous empirical research to determine the equity and efficiency effects of revising existing land ceilings. Finally, all states consider other more practicable non-ceiling approaches to broaden access to land ownership. One approach that deserves consideration is a land purchase approach, especially if implemented through women's self-help group activities. The government of Andhra Pradesh has recently initiated such land purchases in partnership with civil society organisations as part of its IKP project (formerly called Velegu project), and the early experience is promising. Mindful of issues and challenges faced by other land purchase schemes and as the description of the steps above reflect, Andhra Pradesh designed the land purchase activity with the following features:

- *Beneficiary-driven Process:* In contrast to schemes in which bureaucrats initiate the process of identifying land and negotiate for the purchase before identifying beneficiaries, Andhra Pradesh's land purchase activity is initiated by the beneficiaries. Self-selected beneficiaries that have demonstrated capacity for a land purchase identify the land, negotiate a price, and develop a business plan for farming the land.
- *Purchase Plus Improvements:* Andhra Pradesh requires beneficiaries to consider what improvements (such as irrigation) are necessary and to include the costs of and plan for such improvements in their business plan. This

consideration and budgeting for necessary improvements avoids the problems inherent in schemes that allow land purchases without factoring in the costs of necessary improvements essential to successful farming of the land.

- *Business Plan Requirement:* Andhra Pradesh's requirement of a business plan prior to purchase focuses the beneficiaries on the economic feasibility of their land purchase and requires consideration of options. Schemes that do not identify beneficiaries until after land purchase cannot benefit from this kind of essential business planning.
- *Integrated Technical Assistance:* Andhra Pradesh's land purchase scheme includes technical assistance as an aspect of the purchase plan. Because technical assistance is integrated into the purchase option, beneficiaries do not need to look to other government schemes and resources for the necessary technical assistance.
- *Cost Recovery Plan:* Andhra Pradesh's land purchase scheme includes a substantial grant component and reasonable repayment terms so beneficiaries are not saddled with an unmanageable debt and unrealistic repayment plan. The repayment plan is included in the pre-purchase business plan so beneficiaries can evaluate the extent of their obligation and understand how the repayment obligation factors into the overall economics of the land purchase option.

Including those features in a project aimed at broadening land ownership through purchase will help avoid problems that have plagued land purchase projects implemented by Scheduled Caste Development Corporations.

Such schemes have achieved some access, but have also faced significant problems, including allowing the landowners seeking to sell land to initiate and control the process, failing to anticipate the need for improvements and technical assistance and to include those costs in budgeting, identifying beneficiaries after the land is purchased, permitting beneficiaries to take on unmanageable debts and establishing often unreasonable repayment schemes.

Allocation of Government Wasteland

India's land reform efforts are typically described as comprising only the three categories of reforms discussed above-abolition of intermediaries, tenancy reform, and ceiling-surplus redistribution. The reforms, however, also included other significant and sometimes overlapping measures. These include the allocation of government wasteland (discussed in this section) and the allocation or regularisation of land for house sites (covered in the following section VI).

Table 3: Distribution of Government Wastelands as of March, 2002

Name of State/UT	Area Distributed (in thousands acres)
Andhra Pradesh	4,202
Assam	589
Bihar[1]	1,321
Gujarat	1,381
Haryana	0
Himachal Pradesh	17
Karnataka	1,372
Kerala	457
Madhya Pradesh[2]	79
Maharashtra	1,023
Manipur	32
Punjab	110
Orissa	726
Tamil Nadu	207
Tripura	132
Uttar Pradesh[3]	2,489
West Bengal	432
Goa	5
Mizoram	74
Rajasthan	93
Delhi	6
Total	14,747

1. Including Jharkhand
2. Including Chhattisgarh
3. Including Uttaranchal.

The poverty alleviation potential inherent in allocating government wasteland and house sites are often not recognised, but significant opportunities exist for Indian states. These opportunities generally do not require legislative change and are summarised below. The opportunities relating to allocation of government wasteland involve fully implementing already reported allocations. The opportunities relating to house sites arise due to the increasing recognition that if those house sites are 0.05 acre (five cents) or larger, they can provide important supplementary nutrition and income to the household.

"Wastelands" are lands that are either entirely barren or are producing significantly below their economic potential. An estimated 150 million acres of India's total land mass of 810 million acres are wastelands. These include wastelands under the Forest Department, wastelands under the control of the Revenue Departments, common grasing lands managed by villages or local governments, and private wastelands.

Various state governments report allocating 14.7 million acres of government "wasteland" to poor rural households (see Table 3, below). The national government does not maintain statistics on how many households have received such land. Six states report allocating 80 percent of this land, led by Andhra Pradesh (28 percent of the national total) and Uttar Pradesh (17 percent of the national total). In terms of total acreage, the reported amount of allocated government wastelands is nearly three times the amount of ceiling-surplus land redistributed. However, in contrast to the studies and literature devoted to ceiling-surplus redistribution, the topic of government wasteland allocation is rarely mentioned in the literature, perhaps because the quality of such allocated wastelands is often very poor. In isolated studies, researchers have typically found that a majority of the government wastelands allocated are not utilised. Another problem is that the government figures on wasteland allocation are likely over-stated. Field investigations in Andhra Pradesh, for example, indicate that perhaps as much as 30 percent of the reported beneficiaries do not have both legal and physical possession of the allocated land. The gaps between the reported numbers and secure land rights occur for a variety of reasons, including: (1) assignment of land is on paper only and the physical possession has not been given; (2) the beneficiaries have been evicted from their lands; and (3) in numerous cases, especially in Telangana where large compact blocks have been assigned to the poor, the survey subdivision work has not been done so the beneficiaries have not received their individual parcels of land. Similar circumstances concerning past government land "allocations" have been reported in other states.

These "gaps" represent both a problem and an opportunity. The well-recognised problem is that past allocations of government allocation did not always result in secure land rights for the intended beneficiaries. The opportunity for state governments is to now address those "gaps" and thus broaden access to secure land rights. Andhra Pradesh's recent efforts to address the shortcomings in earlier "allocations" of government provide a model for other states to consider. These efforts, through the IKP project (formerly called Velegu) are the subject of a recent paper by K. Raju and Karuna Akella. The experience is notable and deserves a short summary here. Andhra Pradesh's IKP project identifies-often with the help of community-based organisations—specific, local opportunities for enhancing the poor's rights to government land (as well as other land). Once those opportunities are identified, the Project (under the Rural Development Department) works with the Revenue Department and local communities to facilitate the actions necessary to enhance those land rights. To date, the combined efforts of the Revenue Department, IKP, and numerous state officials and local communities have put secure rights to at least tens of thousands of government land into the hands of the rural poor.

The model starts with multi-faceted and decentralised efforts to identify "gaps" of the type listed above 78 or other opportunities to allocate unallocated government land. These gaps or opportunities are then classified by project officials, after which they determine the most appropriate approach, select a course of action, and see that action to completion.

This Andhra Pradesh project (under the Rural Development Department) takes a multi-faceted, flexible, decentralised approach—coupled with the support of the Revenue Department and community-based organisations. It has brought new life to government efforts to broaden land access by taking advantage of the land-related circumstances unique to each setting and tailoring programmes to take advantage of specific opportunities. Adopting an approach modelled upon Andhra Pradesh's recent experience will not likely require changes in legislation. However, states who currently permanently prohibit the sale of wasteland (other land) allocated by the government should change this to a time-limited restriction of perhaps 10 to 15 years.

Allocation or Regularisation of House Sites

Another special feature of the land reform measures in some states is the provision of house sites or homestead plots to landless labourers or other land-poor households. Such land has been provided in various ways, including: (1) allocating state government land; (2) allocating vested ceiling-surplus land; (3) allocating land under the control of the panchayats; (4) allocating ownership of land held by residential tenants; and (5) regularising the possession of illegally occupied land. Some states, such as West Bengal and Bihar, have enacted separate laws for one or more of these purposes, but most states have incorporated provisions in their land reform laws, land revenue laws, or both. Neither the state nor national governments maintain systematic data on the numbers of households that have received ownership of house sites by all the various means. It is estimated that at least 4 million households have received such land. The plots typically have ranged in size from 0.02 acre (about 900 square feet) to 0.10 acre (about 4,300 square feet). The primary purpose of such allocations has been to provide land for a residence and (sometimes) to free agricultural labourers from the power of their employers who are also their residential landlords. Recent studies have also shown that the allocation of such small plots also provides important non-residential benefits (income, nutrition, status, credit access, etc.), particularly when the plots are large enough to include a garden and space for a few animals.Past land reform programmes in India have been based on the assumption that the government should give poor rural households at least two to three acres of land. However, experience in numerous countries as well as recent research findings in India suggest that poor, rural households can significantly improve their well being on house plot land if the plots are larger than 0.03 acre. The research, conducted by the

Rural Development Institute (USA) and the University of Agricultural Sciences, Bangalore, includes several findings worth consideration:

> *Functionally landless, agricultural labourer families that own a house plot typically derive substantial non-housing benefits from the plot including increased nutrition, income, status, wealth generation, and access to credit.*
>
> *Those benefits increase very substantially with relatively small increases in house plot size, especially as the house plot increases above 3 cents (about 1300 square feet) to about seven cents (about 3,000 square feet).*
>
> *Families with house plots larger than 3 cents were more than twice as likely as those with smaller plots to report that their house plot had resulted in increased family income; three times as likely to report that the plot had resulted in improved nutrition; and almost twice as likely to report that receiving the plot had increased their access to credit.*
>
> *Rural families with well-developed house-and-garden plots of about seven cents were producing enough vegetables, fruit, and milk on their homestead plots to meet or significantly exceed their household nutritional needs of these products. Apart from direct household consumption, these households received about Rs 11,000 of annualised income from the sale of products from their house-and-garden plots.*

These findings from India are consistent with evidence from a variety of developing country settings showing that small homestead or garden plots have conferred multiple important benefits in terms of food, income, status, fuel wood, and economic security to poor households. Moreover, many of these important benefits accrue specifically to women. We recommend that state governments further explore the allocation of relatively "large" house sites as a means for creating a buffer against poverty. Several localised initiatives to provide "large" house sites offer lessons on how larger-scale efforts might be operationalised. RDI, with FAO support, has recently conducted a field review of six projects that involved providing relatively large house sites to poor beneficiaries in six different states (Gujarat, West Bengal, Karnataka, Orissa, Andhra Pradesh, and Kerala) in order to distill success factors and other lessons to inform the design of future government and NGO schemes to allocate house sites. The land was obtained through a variety of mechanisms including purchase, acquisition, and expropriation. The review distilled the following as important success factors:

- Relatively large, compact blocks of land that accommodate house sites for at least 20 households.
- Land that is either adjacent to or within close proximity to an existing habitation area.
- Assistance with housing construction and garden development integrated as part of the project or links to other projects that offer such assistance.
- Access to water for domestic and garden use.
- Beneficiary participation in the design, implementation, and cost-sharing, either through NGOs or panchayats.
- Land titled either in the joint names of husband and wife or independently in name of women.
- Suitability of land in terms of quality and location was better when land was purchased.

Homestead Plot Recommendations

Allocating one-fifteenth to one-tenth acre house-and-garden plots may be the most practicable method of providing meaningful land rights to India's seventeen million rural families that are completely landless. Because land in most village habitation areas is scarce and expensive, the government should consider purchasing land parcels of one or more acres within one kilometre of a village, dividing the parcel into one-tenth acre house-and-garden plots, providing some basic infrastructure to this new colony (a road, drinking water, and an electricity line), and distributing the plots to landless labourers.

The land costs per family are affordable. If non-irrigated agricultural land is targeted, typical costs of such land range from Rs 20,000 to Rs 50,000 per acre or Rs 2,000 to Rs 5,000 to benefit each family with a one-tenth acre plot. With land purchase as a feasible option, the government need not be limited by insufficient existing government land or face the political and administrative difficulties of expropriating land. The amount of land needed is not substantial. Allocating such plots to each of the 17 million landless families in India would require less than 0.5 percent of India's agricultural land. Such efforts can take the form of new government schemes or can be incorporated into existing rural housing or rural poverty alleviation schemes. The existing government rural housing schemes currently face two limitations in this regard. First, they typically limit the size of qualifying house sites to 1200 square feet or less, which is not large enough to provide sufficient space for a garden and livestock. Government planners should aim to provide at least 3,000 square feet to each family. Second, housing schemes rarely include resources for land purchase. Thus, those receiving benefits must already have their own land: the poorest often do not qualify because they do not own a house site. Rural housing programmes could address this by devoting some significant portion of existing resources for obtaining land.

Conclusion

India should both rethink and go beyond the twin pillars of past land reform efforts: tenancy reform and land ceilings. Other new and feasible methods exist for improving the poor's secure access to land. Much of the legal framework already exists. What is most needed is the political will of Indian leaders at the Union and state level to reform land policy and laws in a manner that advances the interests of the poor and marginalised. The reforms can be both pro-poor and market friendly, and the required costs are not unthinkable.

At bottom, the legislative foundations of land law and policy reform in India (abolition of intermediaries, tenancy reform, and land ceilings) were designed to increase the poor's access to rural land. To date, the effectiveness of the legislation has been mixed and progress over the last few years has slowed. The following approach, which involves selected revision to existing legislation and adoption of new methods of increasing land access, will help achieve the original equitable objectives of the legislation:

- Revitalize tenancy reform by: (1) solidifying the gains of past tenancy reform by converting protected tenants into owners; and (2) selectively liberalising excessive tenancy regulation and restrictions;

- Assist beneficiaries of ceiling legislation in realising the benefits by removing obstacles to land distribution and relaxing moratoriums on the transfer of ceiling surplus land;
- Consider adopting the decentralised IKP project approach in AP as a model for solidifying the gains of past wasteland allocation and otherwise providing secure land rights to the poor; and
- Explore using land purchase and existing government land to create new colonies of one-tenth acre house-and-garden plots for distribution to landless labourers.

The work required on India's land laws and policies in order to broaden access is significant, but should not be paralysing. The existing legal framework provides a solid starting point. With an open mind, a commitment to benefit the poorest, exploration and piloting of new approaches and an emphasis on implementation the objectives of land reform are achievable. India's poor deserve nothing less.

6

The Colonial Legacy-Myths and Popular Beliefs

While few educated South Asians would deny that British Colonial rule was detrimental to the interests of the common people of the sub-continent several harbour an illusion that the British weren't all bad.

Didn't they, perhaps, educate us-build us modern cities, build us irrigation canals-protect our ancient monuments-etc. etc. And then, there are some who might even say that their record was actually superior to that of independent India's! Perhaps, it is time that the colonial record be retrieved from the archives and re-examined-so that those of us who weren't alive during the freedom movement can learn to distinguish between the myths and the reality.

Literacy and Education

Several Indians are deeply concerned about why literacy rates in India are still so low. So in the last year, I have been making a point of asking English-speaking Indians to guess what India's literacy rate in the colonial period might have been. These were Indians who went to school in the sixties and seventies (only two decades after independence)-and I was amased to hear their fairly confident guesses.

Most guessed the number to be between 30% and 40%. When I suggested that their guess was on the high side-they offered 25% to 35%. No one was prepared to believe that literacy in British

India in 1911 was only 6%, in 1931 it was 8%, and by 1947 it had crawled to 11%! That fifty years of freedom had allowed the nation to quintuple it's literacy rate was something that almost seemed unfathomable to them. Perhaps-the British had concentrated on higher education....? But in 1935, only 4 in 10,000 were enrolled in universities or higher educational institutes. In a nation of then over 350 million people only 16,000 books (no circulation figures) were published in that year (*i.e.* 1 per 20,000).

Urban Development

It is undoubtedly true that the British built modern cities with modern conveniences for their administrative officers. But it should be noted that these were exclusive zones not intended for the "natives" to enjoy. Consider that in 1911, 69 per cent of Bombay's population lived in one-room tenements (as against 6 per cent in London in the same year). The 1931 census revealed that the figure had increased to 74 per cent-with one-third living more than 5 to a room. The same was true of Karachi and Ahmedabad. After the Second World War, 13 per cent of Bombay's population slept on the streets. As for sanitation, 10-15 tenements typically shared one water tap!

Yet, in 1757 (the year of the Plassey defeat), Clive of the East India Company had observed of Murshidabad in Bengal: "This city is as extensive, populous and rich as the city of London..." (so quoted in the Indian Industrial Commission Report of 1916-18). Dacca was even more famous as a manufacturing town, it's muslin a source of many legends and it's weavers had an international reputation that was unmatched in the medieval world.

But in 1840 it was reported by Sir Charles Trevelyan to a parliamentary enquiry that Dacca's population had fallen from 150,000 to 20,000. Montgomery Martin-an early historian of the British Empire observed that Surat and Murshidabad had suffered a similiar fate. (This phenomenon was to be replicated all over India-particularly in Awadh (modern U.P) and other areas that had offered the most heroic resistance to the British during the revolt of 1857.)

The percentage of population dependant on agriculture and pastoral pursuits actually rose to 73% in 1921 from 61% in 1891. (Reliable figures for earlier periods are not available.)

In 1854, Sir Arthur Cotton writing in "Public Works in India" noted: "Public works have been almost entirely neglected throughout India... The motto hitherto has been: 'Do nothing, have nothing done, let nobody do anything....." Adding that the Company was unconcerned if people died of famine, or if they lacked roads and water.

Nothing can be more revealing than the remark by John Bright in the House of Commons on June 24, 1858, "The single city of Manchester, in the supply of its inhabitants with the single article of water, has spent a larger sum of money than the East India Company has spent in the fourteen years from 1834 to 1848 in public works of every kind throughout the whole of its vast dominions."

Irrigation and Agricultural Development

There is another popular belief about British rule: 'The British modernised Indian agriculture by building canals'. But the actual record reveals a somewhat different story. " The roads and tanks and canals," noted an observer in 1838 (G. Thompson, "India and the Colonies," 1838), "which Hindu or Mussulman Governments constructed for the service of the nations and the good of the country have been suffered to fall into dilapidation; and now the want of the means of irrigation causes famines." Montgomery Martin, in his standard work "The Indian Empire", in 1858, noted that the old East India Company "omitted not only to initiate improvements, but even to keep in repair the old works upon which the revenue depended."

The Report of the Bengal Irrigation Department Committee in 1930 reads: "In every district the Khals (canals) which carry the internal boat traffic become from time to time blocked up with silt. Its Khals and rivers are the roads end highways of Eastern Bengal, and it is impossible to overestimate the importance to the economic life of this part of the province of maintaining these in proper navigable order....... " "As regards the revival or maintenance of minor routes,... practically nothing has been done, with the result that, in some parts of the Province at least, channels have been silted up, navigation has become limited to a few months in the year, and crops can only be marketed when the Khals rise high enough in the monsoon to make transport possible".

Sir William Willcock, a distinguished hydraulic engineer, whose name was associated with irrigation enterprises in Egypt and Mesopotamia had made an investigation of conditions in Bengal. He had discovered that innumerable small destructive rivers of the delta region, constantly changing their course, were originally canals which under the English regime were allowed to escape from their channels and run wild. Formerly these canals distributed the flood waters of the Ganges and provided for proper drainage of the land, undoubtedly accounting for that prosperity of Bengal which lured the rapacious East India merchants there in the early days of the eighteenth century.. He wrote" Not only was nothing done to utilise and improve the original canal system, but railway embankments were subsequently thrown up, entirely destroying it. Some areas, cut off from the supply of loam-bearing Ganges water, have gradually become sterile and unproductive, others improperly drained, show an advanced degree of water-logging, with the inevitable accompaniment of malaria. Nor has any attempt been made to construct proper embankments for the Gauges in its low course, to prevent the enormous erosion by which villages and groves and cultivated fields are swallowed up each year." "Sir William Willcock severely criticizes the modern administrators and officials, who, with every opportunity to call in expert technical assistance, have hitherto done nothing to remedy this disastrous situation, from decade to decade." Thus wrote G. Emerson in "Voiceless Millions," in 1931 quoting the views of Sir William Willcock in his "Lectures on the Ancient System of Irrigation in Bengal and its Application to Modern Problems" (Calcutta University Readership Lectures, University of Calcutta, 1930).

Modern Medicine and Life Expectancy

Even some serious critics of colonial rule grudgingly grant that the British brought modern medicine to India. Yet-all the statistical indicators show that access to modern medicine was severely restricted. A 1938 report by the ILO (International Labour Office) on "Industrial Labour in India" revealed that life expectancy in India was barely 25 years in 1921 (compared to 55 for England) and had actually fallen to 23 in 1931! In his recently published "Late Victorian Holocausts" Mike Davis reports that life expectancy fell by 20% between 1872 and 1921.

In 1934, there was one hospital bed for 3800 people in British India and this figure included hospital beds reserved for the British rulers. (In that same year, in the Soviet Union, there were ten times as many.) Infant mortality in Bombay was 255 per thousand in 1928. (In the same year, it was less than half that in Moscow).

Poverty and Population Growth

Several Indians when confronted with such data from the colonial period argue that the British should not be specially targeted because India's problems of poverty pre-date colonial rule, and in any case, were exacerbated by rapid population growth. Of course, no one who makes the first point is able to offer any substantive proof that such conditions prevailed long before the British arrived, and to counter such an argument would be difficult in the absence of reliable and comparable statistical data from earlier centuries. But some readers may find the anecdotal evidence intriguing. In any case, the population growth data is available and is quite remarkable in what it reveals. Between 1870 and 1910, India's population grew at an average rate of 19%. England and Wales' population grew three times as fast-by 58%! Average population growth in Europe was 45%. Between 1921-40, the population in India grew faster at 21% but was still less than the 24% growth of population in the US! In 1941, the density of population in India was roughly 250 per square mile almost a third of England's 700 per square mile. Although Bengal was much more densely inhabited at almost 780 per square mile-that was only about 10% more than England. Yet, there was much more poverty in British India than in England and an unprecedented number of famines were recorded during the period of British rule.

In the first half of the 19th century, there were seven famines leading to a million and a half deaths. In the second half, there were 24 famines (18 between 1876 and 1900) causing over 20 million deaths (as per official records). W. Digby, noted in "Prosperous British India" in 1901 that "stated roughly, famines and scarcities have been four times as numerous, during the last thirty years of the 19th century as they were one hundred years ago, and four times as widespread." In Late Victorian Holocausts, Mike Davis points out that here were 31 (thirty one) serious famines in 120 years of British rule compared to 17 (seventeen) in the 2000 years before British rule. Not surprising, since the export of food grains had increased by a factor of four just prior to that period. And export of other agricultural raw materials had also increased in similar proportions. Land that once produced grain for local consumption was now taken over by former slave-owners from N. America who were permitted to set up plantations for the cultivation of lucrative cash crops exclusively for export. Particularly galling is how the British colonial rulers continued to export foodgrains from India to Britain even during famine years. Annual British Government reports repeatedly published data that showed 70-80% of Indians were living on the margin of subsistence. That two-thirds were undernourished, and in Bengal, nearly four-fifths were undernourished. Contrast this data with the following accounts of Indian life prior to colonisation:-

> *"....even in the smallest villages rice, flour, butter, milk, beans and other vegetables, sugar and sweetmeats can be procured in abundance.... Tavernier writing in the 17th century in his "Travels in India".*

Manouchi-the Venetian who became chief physician to Aurangzeb (also in the 17th century) wrote: "Bengal is of all the kingdoms of the Mughal, best known in France..... We may venture to say it is not inferior in anything to Egypt-and that it even exceeds that kingdom in its products of silks, cottons, sugar, and indigo. All things are in great plenty here, fruits, pulse, grain, muslins, cloths of gold and silk..."

The French traveller, Bernier also described 17th century Bengal in a similiar vein: "The knowledge I have acquired of Bengal in two visits inclines me to believe that it is richer than Egypt. It exports in abundance cottons and silks, rice, sugar and butter. It produces amply for it's own consumption of wheat, vegetables, grains, fowls, ducks and geese. It has immense herds of pigs and flocks of sheep and goats. Fish of every kind it has in profusion. From Rajmahal to the sea is an endless number of canals, cut in bygone ages from the Ganges by immense labour for navigation and irrigation."

The poverty of British India stood in stark contrast to these eye witness reports and has to be ascribed to the pitiful wages that working people in India received in that period. A 1927-28 report noted that "all but the most highly skilled workmen in India receive wages which are barely sufficient to feed and clothe them. Everywhere will be seen overcrowding, dirt and squalid misery..." This in spite of the fact that in 1922-an 11 hour day was the norm (as opposed to an 8 hour day in the Soviet Union.)

In 1934, it had been reduced to 10 hours (whereas in the Soviet Union, the 7 hour day had been legislated as early as in 1927) What was worse, there were no enforced restrictions on the use of child labour and the Whitley Report found children as young as five-working a 12 hour day.

Ancient Monuments

Perhaps the least known aspect of the colonial legacy is the early British attitude towards India's historic monuments and the extend of vandalism that took place.

Instead, there is this pervasive myth of the Britisher as an unbiased "protector of the nation's historic legacy". R. Nath in his 'History of Decorative Art in Mughal Architecture' records that scores of gardens, tombs and palaces that once adorned the suburbs of Sikandra at Agra were sold out or auctioned. "Relics of the glorious age of the Mughals were either destroyed or converted beyond recognition..". "Out of 270 beautiful monuments which existed at Agra alone, before its capture by Lake in 1803, hardly 40 have survived".

In the same vein, David Carroll (in 'Taj Mahal') observes: " The forts in Agra and Delhi were commandeered at the beginning of the nineteenth century and turned into military garrisons. Marble reliefs were torn down, gardens were trampled, and lines of ugly barracks, still standing today, were installed in their stead. In the Delhi fort, the Hall of Public Audience was made into an arsenal and the arches of the outer colonnades were bricked over or replaced with rectangular wooden windows." The Mughal fort at Allahabad (one of Akbar's favourite) experienced a fate far worse. Virtually nothing of architectural significance is to be seen in the barracks that now make up the fort. The Deccan fort at Ahmednagar was also converted into barracks. Now, only its outer walls can hint at its former magnificence.

Shockingly, even the Taj Mahal was not spared. David Carroll reports: "..By the nineteenth century, its grounds were a favourite trysting place for young Englishmen and their ladies. Open-air balls were held on the marble terrace in front of the main door, and there, beneath Shah Jahan's lotus dome, brass bands um-pah-pahed and lords and ladies danced the quadrille. The minarets became a popular site for suicide leaps, and the mosques on either side of the Taj were rented out as bungalows to honeymooners. The gardens of the Taj were especially popular for open-air frolics....."

"At an earlier date, when picnic parties were held in the garden of the Taj, related Lord Curzon, a governor general in the early twentieth century, "it was not an uncommon thing for the revellers to arm themselves with hammer and chisel, with which they wiled away the afternoon by chipping out fragments of agate and carnelian from the cenotaphs of the Emperor and his lamented Queen." The Taj became a place where one could drink in private, and its parks were often strewn with the figures of inebriated British soldiers..."

Lord William Bentinck, (governor general of Bengal 1828-33, and later first governor general of all India), went so far as to announce plans to demolish the best Mogul monuments in Agra and Delhi and remove their marble facades. These were to be shipped to London, where they would be broken up and sold to members of the British aristocracy. Several of Shahjahan's pavilions in the Red Fort at Delhi were indeed stripped to the brick, and the marble was shipped off to England (part of this shipment included pieces for King George IV himself).

Plans to dismantle the Taj Mahal were in place, and wrecking machinery was moved into the garden grounds. Just as the demolition work was to begin, news from London indicated that the first auction had not been a success, and that all further sales were cancelled—it would not be worth the money to tear down the Taj Mahal.

Thus the Taj Mahal was spared, and so too, was the reputation of the British as "Protectors of India's Historic Legacy" ! That innumerable other monuments were destroyed, or left to rack and ruin is a story that has yet to get beyond the specialists in the field.

India and the Industrial Revolution

Perhaps the most important aspect of colonial rule was the transfer of wealth from India to Britain. In his pioneering book, India Today, Rajni Palme Dutt conclusively demonstrates how vital this was to the Industrial Revolution in Britain. Several patents that had remained unfunded suddenly found industrial sponsors once the taxes from India started rolling in. Without capital from India, British banks would have found it impossible to fund the modernisation of Britain that took place in the 18th and 19th centuries.

In addition, the scientific basis of the industrial revolution was not a uniquely European contribution. Several civilisations had been adding to the world's scientific database-especially the civilisations of Asia, (including those of the Indian sub-continent). Without that aggregate of scientific knowledge the scientists of Britain and Europe would have found it impossible to make the rapid strides they made during the period of the Industrial revolution. Moreover, several of these patents, particularly those concerned with the textile industry relied on pre-industrial techniques perfected in the sub-continent. (In fact, many of the earliest textile machines in Britain were unable to match the complexity and finesse of the spinning and weaving machines of Dacca.)

Some euro-centric authors have attempted to deny any such linkage. They have tried to assert that not only was the Industrial Revolution a uniquely British/European event-that colonisation and the phenomenal transfer of wealth that took place was merely incidental to it's fruition. But the words of Lord Curzon still ring loud and clear. The Viceroy of British India in 1894 was quite unequivocal, "India is the pivot of our Empire.... If the Empire loses any other part of its Dominion we can survive, but if we lose India the sun of our Empire will have set."

Lord Curzon knew fully well, the value and importance of the Indian colony. It was the transfer of wealth through unprecedented levels of taxation on Indians of virtually all classes that funded the great "Industrial Revolution" and laid the ground for "modernisation" in Britain. As early as 1812, an East India Company Report had stated "The importance of that immense empire to this country is rather to be estimated by the great annual addition it makes to the wealth and capital of the Kingdom....."

Unfair Trade

Few would doubt that Indo-British trade may have been unfair-but it may be noteworthy to see how unfair. In the early 1800s imports of Indian cotton and silk goods faced duties of 70-80%. British imports faced duties of 2-4%! As a result, British imports of cotton manufactures into India increased by a factor of 50, and Indian exports dropped to one-fourth! A similiar trend was noted in silk goods, woollens, iron, pottery, glassware and paper. As a result, millions of ruined artisans and craftsmen, spinners, weavers, potters, smelters and smiths were rendered jobless and had to become landless agricultural workers.

Colonial Beneficiaries

Another aspect of colonial rule that has remained hidden from popular perception is that Britain was not the only beneficiary of colonial rule. British trade regulations even as they discriminated against Indian business interests created a favourable trading environment for other imperial powers. By 1939, only 25% of Indian imports came from Britain. 25% came from Japan, the US and Germany.

In 1942-3, Canada and Australia contributed another 8%. In the period immediately before independence, Britain ruled as much on behalf of it's imperial allies as it did in it's own interest. The process of "globalisation" was already taking shape. But none of this growth trickled down to India. In the last half of 19th century, India's income fell by 50%. In the 190 years prior to independence, the Indian economy was literally stagnant-it experienced zero growth. (Mike Davis: Late Victorian Holocausts).

Those who wish India well might do well to re-read this history so the nation isn't brought to the abyss once again, (and so soon after being liberated from the yoke of colonial rule). While some Indians may wax nostalgic for the return of their former overlords, and some may be ambivalent about colonial rule, most of us relish our freedom and wish to perfect it-not gift it away again.

Problems of Indian Agriculture

Indian Agriculture in a Historical Context

An important aspect to note about Indian agricultural production (in most parts of the country) is its relationship (even dependency) on skilful and wise water-management practices. One of the unique features of the Indian Subcontinent is how almost its entire rainfall is concentrated in the few monsoon months. During the monsoons, the Indian Subcontinent is usually gifted with bountiful rains, although not infrequently, this bountiful monsoon can turn into a terror, causing uncontrollable floods in parts of the country. Conversely, every few years, the monsoon can be erratic and deficient, leading to drought and the possibility of famine.

Thus, all through history the development of Indian agriculture has been inextricably linked with effective water-management practices that have either been taken up by the state, or by local village communities. Water management has necessitated a certain degree of cooperation and collective spirit in the Indian countryside, and until the imposition of colonial rule, it precluded any widespread development of private property in India.

Regional rulers, or local representatives of the state were generally obliged to allocate a certain percentage of the agricultural taxes on building and managing water-storage, water-harvesting and/or water-diverting structures which facilitated a second crop, and provided water for drinking and other purposes in the long dry season.

Only a small percentage of Indian farmers have enjoyed the luxury of natural irrigation, although there are reports that in certain parts of the country, the soil used to retain enough moisture well beyond the monsoon months. However, it is equally true that the drying up of wells led to mass migrations, and sudden depopulation of old towns and villages. In Assam, Bengal and Bihar-all flood-prone states, there is evidence of a massive network of canals that allowed both effective drainage to prevent flooding during the heavy monsoon months, and also provide for fishing, transportation and irrigation arteries in the dry seasons. Intelligent water-management thus allowed for the growth of a healthy agricultural surplus, that in turn facilitated steady urbanisation (albeit at a much slower pace than seen in the industrial era), and the development of a variety of pre-industrial manufacturing in areas such as textiles, jewellery, wood/metal-working etc.

Because of the immense importance of effective water-management, the entire revenue system of the state was structured so as to take into account both the necessity of water-management and the inherent dependency that existed between Indian agriculture and the availability of water. Most Indian states attempted to collect revenues in a manner that did not entirely destroy the village solidarity that was essential in proper sharing and management of common water-resources. At the same time, urban tax collectors had to deal with mediating entities from the villages, so that they did not tax at a rate that might lead to the destruction of water-management facilities so essential for life and sustainable agriculture.

By and large, taxes were imposed on villages collectively (not on individual farmers directly), and the village elites (whether Brahmins or others) were obliged to ensure that the burden of taxes did not destroy the complete viability of agriculture. Taxes were also adjusted keeping in mind whether the land was well-irrigated or not. When ruling dynasties became utterly corrupt and decadent, and failed to tax within limits, or neglected the construction and maintenance of collective water-management facilities, they were confronted with revolts and rebellions, and even risked being overthrown. There is evidence that whenever the tax collectors of a certain regime became too greedy (such as what happened in certain villages/districts during the reigns of some of Northern India's more rapacious invading conquerors), entire villages would be abandoned to escape the burden of heavy taxes. As long as India was not very densely populated and there was the potential of new lands to cultivate, (and the reach of the armed state was not absolute and all-encompassing), this was one of the means by which Indian villagers-both artisans and peasants were able to escape the burden of back-breaking taxes. But as the population grew and states became more powerful, this escape route was gradually sealed off, and this then led to regional peasant rebellions-most significant of which were the Sikh and the Maratha revolts against the Mughals.

Thus, the British arrived in India at a time when peasant rebellions were beginning to eat away at the invincibility of the might of the Mughal empire. However, even as the decentralisation that resulted from the break-up of the widely resented Mughal empire eased slightly the burden on the peasantry in most instances, it also provided an opportunity for the increasingly cunning and shrewd Britishers in India to seize the opportunity, and exploit the widening cleavages in Indian society for their own nefarious ends.

Colonial Aspects of Exploitation in the Indian Countryside

The imposition of Colonial Rule in India led to a drastic break with the past, in that not only did the scale and intensity of the exploitation of the village communities greatly increase, it also led to the introduction of new, and almost entirely parasitic intermediaries between the state and the tax paying masses-intermediaries who were typically induced (or pressurised) to abandon traditional restraint, and discard the old formulae that helped mediate the burden on the typical village peasant or artisan.

(It is notable that whereas ancient texts such as the Manusmriti put a cap on agricultural taxes at one-sixth of the produce, and taxes during Mughal rule had risen to something between a third and almost half the produce, during British rule, the peasant was often left with barely a third of the crop.)

Not only were these intermediaries under no pressure to build or maintain traditional water-management structures, the manner in which they were chosen by the British to collect the taxes actually discouraged any diversion of the taxes towards any capital upkeep. Over time, this not only led to the destruction of century-old water management structures, but also to the virtual destruction of the knowledge systems and cultural traditions that had helped build and preserve these water-management techniques over the centuries in states such as Bihar, Bengal, Karnataka, Tamil Nadu and others. (Note that this has been highlighted not only by Rajni-Palme Dutt in India Today, but also by several other authors such as Margaret Bourke-White in the 'Famine in South India' chapter in her book: "Halfway to Freedom"). In addition, the British obliged these intermediaries to collect the taxes not in kind, but in cash. Since the peasant had little experience or understanding of a cash economy (or any control on the price of grain and agro-inputs), this put a further burden on the peasant, who now also had to face the thuggery of unscrupulous grain traders and usurious money-lenders who took full advantage of the highly diminished status of the Indian peasant in the colonial dispensation. (Note that the existence of money-lenders and traders is documented from at least Ashokan times, but the traditional Indian state typically insisted on a cap on interest payments and profits. Moreover, money-lenders and traders were traditionally active mostly in towns, not in villages. The encroachment of the cash economy and the growth of usury in the countryside began to adversely affect the peasants during the later Mughal period, but the problem grew very dramatically during colonial rule.)

As a result, not only was the typical Indian peasant reduced to a state of utter degradation, social relations within the village also became highly distorted. The traditional solidarity that had existed between villagers was now subject to the divisive and ruinous tactics of the parasitic intermediaries who had the protection and support of the colonial state.

As colonial rule progressed, the typical Indian peasant (and village artisan) faced a dual burden. Not only did the traditional feudal form of exploitation greatly intensify (in comparison to traditional Indian practices), the typical Indian villager was now also subject to the merciless forces of mercantile capitalism, who attempted to extract every ounce of savings or assets that any villager might still possess. Eventually, the typical Indian villager was stripped of all savings, and driven to mortgaging a considerable portion of any assets-whether personal jewellery, land and livestock, or tools and equipment.

But even as the Indian money-lenders and grain traders fleeced the village artisans and peasants, their accumulated wealth was not especially significant in comparison to the British mercantile capitalists of the East Indian Company who kept a lion's share of the loot.

It is especially important to note that whereas a share of the village surplus went to a few Indian intermediaries (who served as a buffer between the British colonial overlords and the Indian masses, and generally acted to quash the class struggle), it was the British who expropriated the bulk of the peasant's assets and annual agro-produce, and transferred most of this looted wealth to the British homeland where it was turned into industrial capital and urban development.

This point is of special significance in understanding the unique nature of class contradictions in the Indian countryside (as compared to elsewhere in the non-colonised world.) For instance, almost throughout Europe, the peasantry was also subject to exploitation by the feudal landlords, but the expropriated surplus from the countryside eventually found its way into the urban banking system, and ultimately facilitated in the growth of industrial capitalism. Sections of the impoverished peasantry then had the chance to gradually move into industrial occupations.

But India was subject to an especially tragic plight. Its masses were thoroughly impoverished, but their immediate exploiters were able to keep only a very small share of what had been extracted from the peasantry. This meant that even when a transformation into industrial capitalism became possible (after freedom from British colonial rule)-there was simply not enough accumulated savings to fund the rapid expansion of industry that could eventually transform the countryside.

When the British left, they left India with extremely limited material means to industrialize, but a sizeable class of parasitic intermediaries who would serve as a constant drag on future development. Unlike India's pre-colonial mercantile classes and the more nationalist sections of India's traditional feudal nobles and intermediaries (who were mostly neutralised or exterminated in 1857) this new colonial era mercantile class was extremely backward in cultural terms and was generally lacking in nationalist spirit. In comparison, the mercantile classes in Europe of the late 18th and 19th centuries were not only wealthier, but also more urbane, and displayed a much higher level of cultural, scientific and technological openness and curiosity. This was also generally true of Japan, and to a somewhat lesser degree, of mercantile classes in other parts of Asia that escaped direct European colonial rule (such as in Korea, Thailand and even China). It should also be noted that whereas the mercantile classes in Europe, Japan, Korea and China were moving in a broadly secular direction, the Indian mercantile classes were excessively weighed down by sentiments favouring religious revivalism or extreme sectarianism (a trend that was especially strong amongst Muslims, but also posed a serious problem amongst Sikhs and Hindus).

It is thus important to understand that not only was the Indian countryside weighed down by a new and more intensified feudal oppression in the colonial era (such as through the Zamindari or Mahalwari systems), it was also oppressed by a highly reactionary and socially conservative intermediary class of petty mercantile capitalists who would pose as the biggest obstacle to any radical or revolutionary developments in the Indian countryside.

Finally, it should be noted that colonial rule exacerbated the problems of the Indian countryside in yet another way. Prior to colonisation, India was steadily becoming more urbanised, with some estimates suggesting that as much as a third of the Indian population may have been living in large or small towns. In addition, even in the villages, a considerable proportion of the population comprised of skilled artisans-weavers, potters, carpenters, metal-workers, painters etc. The proportion of the population that was exclusively engaged in agricultural production was steadily decreasing.

But in the colonial regime, several laws were passed that led to a catastrophic de-urbanisation and de-industrialisation of India. Trade tariffs and excise duties were set so as to destroy Indian industries, and squeeze domestic trade. In states like Bihar and Bengal, severe restrictions were placed on the use of inland waterways-causing fishing and inland shipping and transportation to suffer. This led to even greater pressures on agriculture since large categories of highly skilled artisans and non-agricultural workers were thrown out of work.

Effects of Partition

The problem for India was compounded further by the demands for partition, and the insistence of the Muslim League in splitting the country on communal lines. It is important to note that prior to partition, the best naturally irrigated and most productive lands in Northern India were in North Western Punjab (now Pakistan). Fed by a network of all-weather rivers, no other part of the Indian sub-continent was capable of producing more grain with relatively little capital investment. Similarly, Bangladesh was a much better irrigated land than West Bengal (although it faced far greater risks of flooding than Pakistan Punjab).But in any case, it is worth pointing out that the bulk of pre-partition India's wheat, cotton and jute were grown in what are now Pakistan and Bangladesh. Not only did partition provide India with a smaller share of the land (relative to the ratios of the Hindu, Sikh and Muslim populations), it also left India without the means to feed itself, and without some of the essential raw materials for industry.

(Although India did inherit bulk of the cotton and jute mills, India was unable to take full advantage of this until it had increased its own production of jute and cotton to supply these mills, whereas the raw material producers in West and East Pakistan could at least export their raw materials)

It should also be noted that partition disrupted what had been a somewhat natural distribution of labour between what became Pakistan and India. Since West Punjab and Sindh were better suited to agriculture, the relatively arid states of Rajasthan and Gujarat specialised in all manner of cottage industries and manufacturing that needed the raw materials and markets of West Punjab and Sindh to flourish. In the same way, there was considerable co-dependencies not only between Western and Eastern Bengal, but also between undivided Bengal and its neighbouring states such as Assam, Orissa and Bihar.

The artificial vivisection of Bengal virtually destroyed the potential of regenerating the traditional trade linkages that had been so vital to the prosperity of the Eastern half of India. Geographically, it should be evident that the management of water and other natural resources cannot be efficiently undertaken without the effective coordination and active involvement of all the states in the Ganga-Brahmaputra region. But the vitiated atmosphere under which partition took place meant that the possibilities of mutually beneficial cooperation in matters of resource-sharing, trade, transportation and agriculture were practically foreclosed. (To this day, communal forces in Bangladesh have resisted attempts by India to expand cooperation since they would rather see India suffer more rather than see both India and Bangladesh make more rapid progress.)

Thus, when the British left, India had become a much more village-based agricultural economy than it had been earlier-it is likely that the British had pushed India back by several centuries in this respect. Yet, its prospects for rapid industrialisation were also quite bleak.

India had inherited one of the most depressing scenarios in Asia-a fairly densely populated nation with a pitiful urban base, a rural infrastructure in wrecks, a huge mass of population forced to survive exclusively on agricultural production-yet cynically oppressed by petty mercantile capitalists and feudal intermediaries. Moreover, it had also been left artificially divided on communal lines that meant that important historical linkages might never be revived (or revived only with great difficulty).

No civilised nation could have faced a worse set of circumstances.

The Indian Political Situation Post-1947

The Indian National Congress conducted a dual (and somewhat contradictory) policy relative to Indian agriculture. On the one hand, it attempted to ameliorate the problems of the Indian countryside by investing in irrigation, agro-research, agro-modernisation and mechanisation, but on the other hand, it was only half-hearted (at best) in implementing its own platform of land reforms because it was reluctant to hurt the interests of the feudal and mercantile intermediaries that oppressed most peasants.

Where the struggle for 'land to the tiller' became very intense, it was obliged to make concessions to the impoverished peasants, and move against the parasitic forces, but wherever the demands for land reform were not backed up by strong and effective people's movements, it chose to drag its feet.

It is only in the sixties, when India's Naxal movement began to spread and acquire a certain degree of political depth did the Indira Congress feel the threat and necessity of clipping the wings of the Zamindars, taking away the privy purses of the Maharajas, and assisting farmers more actively. Even as the Naxal movement was harshly repressed, banks were nationalised and were required to set up more branches in rural areas so that loans for seeds and farm equipment (and inputs such as fertilizers and pesticides) could be purchased through loans at more reasonable interest rates. The state also actively intervened in the buying and selling of grain.

Although these measures did not help all sections of the peasantry, it did allow a section of the country's farmers to gradually liberate themselves from the clutches of the old parasitic intermediaries, and move towards mechanised farming. Over time, peasants struggles put further pressure on the government leading to periodic waiving of loans, and easing of credit norms so that even middle farmers could get loans from government banks and rural credit unions. Subsidies were also provided for electricity and water use, as well as on the sale price of fertilizers and pesticides.

Thus, a combination of people's pressure and the gradual expansion of industrial capitalism has brought about significant changes in the Indian countryside. Whereas a section of Indian farmers (at least in some states) have become rich capitalist farmers, a large middle layer of farmers has also developed which is able to survive (even eke out a small surplus) in the good agricultural years (when the monsoon and market conditions happen to be favourable). These middle-income farmers also hire seasonal labour-and this further distinguishes them from the poorest farmers who can't even survive in the good years. Thus today, there is a growing differentiation in the Indian countryside, and this is not too different from what has been seen in many other relatively mature capitalist countries. However, the increasing subdivision of land, and the rising costs of agricultural inputs is a constant source of problems and tensions in the countryside.

Comparisons with Europe

In many respects, developments in Indian agriculture have paralleled developments in the Germany and Italy in an earlier century. In both Germany and Italy, the transformation towards a modern industrial society took place slowly, and through a series of evolutionary steps-as is occurring in India today.

The main differences between India and Germany and Italy are simply that not only did Germany and Italy escape the horrors of colonisation, they indirectly benefited from the colonial loot.

This meant that as their urban industrial economies expanded, these nations were able to absorb their landless populations in their rapidly expanding industrial and services sectors.

When industrial expansion wasn't fast enough, Europe's landless had another escape route-external migration. For more than a century, Europe's unemployed and poor escaped to the US, Canada, South America, South Africa, Australia and New Zealand-where the indigenous populations were killed (or displaced from the best agricultural lands).

Whereas Europe had the distinct advantage of being able to export away its rural poor to land it grabbed from indigenous communities (who were not well-armed or skilled in modern warfare), India cannot simply wish away its excess rural population.

Solutions to the Problems of Indian Agriculture

The subdivision of already small farms in an agricultural model whose profitability is greatly linked to economies of scale makes the survival of the small farmer very difficult. Although the introduction of tractors and other industrial implements, of chemical fertilizers and pesticides, greatly increased the productivity of land and labour, it has not come without considerable burdens for the small farmer who is finding it very hard to compete with large and medium farmers. In most industrial nations, the introduction of such practices in the countryside has been accompanied by a gradual reduction in the rural population so that those who remain on the land can enjoy so.

7

Labour and Peasant Movements

The First Factories Act

In 1875, the first committee appointed to inquire into the conditions of factory work favoured legal restriction in the form of factory laws. The first Factories Act was adopted in 1881. The Factory Commission was appointed in 1885. The researcher takes only one instance, the statement of a witness to the same commission on the ginning and processing factories of Khandesh: "The same set of hands, men and women, worked continuously day and night for eight consecutive days. Those who went away for the night returned at three in the morning to make sure of being in time when the doors opened at 4 a.m., and for 18 hours' work, from 4 a.m. to 10 p.m., three or four annas was the wage. When the hands are absolutely tired out new hands are entertained. Those working these excessive hours frequently died." There was another Factories Act in 1891, and a Royal Commission on Labour was appointed in 1892. Restrictions on hours of work and on the employment of women were the chief gains of these investigations and legislation.

Peasant Movement

Peasant movement is a social movement involved with the agricultural policy.

Peasants movement have a long history that can be traced to the numerous peasant uprisings that occurred in various regions of the world throughout human history. Early peasant movements were usually the result of stresses in the feudal and semi feudal societies, and resulted in violent uprisings. More recent movements, fitting the definitions of social movements, are usually much less violent, and their demands are centred around better prices for agricultural produce, better wages and working conditions for the agricultural labourers, and increasing the agricultural production.

The Kisan Sabha movement started in Bihar under the leadership of Swami Sahajanand Saraswati who had formed in 1929 the Bihar Provincial Kisan Sabha (BPKS) in order to mobilise peasant grievances against the zamindari attacks on their occupancy rights. Gradually the peasant movement intensified and spread across the rest of India. All these radical developments on the peasant front culminated in the formation of the All India Kisan Sabha (AIKS) at the Lucknow session of the Indian National Congress in April 1936 with Swami Sahajanand Saraswati elected as its first President. D. D. Kosambi and R.S. Sharma, together with Daniel Thorner, brought peasants into the study of Indian history for the first time."

Anthony Pereira, a political scientist, has defined a peasant movement as a "social movement made up of peasants (small landholders or fram workers on large farms), usually inspired by the goal of improving the situation of peasants in a nation or territory".

Peasant Movements by Country or Region

India: Peasant movement in India arose during the British colonial period, when economic policies resulted in the ruin of traditional handicrafts leading, change of ownership and overcrowding of land, and massive debt and impoverishment of peasantry. This led to peasant uprisings during the colonial period, and development of peasant movements in the post-colonial period.

Fifty Years of Organised Peasant Movement

Today, the Kisan Sabha is the biggest organisation of the peasantry with 8.4 million members, and if the membership of the All India Agricultural Workers Union is also included, the figure goes up to 9.5 million. Not a day passes without some struggle or movement being conducted somewhere in India. In many areas of the country the Kisan Sabha symbolises the aspirations and hopes of the multitude of poor and the collective will of the peasantry. The organisation is growing everywhere, and more and more peasants are joining it and taking part in its activities and struggle.

Fifty years ago, when it was founded in a Conference in Lucknow, the AIKS was a small organisation, and very few people heard about its formation. During these intervening years many heroic battles have been fought and won. The battles which were lost, also left their imprint on the organisation. Thus a great deal of blood has been shed, and many martyrs have given their lives fighting for the democratic rights of the peasants. Many comrades have sacrificed the better part of their youth in the underground or prison.

The entire history of the past fifty years has been a long history of severe repression against the organisation and its workers. But none of the sacrifices have gone waste. Each ounce of blood, energy and time given has strengthened the body and the soul of the organisation. The Kisan Sabha which we see today, with its large membership and an elaborate network of units reaching down to the village level, is a product of this history. It was founded to play a distinct role in the history of the country. For an assessment of the role played by the organised peasant movement in the last fifty years under the leadership of the Communists, it is essential to understand the actions of the peasantry, first under the feudal leadership and the later under the leadership of the bourgeoisie, and the class limitations imposed on the peasant movements by these leadership.

Peasant Struggles in Nineteenth Century

Though the AIKS was formally established on April 13, 1936, it had not been built in a day. The peasant movements in different parts of the country had existed for the past century. Many of the peasant struggles fought in those days were spontaneous in character, lacked proper direction and in many cases were badly organised. Still they played a role in raising the consciousness of the peasantry to fight against oppression and in defence of their rights.

The first half of the nineteenth century witnessed uninterrupted anti-colonial activity on the part of the peasantry, and tribesmen led by feudal lords who had lost their privileges. The feudal lords in the Northern *Sarkars* had been strongly resisting British domination ever since the beginning of the nineteenth century. In 1807 the whole Delhi regime took up arms; in 1814 at Tuppan of Muneer (near Varanasi). Rajput peasants secured the abolition of the sale of land by public auction of a large village community to a stranger. In 1817 the peasants of Orissa led by local feudal lords, rose up in protest against the introduction of taxation of their rent free service lands. Poona district witnessed the uprising of the peasantry from 1826 to 1829 when the authorities were obliged to cede to them holding subject to low revenue charges. In 1830-31 British troops were sent to suppress a peasant uprising in Bedsore district of Mysore State against the tax increase. In 1835-37 there was an uprising in Gumsur in Madras Presidency. In 1842 an uprising flared up in Sagar. In 1846-47 the peasants in Karnal rose up in revolt. In 1848 Rohillas in Nagpur took up arms. In 1844 in the Kolhapur and Santavadi State bordering Bombay Presidency, there was a large-scale revolt in protest against the British decisions increasing the land revenue to pay the princes' tribute. The peasants of Khandeth in Bombay Presidency rose up in protest against the land settlement which resulted in the increase of land tax.

There were also innumerable uprisings of tribals in this period – of the Bhils in 1818-1831 and Kolis in 1824 in Bombay Presidency, unrest in Kutch in 1815 and 1832 and revolt in Kittur in 1824-1829. In 1820, there was an uprising of the Mers in Rajputana, and of the Hos tribe in Chote Nagpur in 1831-32.

In 1846 the Khonds rose up in Orissa and 1855 witnessed the Santhal revolt in Bihar.

There was also unrest in the Indian towns usually resulting from the introduction of new taxes, which generally took the form of hartals.

These heroic struggles culminated in the First War of Independence of 1857, when the leadership of the movement was taken up by Sepys. Explaining the significance of their rebellion Karl Marx wrote:

"Before this there had been mutinies in the Indian Army, but the present revolt is distinguished by characteristic and fatal features. It is the first time that Sepoy regiments have murdered their European Officers: that Mussulmans and Hindus, renouncing their mutual antipathies, have combined against their common master; that disturbances beginnings with the Hindus, have actually ended in placing on the throne of Delhi a Mohammedan Emperor', That the mutiny has not been confined to a few localities and lastly, that the revolt in the Anglo-Indian army has coincided with a general disaffection exhibited against English supremacy on the part of the great Asiatic nations, the revolt of the Bengal army being, beyond doubt, intimately connected with the Persian and Chinese wars."

The uprisings were confined to northern and central India. The peasants after driving out the local representative of the colonial administration set up armed detachments for their own defence and defended the village communal lands, which had been expropriated by the British conquerors. The population in the town played an active par in the uprising. They not only liberated a number of large cities like Aligarh, Bareilly, Lucknow, Kanpur and Allahabad but set up a government in each of them.

This popular uprising of 1857-59 was defeated for various reasons the most important being that although the fighting forces had consisted of peasants and artisans, they were led by the feudal nobility, who showed themselves incapable of leading the national liberation struggle. They could not evolve a united strategy and a united command. The centres of uprising which emerged spontaneously, acted independently of each other. Moreover, the feudal lords did not take any measure to alleviate the lot of the peasantry. When the British Government made concessions to the feudal lords, they dissociated themselves from the uprising. The Sepoy commanders were not able to wage a complex war.

After the British succeeded in suppressing the uprising, they had to learn a lesion and change their tactics. The East India Company was liquidated and India became a colony of the British government. They also made a lot of concessions to the feudal lords thereby winning their sympathy and support. In spite of all this the uprisings left their imprint on the national liberation struggle, which developed in subsequent years. Then followed the period of intensified exploitation of the country. This exploitation of India as a source of cheap raw materials as well commodity market for British manufactures constituted the main form of colonial loot. It helped to promote the development of commodity-money relations in both the towns and villages, and this growth of simple commodity production in a period of formation helped in the further penetration of trading and usury capital into the spheres of agriculture and handicrafts.

Bourgeois Leadership Takes Over

Discontentment among the people, especially the peasantry, was rapidly growing; the defeat of Czarism by Japan gave encouragement to the feelings national liberation; and the Russian Revolution of 1905 also made its own impact on the country. The immediate issue which galvanised the atmosphere, was the partition of Bengal which aroused universal indignation throughout the land, leading to the movement for boycott of foreign goods which began on August 7, 1905. Simultaneously, the Punjab was witnessing great unrest among the peasantry on the question of the Colonisation Act. A powerful movement developed against it, led by Lajpat Rai, Ajit Sigh and Banke Dayal.

These movements in which the peasantry participated in large numbers, were accompanied by trade union struggles in Bombay Calcutta and other places. The revolutionaries who at this time took to the path of armed struggles against imperialism helped radicalise the politics of those days. To meet the situation the British rulers resorted to repressive measures; heavy sentences, deportation banning of meetings, detention without trial, etc. But this did not deter the people from their path. The Government had to announce a review of the partition of Bengal and withdrew the Punjab Colonisation Act. These developments and their outcome signified that a new class had come onto the scene, i.e., the bourgeoisie. It was providing leadership to the movement and was able to get concessions.

The outbreak of the imperialist world war in 1914 raised hopes among the people for the liberation of all colonial peoples and Indian revolutionaries abroad, who were mostly peasants, took the initiative to organise a revolt in the Indian Army. They formed the Gadhar Party with headquarters in San Francisco. They raised the slogan of complete independence and sent hundreds of revolutionaries to India to organise a revolt against the British. Many of them were caught and hanged, large numbers had to undergo life imprisonment, and face tortures and deprivation. Although they did not succeed in their mission their impact in arousing the peasantry during the war period should not be underestimated. An overwhelming majority of them later on joined the Kisan sabha when it was formed.

By contrast with the activities and goal of these revolutionaries, the Indian National Congress for its part had expressed its loyalty to the imperialist war in all its sessions held in this period. Even on 1918 at the close of the war at its session in Delhi the Congress Party passed a resolution expressing loyalty to the King and conveying its congratulations at the successful termination of the war.

Postwar Upsurge and the Impact of the Russian Revolution

By December 1917 news of October Revolution in Russia was beginning to filter through to India and the not-too-efficient censorship allowed it to appear in the Press. Many articles appeared and demobilised soldiers returning from the fronts also brought the news. It had a tremendous impact on the Indian people, who welcomed the success of the Russian Revolution with understandable enthusiasm in particular, its slogan of the right to self-determination of a nation. At the Calcutta Session of the Congress in December 1917, Annie Besant spoke of the Russian Revolutions as one of the factors that fundamentally changed the previously existing situation in India.

As the war neared its end, having cost almost ten million lives, the Indian soldiers began returning home, by sea, on foot, through the endless expanses of the Himalayan passes, covered with blinding white snow. But these were no longer the timid downtrodden peasants and craftsmen who had cowered before the arrogant Englishman, or a conceited zamindar. They had forgotten the smell of freshly turned earth; their hands were no longer accustomed to the plough. Instead they brought with them the smell of fire bayonet, and slash with a sabre. They had acquired a sense of their own worth and dignity and came to believe in their own strength. In their native villages and hamlets they found their holdings ruined or falling into decay, and the land, which had once been fruitful, dried and barren. Clenching their teeth in anger they listened to heart-rending stories, broken by sobs, of the death from hunger of their children, wives and aged parents. They had come to understand that their trouble was caused by the greed and cruelty of the colonialists and landlords. It was no by chance that India was in the throes of an unprecedented upsurge in the postwar period.

Lenin had taken note of the situation. Addressing the Second Congress of the Communist Organisations of the East on November 22, 1919, he stated:

"In this respect you are confronted with a task which has not previously confronted Communists of the world; relying upon the general theory and practice of Communism, you must adapt yourself to specific conditions such as do not exist in European countries, you must be able to apply that theory and practice to conditions in which the bulk of the population are peasants and in which the task is to wage a struggle against medieval survivals and not against capitalism..." (emphasis added)

On February 17, 1920, the Indian Revolutionary Associations headed by émigrés like Raja Mohinder Pratap, Maulana Mohammed Barkatullah and Maulana Obeidullah Sindhi, in an Assembly held in Kabul, adopted the following resolution addressed to Lenin.

"Indian revolutionaries express their deep gratitude and their admiration of the great struggle carried on by Soviet Russia for the liberation of all oppressed classes and peoples, and especially for the liberation of India. Great thanks to Soviet Russia for her having heard the cries of agony from the 315,000,000 people suffering under the yoke of imperialism. This mass meeting accepts with joy the hand of friendship and help extended to oppressed India."

In reply to this message Lenin wrote: "I am glad to hear that the principles of self-determination and the liberation of oppressed nations from exploitation by foreign and native capitalists, proclaimed by the workers' and Peasants' Republic, have met with such a ready response among progressive Indians, who are waging a heroic fight for freedom. The working masses of Russia following with unflagging attention the awakening of the Indian workers and peasants. The organisations and discipline of the working people and their perseverance and solidarity with the working people of the world are an earnest of ultimate success. We welcome the close alliance of Muslim and non-Muslim elements. We sincerely want to see this alliance extended to all the toilers of the East. Only when the Indian, Chinese, Korean, Japanese, Persian and Turkish workers and peasants join hands and march together in the common cause of liberation – only then will decisive victory over the exploiters be ensured. Long lives a free Asia."

Peasantry in Action for National Liberation

Lenin's prediction proved to be true. The peasantry in India was drawn into action in a big way. With the starting of the non-cooperation movement the peasantry in various parts of the country became very active. Though not strictly a part of the non-cooperation movement, at the same time, their activities cannot be separated from the movement for national liberation. Peasant struggles became linked up with the struggle for independence since it was the imperialist system of exploitation, which was the main protector of the feudal exploitation in the countryside.

In northern India the Gurudwara Reforms Movement, which started with the Nankana Massacre, brought the vast Sikh peasant masses into action against British rule, thus making it a part of the liberation movement. In UP had begun the Eka Movement of tenants who were fighting against the extortions and oppression of the landlords. In the south there was the Moplah Rebellion in Malabar (Kerala) an uprising tenants against the oppression of *jenmies* (landlord).

The main slogan of the Gurudwara Reforms Movement was the liberation of Gurudwaras from the control of Mahants who had the patronage of the British imperialists. Bringing the Sikh peasantry into the national mainstream, it soon took the form of an anti-imperialist movement. The Eka Movement was also widespread and militant. It raised the demands of fixed rents, receipts for payments, stoppage of *beggar* for the landlord, free use of water from ponds, and the freedom to graze cattle in the jungles.

It was a revolt of the tenants against the unbearable oppression of the landlord.

The Moplah rebellion, again essentially an uprising of the tenants in Malabar, began on August 20 1921. The tenants were Muslims while the *jenmies* were Hindus. The main targets of the attack of the rebellion were the police, military, landlords and moneylenders. The police and military suppressed the rebellion with brutal violence in which 3,266 Moplahs were killed.

The period also witnessed big working class actions-in the textile and jute Mills in Calcutta, Bombay, Madras; in the North Western and Eastern Railway, the coal-fields of Jharia, the P & T Department of Bombay; plantations of Assam; tramways of Calcutta, etc.

C.I. Notes Development

The Fourth Congress of the communist International took note of the situation and drew attention to mobilising the peasantry in the struggle for independence. The Congress emphasised that *"the revolutionary movement in the colonial countries would achieve no success unless it gets the support of the peasant masses.* The *agrarian programme of the Communist in the counties of the East demands the complete elimination of feudalism and all its survivals and aims at drawing in the peasant masses in the struggle for national liberation."*

The thesis on the Eastern question adopted at the Congress stated that the Communists must see to it that the national revolutionary parties adopt a radical agrarian programme.

Dealing with the agrarian question and describing the situation of the peasantry in the colonial countries the Congress came to the conclusion that

"Only the agrarian revolution aiming at the expropriation of large land owners can rouse the vast peasant masses destined to have a decisive influence in the struggle against imperialism. The fear of agrarian watchwords on the part of the bourgeois nationalists (India, Persia and Egypt) is evidence of the close ties existing between the native bourgeoisie and the large feudal and feudal bourgeois landowners and their ideological political dependence on the latter. The hesitation and wavering of this class must be used by the revolutionary elements for systematic criticism and exposure of

the lack of resolution of the bourgeois leaders of the national movement. It is precisely this lack of resolutions that hinders the organisations of the toiling masses as is proved by the bankruptcy of the tactics of non-cooperation in India.

"The revolutionary movement in the backward countries of the East cannot be successful unless it is based on the action of the masses of the peasantry. For the reason the revolutionary parties in all Eastern countries must define their agrarian programme which should demand the complete abolition of feudalism and its survivals, expressed in the forms of large landownership and farming.

"In order that the peasant masses may be drawn into active participation in the struggle for national liberation, it is necessary to proclaim the radical reform of the bourgeois nationalist parties to the greatest extent, possible to adopt this revolutionary agrarian programme." (Documents of the History of the C.I. vol. Pp. 550).

Chauri Chaura Incident: Betrayal by Bourgeois Leadership

When in 1922 Mahatma Gandhi launched a mass civil disobedience movement in one district of Bardoli, it gave encouragement to the people in the rest of the country. A few days later in a little village. Chauri Chaura in UP angry peasants stoned and burnt the village police station, and the unpopular village constabulary was burnt in the flames. This unrest of the peasantry crucial to the Indian Revolution was not to the liking of Mahatma Gandhi. He lost no time in announcing the withdrawal of the movement, disappointing even congress leaders who were then in prison. The reality of the situation was that the reformist control of the movement was weakening.

This concern was reflected in the message telegraphed by the Viceroy to London on February 9, only three days before the withdrawal of the movement:

"The lower classes in the towns have been seriously affected by the non-cooperation movement.... In certain areas the peasantry have been affected, particularly in parts of the Assam Valley, United Provinces, Bihar Orissa and Bengal. As regards the Punjab, the Akali agitation.... has penetrated to the rural Sikhs. A large proportion of the Mohammedan population throughout the country are embittered and sullen... grave possibilities. The government of India are prepared for disorder of more formidable nature than has in the past occurred and do not seek to minimise in any way the fact the great anxiety is caused by the situation."

The resolution adopted by congress Working Committed on the withdrawal of the movement, on February 12, 1922, makes clear as daylight that Mahatma Gandhi and the Congress leadership were afraid of the agrarian revolution and opposed to it. They were not interested in drawing in the working class and peasantry as classes, into the movement. After deploring the activities of the peasants of Chauri Chuara as inhuman, the working committee resolution instructed the local congress committee "to advise the cultivators to pay land revenue and other taxes due to the government and to suspend every other activity of an offensive character."

In order that there should be no ambiguity on this question, it further stated.

"The working committee advices congress workers and organisations to inform the *ryots* (peasants) that withholding of rent payment to the zamindars (landlords) is contrary to the Congress Resolutions and injurious to the best interests of the country."

The resolution then ended by coming out in open defence of the landlords as against the peasants:

"The working committee assures the Zamindars that the Congress movement is in no way intended to attack their legal rights, and that even where the ryots have grievances, the Committee desires that redress be sought by mutual consultation and arbitration."

It is clear from the above resolution that the question here was not one of violence or non-violence. It was instead a clear question of defence of the class interests of the landlords-the exploiters against the exploited. Gandhi and the dominant leadership of the Congress called off the movement because it was beginning to threaten those propertied class interests with which they themselves were closely linked.

Thus the class limitations of the bourgeois stood revealed: though it wanted the peasantry to be drawn into the national liberation struggle, did not want the peasantry to come into action as a class. And thus began the struggle between the two approaches, the approaches of the working class, which had by now emerged on the scene, and that of the bourgeoisie.

Working Class Leadership

By contrast March 1923, the Executive Committee of the Communist Internation issued a manifesto on the Chauri Chaura sentences where 172 peasants had been given death sentences, asking for protest meetings and a movement for their release.

The peasantry had already had the experience of betrayal by the landlords during the struggles of the 19 century. In the Chauri Chaura struggle they were able to se the betrayal by the bourgeoisie. The Communists and the Left in the Congress learnt from the experience of these two betrayals by the two classes, who were considered their natural leaders, and decided to organise the peasantry independently, as a class, though working in cooperation with other anti-imperialist classes and strata including the bourgeoisie.

In May 1923, the formation of the Labour and Kisan Party was announced and its action programme for the peasants included protection against eviction, 20 per cent reduction on all economic rent in ryotwari settlement areas, eventual abolition of Permanent settlement abolition of *beggar*, protection against oppression of zamindars, abolition of salami, free irrigation, abolition of dowry, etc. loans in seed or money without interest, etc.

This was the beginning of the preparations for a platform of action for the peasantry. Subsequently, peasant organisations also came into existence in various places. A Note of Satya Bakta, Secretary, Indian Communist Party dated June 18, 1925, states:

"In order to organise the Indian peasants, labourers and other working people and with a view to bettering their condition, the Indian Communist Party resolves to adopt the following programme:

"In these days *there are several kisan sabhas (peasants' unions) in UP and other provinces.* They are striving after some reforms. But as long as landlordism exists in India, peasants cannot become happy and prosperous. That they should pay something to the

Government is after all acceptable. But there is no reason why middlemen or commission agents should be allowed to exist. But until the victory of the proletarian class, landlordism cannot be abolished entirely.

"Even now the government and leaders of our country, if they really desire the betterment of the peasants can improve the present conditions to a great extent. In our opinion peasants should be entitled to pay their rent direct to the Government who may pay to the landlord their share. They should not be allowed to have any other connection with or control over the peasants. In this way while landlords will loss nothing of their legitimate income, they and especially their servants will no longer be able to rob peasants in the shape of unlawful taxes and gratuities. For this purpose the Indian Communist Party will agitate among the peasants and will *urge upon all new and old kisan sabhas to work in the suggested manner."*

It is clear from this that kisan sabhas had already come into existence in many parts of the country. Subsequently the Labour Swaraj Party was formed in Bengal, on November 1, 1925. It was called the Labour Swaraj Party of the Indian National Congress. Its programme for the peasantry stated:

Land taxes to be reduced to a fixed maximum and fixity of the interest rate of the Imperial Bank on arrears of rents; fixity of tenure, no ejection cessation of illegal and extra taxation, right of transference, right of felling trees, sinking wells, excavating tanks and erecting pucca structure; fixed term of fishery rights in *jolkars;* fixity of maximum rate of interest to be levied by moneylenders; agricultural cooperative banks to be established to provide credit to the peasants and to free them from the clutches of moneylenders and speculating traders; agricultural machinery to be sold or lent to the cultivators on easy terms through the cooperative banks.

This organisation was a forerunner of the Workers and Peasants Party. On February 6-7, 1926 the Second Session of the All Bengal Kisan Conference was held in Krishna Nagar (Nadia District). It decided to organise a peasants and Workers Party called the Bengal Peasants and Workers Party. While the basic demand mentioned that the ultimate ownership of land would vest in a self-contained autonomous village community, it put forward the following immediate demands:

1) Fixity of rates in relation to the rents payable by the tenants: the interest charged on arrears of rent to be equal to the rate of interest charged by the Imperial Bank.
2) Cultivator's undivided ownership be recognised on the land he tills.
3) Permanency of tenure in land (which the cultivator tills), banning of evictions.
4) Stopping of all unjust and illegal cesses.
5) Right freely to transfer the land to another without payment of *salami.*
6) Right to cut the trees, to dig wells and cut canals and build a house on his land without paying any *salami.*
7) Fixing conditions for catching fish in the ponds on the land.
8) The highest rate of interest to be charged by the mahajan to be fixed at a rate not more than 12 per cent.
9) Establishing cooperative agricultural banks to give credit to the peasant and thus to release him from the grip of the greedy and professional moneylender.
10) Machinery needed for cultivation etc. to be sold outright to the peasant or to be given to him on rent for use, and the price of the same or the rent amount thereof to be recovered from peasant in easy instalments.
11) To make arrangement for the wholesale sale of jute or other commercial crops so that a just profits rate is guaranteed to the peasant.

It was on February 24, 1927 that the Workers And Peasants Party was formed in Bombay.

It resolved that "a political party of workers and peasant be established to voice the demands of these classes within the National Congress, to promote the organisation of trade unions to wrest them from their alien control, to advance the organisation of peasants on the basis of their economic and social requirements and to present a determined and pertinent opposition to the government and thus secure the social, economic and political emancipation of these classes."

In formulating the economic demands it proposed:

12) The abolition of indirect taxation and the introduction of graded income tax on all income exceeding Rs 250 per mensem.
13) Nationalisation of land wherein all cultivable land will be leased by Government to cultivator.
14) Nationalisation of means of production, distribution and exchange.
15) Rent of land holding not to be excessive.
16) Establishment by the government of State-aided cooperative banks controlled by local organisations for the provision of credit to peasants, at a rate of interest not exceeding seven per cent.

In a programme formulated for the All India Congress Committee it proposed: 70 per cent of the population which is engaged in agriculture is to be organised into peasant societies, by district, taluk, and village, on the lines of the village panchayat, based on universal suffrage aiming to secure control of the economic life of the rural areas. Through the agricultural cooperative banks to be established by the State for the provision of cheap credit to the peasants, whereby they will be enabled to free themselves from the grip of Saukars, and to purchase modern machinery and other equipment; limitation by law of the rate of interest at seven per cent per annum; limitation of rent to 10 per cent of the total produce to be paid direct to the Sate, and brining into cultivation by State aid cultivable land by present unused.

But the bourgeoisie leadership of the Congress was not prepared to take up the peasant demands.

When a proposal was mooted before the Subjects committee of the Congress that it should side with peasants and workers when a conflict arose between them and the zamindars and capitalists. Pandit Motilal Nehru, the then President of the Congress, contended in reply, that the Congress was not the Socialist or Communist Party. The reason for making this statement was that the Congress was by no means ready to stand up for those who produce all things by their labour. J M Sengupta, leader of the Bengal Swarajists, made this even clearer. He said that the party includes many zamindars and that without their help so many men of their party would certainly never be able to enter the Councils. So they could by no means help the peasants, going against those zamindars. They tried to cover this defence of the interest of the landlords under the pretext that no class struggle existed in the countryside, and the congress represented the whole country.

It is not accidental that certain juridical measures of reforms in tenancy rights were introduced in India not at the initiative of the bourgeoisie, but by imperialism often in the face of nationalist bourgeois opposition.

Popularisation of the Agrarian Programme

The formation of the All India Workers and Peasants Party and the subsequent historic Meerut Trial, helped in popularising the agrarian programme among the Indian masses. The Meerut Trial went on for more than four years. The persons involved in the trial in their statements advocated the programme of the Communists in relation to the working class, peasantry and other toiling sections of the Indian population, along with their unflinching opposition to imperialist rule in the country.

This was the period when the economic crisis of the 30s had engulfed the world. India was the worst hit during this crisis and in 1931 the Central Banking Enquiry Committee registered the general conviction that

"Indebtedness leads ultimately to the transfer of land holdings from the agricultural class to the non-agricultural money-lenders leading to the creation of the landless proletariat with a reduced economic status. The result is said to be loss of agricultural efficiency as the moneylenders sub-let at a rate which leaves the cultivators with a reduced incentive."

The 1931 Census report reached the conclusion that;

"It is likely that a concentration of the land in the hands of the non-cultivating owners is taking place."

Similarly, the extent of the collapse in prices of agricultural commodities was such, that whereas in 1928-29 the value of agricultural crops, taken at an average harvest price, was about

Rs 1034 crore, in 1933-34 it was only Rs 473 crore a fall of 55 per cent. In the United Provinces, the number of tenants abandoning their land because they could not pay rent, reached as high as 71 440 in 1931. The burden of debt doubled. Peasants were groaning under their heavy indebtedness, their lands were passing into the hands of moneylenders and they were being forced to live the life of paupers.

The peasant organisations emerging in various States now had a clear-cut programme not only for immediate relief but also directed against the system of landlordism. The peasants had realised the necessity of organising themselves as a class which was numerically not only strong but also the worst exploited under the triple attack of the imperialists landlords and moneylenders and traders. The Indian National Congress was desirous of mobilising them in the struggle for independence since without them it was not possible to bring pressure to bear on the imperialists but it did not want the peasantry to emerge as a class conscious of its rights and determined to put an end to the rule of the landlords.

The Congress started the Civil Disobedience movement but its 11-point charter of demar ds did not contain any demands of the working class and peasantry against the capitalists and the landlords.

The resolution of the Karachi Session of the Congress where fundamental rights were mentioned in relation to the peasant demands it did not stipulate more than a substantial reduction of land revenue and rent, and total exemption only for the necessary period in the case of uneconomic holdings. There was no reference to abolition of landlordism or even the annulment of at least a portion of the rural debt. It was clear that that Indian National congress did not want to rouse the peasantry against feudal oppression.

Gandhi's hopes for a compromise were shattered at the Round Table Conference and he had again to continue the movement, which lasted up to 1934, drawing into its fold huge masses. Once again the movement was withdrawn without achieving its aim, and Gandhi withdrew from the Congress exercising his influence from outside.

Formation of all India Kisan Sabha

The Communist Party was banned in 1934 but continued to exercise its influence on the working class and on the Left in the Congress. The ideas of Socialism wee becoming very popular, and left dements in the Congress, becoming disillusioned with Gandhi formed the Congress Socialist Party, in order to give the Congress a Left orientation.

Coming to realise that the vast masses of the peasantry could be brought into the struggle for independence only by taking up the anti-feudal struggle and their immediate demands they were also realising the necessity of organisation the peasantry as a class. They had already come to the conclusion that the struggle for real political freedom could not be separated from the struggle of the peasantry for an end to landlordism and for radical restructuring of rural society. The Communists were already trying to develop class organisations and had popularised the ideas of independent class organisations of the working class peasants and other sections of the toiling people. Thus it was the Left Congressmen, Congress Socialists and Communists who took the initiative in organising the All India Kisan Sabha.

The First Session was held in 1936, Lucknow to coincide with the holding of the Session of the Indian National congress. The idea was to project the kisan movement as a part of the national movement though maintaining its separate identity as a class organisation.

Broad Based Organisation

The following list of the names of some of the participants in the first All India Kisan Sabha Session is revealing : EMS Namboodiripad, Dinkar Methta, Kamal Sarkar, Sohan Singh Josh, Lal Bahadur Shastri, K D Malaviya, Mohan Lal Gautam, B Sampooranand, Jayaprakash Narain, Swami Sahajanand, NabaKrishna Choudhury, Harekrishna Mahtab, N G Ranga, Indulal Yajnik, R K Khadilkar, Bishnuram Medhi and Sarat Sinha. Many of them became prominent national and state-level personalities in subsequent years. It also suggests how broad-based the Kisan Sabha was from the very beginning and how it tried to attack people of varying political views to join together in defence of the democratic rights of the kisans.

The formation of the AIKS was preceded by a meeting in Meerut in January 1936, where the necessary preparations were made. A clear decision was taken to launch the organisation with a broad-based programme and membership to link it closely with the national movement for independence and to view the fight against imperialism as an integral part of the fight against the feudal social order since the former patronised and provided state support to the latter.

Today with the benefit of hindsight one is struck by the simplicity and directness with which the very first session set out its tasks in the main resolution. To quote:

"The objective of the Kisan movement is to secure compete freedom from economic exploitation and the achievement of full economic and political power for the peasants and workers and all the other exploited classes.

"The main task of the kisan movement shall-be the organisation of peasants to fight for their immediate political and economic demands in order to prepare them for their emancipation from every from of exploitation.

"The kisan movement stands for the achievements of ultimate economic and political power for the producing masses through its active participation in the national struggle for winning complete independence."

It their indicted the zamindari system, "supported by the British government in India", as "iniquitous unjust, burdensome, and oppressive to the kisans", and declared that "all such system of landlordism shall be abolished and all the rights over such lands be vested in the cultivators."

This was the essence of what the kisan movement stood for at the time of the launching of the AIKS. The other issues covered by resolutions included questions of rent, irrigation rates and prices of inputs, prices of marketed agricultural products, indebtedness, forced labour and illegal exactions from the tenants by the landlords and the distribution of landlords land to the landless poor peasants as also the vesting of waste land and grazing land in the village level panchayats. The AIKS also demanded minimum wages for the regulating their unionisation.

Any one reading those resolutions will immediately notice that many of the issues raised by the conference of the AIKS in its first session have remained unresolved till today.

Part of the National Movement

The Bombay session of the Central Kisan Sabha Council (CKC) held in August 1936 further elaborated many of the points raised in the founding session. It categorically stated that, since the kisans constituted more than four-fifths of the population, "no political or economic programme which has the audacity to ignore their needs and demands can by any stretch of imagination, be labelled as a national programme", and called upon the Indian National Congress to make "the solution of the problems of the peasantry the chief plank of its political and economic policy." At the same time the CKC felt the need for a political movement, which draws "its main strength and inspiration from the peasantry."

These two struggles – the kisan movement and the national movement were seen as "inter-dependent, the strength of the one adding to the other."

The CKC meeting also strongly emphasised on the need for peasant unity. The AIKS was an "expression of the awakening of the peasantry", and should represent not only the ryots the tenants and the landless labourers but also all sections of cultivating peasantry – "in other words, it represents, and speaks and fights for those who live by cultivation of the soil. All these different strata among the kisans will have to combine and fight for removal of all the letters imposed by British imperialism and it's allies the landlords."

Fundamental and Minimum Demands

The Bombay Session made a separate listing of "fundamental demands" and "minimum demands". The former included the demands for abolishing intermediary tenures, replacement of existing land revenues by graduated land tax, cancellation of old debts and allocation of land to landless and poor peasants for cooperative farming.

The minimum demands included the cancellation of the rent and revenue arrears; exemption of uneconomic holdings from land revenue; reduction of rent revenue and water rates by half; immediate grant of right permanent cultivation to tenants cultivating land held by zamindars, talukdars, etc., rent remission for these tenants; graduated taxation of agricultural income abolition and penalisation of all feudal and customary dues, forced labour and illegal exactions; a five year moratorium on debts freedom from arrest and imprisonment for debtors and also immunity from attachment for small holdings; licensing for money-lenders; arrangement of credit from the state cooperative and land mortgage banks over a long period of 40 years t five per cent interest lowering the freight on agriculture goods introduction of one paise postcards; abolition of indirect taxes on salt kerosene sugar, tobacco molasses, etc., stabilisation of agricultural prices minimum wages legislation to recognise collective action of the peasants insurance for cattle fire and health adult franchise and establishment of village panchayats for managing civic affairs and communal land among others.

These show the wide range of issues covered by the AIKS in its campaign which catered to the needs and aspirations of various sections of the peasantry. From its very beginning the AIKS was alert and reacted to major national and international events. While striving for the country's independence the AIKS had a distinct concept of independence, which was outlined in various resolution where along with political independence, socio economic independence was emphasised. To quote from the resolution of the Bombay CKC meeting in 1936 again it stated:

"The Kisan must fight for national socioeconomic independence Indian a democratic of Britain must be transformed into a free progressive democratic India of the masses."

There was no room for exploitation and oppression in the concept of the free Indian that the AIKS held. It was never solely concerned with narrow peasant issues and defined the interests of the peasantry in broad terms.

For Workers Peasant Alliance

One of the cornerstones of its policies had always been the unity of the peasants with the workers. In its Gaya Session in 1939 the AIKS talked about the objective of building "a democratic State of the Indian people leading ultimately to the realisation of

Kisan – Mazdoor Raj". Even earlier in its second session at Faizpur the Presodential Address stated: "It is the sacred duty of every of our kisans to fraternise with the workers in the village and in the town... There is much to be achieved by both workers and peasants by common effort for their mutual benefit."

The adoption of the red flag with hammer and sickle, signifying the unity of these two classes, was strongly defended by the General Secretary Swami Sahajananda at the Comilla Session in 1938 on the grounds aspirations of the exploited and the oppressed." Its commitment to anti-imperialism was reflected in the resolutions passed in the earlier years condemning the Italian attack on Ethiopia and the Japanese attack on China, and supporting World War began it doggedly opposed the war efforts championed the cause of world peace and later when the fascist forces of Hitler attacked the USSR it firmly came out with the slogan of defeating the fascist hordes to save humanity from fascist enslavement. It mobilised popular opinion against fascism.

On national issues too, the AIKS conferences not only passed resolutions against the colonial rulers but also fought for a determined struggle against British rule and State organised oppression. In fact, many of the leaders of the AIKS were themselves the stalwarts in the national movement and spent many years in British prisons.

Against Heavy Odds

The formation of the AIKS was greeted with hostility from many sides. Both the Hindu and Muslim vested interests joined hands against the AIKS and tried their best to disrupt the working of the organisation by terrorising the peasants and using communal propaganda. The British government alarmed by its growing hold on the peasantry intensified its repression by arresting key leaders, from time to time and forcing many others to go underground. A report of the intelligence Bureau of the British colonial government in India said in 1937:

"The Communist leaders are developing a strangle hold upon any future agrarian movement as well as inspiring this with their special methods and outlook of which by no means the least is the belief in mass violence and the violent overthrow of British rule."

The right wing of the Congress party led by Sardar Ballavbhai Patel and Dr. Rajendra Prasad fought against the collective affiliation of the Kisan Sabha to the Indian National Congress and strongly opposed the separate existence of the kisan organisation had produced such an atmosphere of violence in the countryside that an explosion may occur at any moment."

In many provinces the Congress leaders took an openly pro-landlord view and used their power in governments formed in the late thirties to suppress the agitation of the peasants. In Bihar they made an alliance with the landlord lobby to fight off AIKS activists. In its formative years therefore the AIKS had to grow fighting against such heavy odds. But it grew nevertheless. The very formation of the organisations inspired peasants all over the country to take up immediate issues and light. As opposed to the path taken by the Indian National Congress, which compromised with landlords and other vested interests, and spoke of nonviolent resistance, the AIKS rallied the peasants to stand up to the attacks by the armed thugs of the landlords and the police. The Gaya Session of the AIKS in 1939 reported that "the past year has witnessed a phenomenal awakening and growth of the organised strength of the kisans in India.

Formation of Ministries

To keep the mass movement under control, congress decided to implement the Constitution of 1935 and formed the ministries. Congress policy was again put to the test and again it was found that it stood by the side of the landlords against the tenant and the landless. But the organised peasant movement supported by the Congress Left was proving capable of exercising influence, and the Congress Ministries were being forced to give some concessions. However, the Congress never defined the meaning and importance of national freedom other than as freedom from British rule. It was the Communists, Socialists and the Congress Left, which were trying to propagate the understanding that freedom from foreign rule could have real meaning only if it was followed by agrarian revolution and completion of the bourgeois democratic tasks.

The masses were getting disillusioned and impatient, and wanted the Congress leadership to launch a final assault on British rule. The leadership wanted to restrain them and use them for pressure and bargaining. The peasant movement thus came again into conflict with the bourgeois leadership of the Congress, especially on the issue of struggle against feudal and semi-feudal relations. The limitations of the bourgeois leadership were starkly revealed and it could be clearly seen that it did not want to come into conflict with the landlord class.

The leadership was prepared to accept and support certain demands of the peasantry, which were directed against the Government, but was not prepared to take up the basic issue of abolition of landlordism. In fact it was afraid of agrarian revolution. Therefore, the kisan sabhas, while supporting the struggle for national independence had not only to strengthen the independent class organisations of the peasantry but also to forge unity with the working class, the most revolutionary class for our society for completion of the agrarian revolution.

Kisan Sabha and the War

As compared to the Indian National Congress, which lent its support to the war efforts of British imperialism the AIKS came out in firm opposition to the war. Here again there were two different class approaches-one supporting the British imperialist power the other expressing its firm opposition to imperialist war being fought with the sole purpose of redividing the world for the continuation of colonial exploitation.

The AIKS gave a call for struggle against British rule and their Indian lackeys, and launched a no rent, no tax movement. The AIKS was naturally subjected to unprecedented police repression and its open functioning became extremely difficult. Its officers in Bengal and other States were raided and put under lock and key, and its main functionaries were either arrested or forced to go underground. However, with the attack on the Soviet Union by the German Fascists in June 1914 the Sabha raised the slogan of defeating fascism to save humanity from fascist enslavement. It took the view that on the victory over fascism depended the survival of the first Socialist State as well as the independence of countries including ours. The AIKS therefore considered it the sacred duty of the organisation to support the cause of defence of Socialist State and defeat of fascism.

While the task of fighting fascism was given the priority it deserved the AIKS in its Session in 1914 reminded its members that "the struggle for India's freedom should not be slackened even temporarily." The CKC meeting at Nagpur in 1942 demanded transfer of power to a national Government and a declaration recognising India's right to freedom. It identified the British colonial regime, which was working "in complete isolation from the millions on the land" as the greatest obstacle to the mobilisation of India's millions in the defence of their country and the successful persecution of the war."

When on August 9, 1942 Gandhi and other leaders of the Congress were arrested leading to violent protests in many parts of the country, the AIKS expressed its full support to the Congress demand for transfer of power, demanded the released of Gandhi and other national leaders, and condemned the "indiscriminate firing and repression that have been let loose by the Government on the people."

Postwar Upsurge

The military defeat of the fascist powers headed by Hitlerite Germany and the decisive role played by the Soviet Union altered the alignment of class forces on a world arena in favour of Socialism. This also resulted in the general weakening of imperialism on a world scale. Inspired by this powerful national liberation struggle swept throughout the countries of Asia.

India the largest country of the British Empire witnessed a mass revolutionary upheaval against British rule-peasant revolts of which the heroic armed struggle of the Telengana peasantry was the most important general strikes of workers, student strikes and the states people mass struggle developed on an unprecedented scale. The demonstrations for the release of INA personnel took the form of a country – wide revolt against British rule. This wave of protest reached a climax with the uprising of the Royal Indian Navy in February 1946 in Bombay, Karachi and Madras. The Union Jack was removed from the ship's masts and the Congress and Muslim League flags hoisted instead. In Bombay the naval ratings carried the Red Flag of the Communist Party along with the other two. The slogans the navy men raised showed the political nature of the action-*Jai Hind, Inquilab Zindabad, Hindu-Muslim Unity.* Release INA *and other political prisoners. Down with British*

Imperialism, Accept our demands. Rajani Palme Dutt, in his outstanding and seminal work, *India Today,* not only captured the spirit of the time, but gave a keen analytical insight into the significance of the event and the class reactions it engendered:

"The Naval rising and popular struggle in the February days in Bombay revealed with inescapable clearness the alignment of forces in the explosive situation developing in India in the beginning of 1946. It showed on the one hand the height of the movement the courage and determination of the people and the overwhelming mass support for Hindu-Muslims unity and Congress-League unity. It showed that the movement had reached to the armed forces and that therefore the basis of British rule was no longer secure. But it showed on the other hand the unreadiness and disunity of the existing national leadership and their consequent inability to lead the national struggle.

"But now when the masses were really in movement when Hindu-Muslim unity was being realised and practised when the armed forces had united with the civilian population in the common national movement and when the real struggle for freedom had opened the gates of British rule, the attitude of the upper leadership of the national movement revealed a marked change. The upper class leadership of the Congress and Muslim league found themselves in opposition to the mass movement and aligned with British imperialism as the representative of law and order against the people. A whole series of statements and denunciations were issued condemning the "violence" not of the imperialist authorities whose firing slaughtered hundreds in three days but of the unarmed people who had been the objects of military firing Vallabhai Patel issued a statement in which he declared that the Naval ratings ought not to have taken to arms and that he endorsed remarks of the Commander-in-Chief that there ought to be discipline in the Navy".

The RIN uprising however was followed by militant struggles in the countryside at the head of which, at the many places stood the Communist Party. And by 1946 the AIKS through militant struggles in Punjab, UP, Bihar, Kerala, Maharashtra and Andhra had drawn the attention of all on the question of abolition of landlordism. The slogan of agrarian revolutions was brought onto the agenda in the armed resistance of the peasants of Vayalar and

Punnapra in the State of Travancore, the militant Tebhaga struggle of the peasants of Bengal the struggle of the Warli peasants in Maharashtra and the struggle of the Tripura peasants.

Crowning all these struggles was the epochal struggle of the peasantry of Telengana, which has no parallel in the history of the country where peasants fought with arms in hands from 1946-1951 for three years, 1948-51 against the armies of the Indian State.

In the course of the movement guerrilla squads were formed from the village to the district level, which met the terror unleashed by the *Razakars,* and in many instances scared away the landlords in the area. At the peak of the struggle almost 3000 villages, with roughly 30 lakh of the people and an area of 16,000 square miles were liberated and brought under the administration of *Gram Raj.* In this area guerrilla squads of 2000 and a people's militia of 10,000 guarded the villages and about10 lakh acres of land were distributed among the landless.

Among the reforms introduced by the revolutionary leadership was the slashing of usurious interests banning of forced labour and fixation of a minimum wage. This was the real alternative developing to bourgeois landlord rule in the countryside and its significance lay in the fact that if it had been allowed to develop a qualitative change would have come about in the situation combining agrarian revolution with the national liberation movement and the course of history would have been entirely different.

Bourgeois Parties Settle with Imperialists

Telengana showed the direction the mass movement could have taken if it had not been checked. The completion of the tasks of the bourgeois democratic revolution had come onto the political agenda with the agrarian revolution as its crux. But though the 'workers and peasants' alliance was being forged and the Communist Party was at the head of some of these struggle it was not in a position to assume the leadership of the national movement, which still remained in the hands of bourgeoisie.

Afraid of this mass upsurge the bourgeoisie realised that if the struggle against imperialism developed into a general revolt the leadership of the mass movement would slip away from is hands. British imperialism also saw that it would no longer be possible to continue their rule. Under these circumstances the leaders of the National Congress and the Muslim League reached a settlement with the British imperialists.

With the outmoded agrarian relations not being radically changed and a path of capitalist development in compromise with imperialism and feudalism being pursued by the ruling Congress party, it was but natural that the tasks of the bourgeois democratic revolution remained incomplete.

Had the bourgeoisie not compromised at this stage, the situation would have gone out of its control. It would have lost its leadership and the working class would have been in a position to lead the movement and complete the tasks of the bourgeois democratic revolution. By now our country would have also taken the road to Socialism as has been done by China, Vietnam, North Korea and other Asian countries.

Existence of Caste and Communal Problem

The existence of the communal and caste problems and threat of divisive forces with which we are faced today also originates from the policies pursued by the Congress party in the pre-independent and post-independent period-its policy of alliance with feudalism instead liquidating it and the weakness of the organised peasant movement in leading the agrarian revolution in alliance with the working class the position which it started acquiring during the postwar period but was not able to bring to a decisive turning point. Historical experience shows that it is only in countries where feudal and semi feudal relations have been put an end to and the agrarian revolution has been led to successful completion that the problem of caste or communalism can be overcome. It is only in the countries where the national liberation struggle was led by bourgeoisie but was not led to its completion that this problem not only remains but gets aggravated to be used by the ruling classes to divert the discontent of the masses and to disrupt the unity of the democratic movement. Experience has also shown that in the areas where the peasant movement was strong in spite of efforts made by the British imperialists riots could not be organised and the unity forged during the struggle between the Hindu-Muslim peasants stood as the guarantee of communal peace. The Kisan Sabha never allowed any scope for communalism and casteism on its platform. It not only maintained its secular character but exposed the communal ideology and fought against this virus during the riots in Punjab, Bihar and Bengal. In pursuing this policy some of its leaders and cadre laid down their lives fighting against the dark forces of communalism. Thus, though the leadership of the national liberation movement was in the hands of the bourgeoisie, alternative political forces represented by the trade unions and kisan and other militant organisations had started emerging as a powerful force at the end of the war to offer a real challenge to the bourgeoisie. This became clear with the results of the first general election in free India. Wherever there had been strong peasant organisations, the combination of Left and other Opposition forces won a magnificent victory, becoming the main opposition in Parliament, the recognised Opposition in four State Assemblies-West Bengal, Hyderabad, Madras and Travancore-Cochin. The struggle for an alternative leadership continues to this day.

Congress Agrarian Policies

In the post-independent period the bourgeoisie continued its alliance with the landlords and the balance sheet of bourgeois agrarian policy is explained in the Programme of the CPI(M).

"In no field is the utter failure of the bourgeois-landlord government's policies so nakedly revealed as in the case of the agrarian question. Nearly two decades of Congress rule has proved beyond any shadow of doubt that the aim and direction of its agrarian policies is not to smash the feudal and semi-feudal fetters on our land relations, and thus liberate the peasantry from age-old bondage, but to transform the feudal landlords into capitalist landlords and develop a stratum of rich peasants. They want to depend upon the landlord and rich peasant section to produce the surplus of agricultural products to meet the requirements of capitalist development. They also want to make these sections the main political base of the ruling class in the countryside."

Although these measures did not bring the desired resulted of making the tiller of the soil the owner of the land it made certain changes in the agrarian relations. Under the impact of the agrarian movement intermediary tenures like zaminidaris, jagirs, imams, etc., which prevailed over quite a large area of the country were abolished in the early 50s and more than 20 million tenants were brought into direct relation with the State. It was these occupancy tenants who directly benefited from the land reforms to become owners of the land they tilled. These rich and middle peasants were no longer interested in radical land reforms.

This has been shown by the subsequent developments also.

The overall result has been that even after four decades of independence the pro-landlord, anti-peasant policies of the Government have resulted in the further deepening of the agrarian crisis, which manifests itself in growing landlessness increase in disparities both inter-regional and inter-sectional in the same region, an extremely low level of consumption of food-grains despite increasing production and bourgeoning stocks held by the Government growing poverty and unemployment despite all the poverty alleviation schemes and growing indebtedness which finds partial reflection in the growth of overdues in institutional credit supplied to the agricultural sector and so on.

In spite of two rounds of Land Ceiling legislations in the 1950s and 1970s only 7.2 million acres have been declared surplus out of which 5.6 million acres have been taken over and 4.4 million acres actually distributed. This is about seven per cent of the surplus estimated i.e., 63 million acres by the Mahalanobis Committee after the first round of ceiling laws were enacted and one fifth of the surplus estimated on the basis of date made available by the NSS 26th Round. Even if we take into consideration the 1981 Agricultural Census land concentration continues. As compared to three per cent land holders holding 10 acres and above and operating a total of 26 per cent of the land in 1976-77 in 1981-82, 2.4 per cent of land holders held 22.8 per cent of the land. It is also estimated by the Planning Commission that even now if a 20-acre ceiling is imposed and all loopholes in ceiling laws plugged about 23 million acres of land can be made available for distribution. But the Seventh Plan makes no mention of amending the ceiling laws nor about breaking the land monopoly. And typically the Central Government took more than five years to give Presidential assent to the West Bengal Land Reforms Legislation, which seeks only to plug certain loopholes.

Peasant Movement after Independence

In the first six years of the post independence period the peasant movement again had to face severe repression at the hands of the Government Afraid of the tempo of the growing revolutionary movement, it unleashed repression making the functioning of various units impossible. The All India Kisan Sabha was not able to hold any session till April 1953. But in spite of this the Kisan Sabha was busy organising the resistance of the peasantry especially on the question of evictions, and militant fights were put up in many States. Subsequently various Congress Government were forced to take measures of land reforms such as ceiling legislations security of tenure and rent reduction, consolidation of holdings, etc., but all failed to fulfil the declared objectives. On the other hand the period witnessed a large-scale eviction offensive throwing millions of tenants into the ranks of agricultural workers.

In the late fifties the Kisan Sabha fought many struggles on the issues of land fair prices for peasants produce, debt relief, in defence of the rights of tribal people and on the issue of the burden of heavy taxation. The most important of these struggles was the heroic struggle of the Punjab peasantry against the imposition of the betterment levy tax in the beginning of 1959. This was the most important struggle fought under the flag of the Kisan Sabha after the epoch-making Telengana struggle. The peasants defied firings lathi-charges, beating and all types of repression. The all in peasant unity forged during the struggle was unparalleled, when peasant united irrespective of their political affiliations. The movement ultimately forced the Government to withdraw the tax amounting to Rs. 136 crore.

The agrarian crisis further aggravated in the 60s. By the mid-1960 stagnation in agriculture and the consequent food crisis worsened. The bourgeois-landlord classes began losing their hold over the mass of the peasantry with the result that in the 1967 elections the Congress monopoly of power was broken in eight States with West Bengal and Kerala giving victory to the Left and democratic force among which the CPI(M) played an important role. Powerful peasant struggle took place in different States on different issues. In Kerala and West Bengal these struggles were most widespread and became intimately connected with political issues.

The United Front Government of West Bengal and Kerala made a big impact on the masses, not only in those States but also in the rest of the country. When the Central Government dismissed these governments hundreds of thousands of peasants actually joined the struggle for democracy in West Bengal combining this with the struggle for defending heir land and crops.

Mid-term elections gave a bigger victory to the United Front in West Bengal and the peasant movement attained wider sweep. Millions of peasants all over the State unleashed an unprecedented struggle with the backing of the United Front Government, for recovering benami land for possession and distribution of surplus lands, for loans in kind and for checking hoarding and black-marketing. In this period more than three lakh acres of land were located taken over and distributed among the landless through village level committees. Many peasants lost their lives in the battles fought on this issue, but it gave a big impetus to the kisan movement and the AIKS spread to all districts.

These struggles achieved important gains and helped in raising the political consciousness of the peasantry. It was because of this that the Kisan Sabha was able to face the semi-fascist terror of 1917 to 1977, fight back the repression and defend their interests though working in semi-legal conditions.

In Kerala, the peasants conducted a statewide movement for agrarian legislation and debt relief legislation for the rights on Government lands against threat of central intervention. As a result of the campaign one lakhs pattas were distributed to erstwhile-unauthorised occupants of the land. The ceiling was revised downwards and made family-based many exemptions were withdrawn and hutment dwellers were given rights on land on which they lived. Tens of thousands of agricultural labourers conducted powerful and successful struggle for better wages and living conditions.

The discontent found powerful expression in other parts of Indian also. In Maharashtra, Andhra Pradesh, Uttar Pradesh, Bihar, Assam, Tripura, etc., widespread struggles took place for occupation of forest or government lands and against eviction from these lands. In Punjab and UP widespread agitations took place on the question of sugarcane prices. Struggle took place against increased taxation on the question of food and relief rent reduction and against unjust levies. Militant struggles of agricultural labourers took place in Tamil Nadu and Andhra Pradesh.

This period also witnessed two splits in the AIKS one from the Right and other from the Left. While they did a lot of harm to the Kisan Sabha, it not only survived these attacks but advanced further. At the same time it also failed to properly understand the changes in the agrarian structure and work out the appropriate tasks on that basis. By 1978-79 it was able to give a new orientation to its policy, which led to its big advance. Membership of the Kisan Sabha, which had never gone beyond ten lakhs till 1968-69 after 1978-79 jumped by millions and now stands at 84 lakhs.

Present Phase of Struggle

In this connection the question may be asked why has the bourgeoisie not been able to implement radical land reforms when the latter would serve its objective interests? The breaking of the feudal and semi-feudal relations would naturally lead to the expansion of the internal market, which would be helpful for expanding industries. The answer lies in the fact that in spite of the objective interests of the bourgeoisie, the latter dies not want the forces of agrarian revolution to be unleashed which, in unity with the working class would pose a threat to its class rule. It was from this angle that it forged an alliance with the landlords and now tries to solve its contradiction through pressure and bargaining. All conflicts and contradictions, which arise between the landlords and the bourgeoisie whether on the question of remunerative prices for agricultural produce cheep agricultural inputs and machinery or on the question of taxation the push and pull between the two remains but the alliance continues.

It is in this context that the Kisan pursues its alternative line, the line of completing the agrarian revolution, in unity with the working class, and continues to lead the mass struggle of the peasantry in this direction. Since independence the situation has changed. Although land monopoly remains a lot of changes have taken place in the agrarian structure, which require a changed approach in building peasant unity and in leading the agrarian revolution to success.

Land to the tiller and total abolition of landlordism have been the basic slogans of the Kisan Sabha since its inception. What bearing do the changes in agrarian sector have on these basic slogans? Before examining these changes, let me state here at the outset that the seizure and distribution of the land of the landlords still remains the central slogan for the kisan sabha to propagate among the peasantry and other democratic classes. Without the victory of this slogan there cannot be any solution to rural poverty unemployment, a fast development of a balanced economy in the country and so on.

But the correlation of class forces, which existed at the time when the Kisan Sabha inscribed these basic aims in its programme are not the same as exist today. It is necessary for us to understand his change since it has great relevance to the chalking out of our immediate slogans and actions.

The land reforms which the Congress Government set about to introduce after independence were not directed to end landlordism and give land to the tiller though this was the pledge the Congress had made to the peasantry during the freedom struggle. These land reforms had only very limited objectives, the main one of which was to reform, not abolish the old type of feudal landlordism by converting the absentee feudal landlords into capitalist landlords personally supervising cultivation in large farms with farms servants and hired agricultural workers. This is the new type of landlord who combines in himself elements of both feudalism and capitalism.

Another objective was to create a stratum of rich peasants. These two sections were to constitute the political base of the ruling party in the rural areas. They were also to produce the surplus food grains necessary for the Government to feed the urban people as well as to produce the raw materials for industry. With thousands of crores of rupees from the public exchequer pumped into agriculture these sections have been helped to adopt modern methods of farming.

Here, we should warn against one tendency. Earlier there was a tendency to altogether ignore the penetration of capitalism into agriculture. Now a reverse tendency is raising its head, which considers that feudal landlordism, and other semi-feudal relations have almost totally been abolished. This is wrong. The extent of capitalism in agriculture varies from State to State and even from region to region inside a State. Here a concrete study of the situation in each area is necessary.

We have also the note the phenomenon of the monetisation of the entire agrarian economy. Today, it is not only those who have a surplus who are taking their produce to the market, even the poor peasant immediately after the harvest for various reasons, sells his produce in the market and later buys even his food grains requirement from the market. It is only if this phenomenon is properly understood can we mount a struggle against the big traders and monopolists.

Even after the abolition of statutory landlordism like zamindari, jagirdari, etc. concentration of land in the hands of big landlords has not been appreciably reduced. Even today 2.5 per cent of top landlords posses 22.8 per cent of the land. The real concentration would be even more if benami transactions are included.

Congress land reforms have also resulted in the eviction of millions of tenants who have either joined the ranks of landless agricultural labourers or become tenants-at-will without any rights or protection. Only a section of the earlier tenants could by a portion of the land on which they were working either by paying compensation in instalments or outright purchase at lowers than market rates.

So, after the Congress land reforms the situation we find in the rural area is that three per cent of big owners have in their possession about one third of the cultivated land.

Another ten per cent consists of rich peasants owning roughly five to ten acres of wet, or ten to twenty acres of dry land, who contribute manual labour and employ a considerable number of farm servants and agricultural workers.

Another 15 per cent consists of middle peasants owning two to five acres of wet, or ten to twelve acres of dry land. They and their families work on the land but also hire labour in busy seasons.

Twenty per cent of the rural households are poor peasants possessing one or two acres of wet, or two to five acres of dry land. Apart from working on their own land, they have to frequently hire themselves out to earn a living.

The last 50 per cent are those who own no land at all, earns their livelihood mainly by hiring themselves out as wage workers or are engaged in handicrafts, villages' services, etc.

Of course, it has to be borne in mind that this categorisation will pay from State to State and region to region.

What has to be noted is that unlike in the pre-Independence days, 25 per cent of peasants, rich and middle peasants are not moved any longer by the slogan of seizure of landlords land and its distribution. At the other end of the scale the 70m per cent of landless and poor peasants are not conscious and organised enough to go into action today for the seizure of landlords lands; even when they are moved into action, it is only for Government waste land, cultivable forest land etc. Regarding even surplus land above the ceiling which the landlords are keeping illegally, the struggle as in Kerala or recently in Andhra Pradesh, could not advance beyond the stage of locating such surplus land and exposing the Government's claims. Only under the United Front Government in West Bengal in 1969, could some of the surplus land be occupied. This we will have to take into consideration when we work out our immediate tasks.

But what we have to note is that the Congress Party, which ruled the country for thirty-five years, while failing to end landlordism, land concentration and growing landlessness has successfully disrupted the pre-independence peasant unity. It is true that unity cantered around the rich and middle peasants, which today we are striving to build peasant unity cantering around the agricultural workers and poor peasants. The ruling class party, whether congress or Janata, also used its control peasantry and the disruption of their unity. The two-year of the cooperatives rural banks etc., to perpetuate the division in the peasantry and the disruption of their unity. The two years of the Janata Party government showed that its policies in regard to land reforms were no different from those of the Congress. In fact, some of the Janata State Governments were proposing to reverse even the Congress legislation to favour the landlords.

Taking note of these structural changes and their multifarious consequences we have to come to the conclusions that the slogan of complete abolition of landlordism and distribution of land of the landless and land-poor continues to be the central slogan of the agrarian revolution a slogan which we have to continue to propagate. But it is a slogan on which we cannot go into action today in most parts of the country.

While continuing to propagate this as the central slogans, while continuing struggles for surplus land, benami lands, waste land etc. the kisan sabha will have to take up for immediate action such issues as the question of wages of agricultural workers, house sites, rent-reduction, 75 per cent of the produce to the sharecroppers evictions, abolition or scaling down of rural indebtedness, remunerative price for agricultural produce, cheap credit, reduction of burdens and heavy levies like water charges, electricity rates, etc., landlord-goonda attacks with the connivance or direct help from the police the social oppression of harijans, corruption in administration etc.,. These are issues which affect all sections of the peasantry-poor, middle, rich, and they can all be drawn into the movement on them. All these currents have to be brought together to build the maximum unity of the peasantry cantering around the agricultural workers and poor peasants to isolate the small stratum of landlords.

All this will, course depend on how successfully we organise the agricultural workers and poor peasants and bring them into action not only on their own specific demands but also on the general demands of the peasantry as a whole, and how far we are able to draw other sections of the peasantry into movements on issues affecting them, and on the general demands of the peasantry. There is no doubt that the middle and rich peasants can be drawn into movement on such issues. It is our task to see that while other sections of the peasantry support the agricultural workers in their struggles, the latter in turn extend support to movements on the demands of the peasantry, thus paving the way for building peasant unity.

Our earlier analyses of the agrarian policies of the Congress Governments have shown them to be anti-peasants, serving the interests of the landlords and the bourgeoisie. As compared to that the Left Front Government of West Bengal and Tripura, and the Left Democratic government of Kerala (for a brief period) with the limit power they enjoy under the constitution, backed by the organised peasant movement, have tried to alleviate the conditions of the peasantry. In West Bengal, land has been distributed to 12 lakh families 13 lakh sharecroppers have been registered and more than two lakh of them receive credit from banks in a year, more than two lakhs have been given rights over homesteads, minimum wages fro agricultural workers are regularly revised. Small farmers have been exempted from land revenue and debt relief has been given.

In Tripura more than one-lakh beneficiaries have been given land, debt relief has been given to poor peasants and artisans, while minimum wages have been fixed and sharecroppers recorded. In Kerala under the Left Democratic Front Government holdings under four acres were exempted from plantation tax, rent arrears for holdings up to 2.5 acres cancelled and subsidies given on inputs and exemptions on gifted land taken away.

This would not have been possible without the strength of the peasant organisation because without the active intervention of the Kisan Sabha, the bureaucracy would never have allowed the implementation of measures, which would have remained on paper as pious declarations. It is because of these alternative policies that the Kisan Sabha has grown so strong in West Bengal with almost 33 per cent of the adult peasant population including agricultural workers joining the organisation.

In other states also the kisan sabha has grown through struggles. Kisan Sabha units in different States have taken up different issues depending on the concrete situation in each state. In Bihar the question of eviction of sharecroppers has remained very acute and struggle fought over it; in some, states against rise in taxation and on remunerative prices in most of the states. The first half of 80s witnessed a tremendous upsurge among the peasantry where even the Congress base was drawn into struggles. This shows the tremendous possibilities for building the peasants movement.

Peasant Movements

Colonial economic policies, the new land revenue system, the colonial administrative and judicial system and the ruin of handicrafts leading to the overcrowding of land, transformed the agrarian structure and impoverished the peasantary. In the vast zamindari areas the peasants were left to the mercies of the zamindar who rack-rented them and compelled them to pay illegal dues and perform beggar. In the ryotwari areas, the government itself levied heavy land revenue. This forced the peasants to borrow money from the moneylenders. Gradually over large areas the actual cultivators were reduced to the status of tenants at will, share croppers and landless labourers while their lands, crops and cattle passed into the hands to landlords, trader moneylenders and such peasants. When the peasants could take it no longer they resisted against the oppression and exploitation and they found whether their target was the indigenous exploiter or the colonial administration that their real enemies after the barriers were down was the colonial state. In 1930s nation wide awakening of peasants was largely the result of the combination of particular economic and political developments.

- The great depression that began to hit India from 1920-30 and
- The new phase of mass struggle launched by the Indian National Congress in 1930.

The depression brought agricultural prices crashing down to half of less of their normal levels dealt a severe blow to the already impoverished peasants burdened with high taxes and rents. Therefore the peasants were placed in a situation where they had to continue to pay taxes, rents and debts at pre-depression rates while their incomes continued to spiral steadily downward. The civil disobedience movement was launched in this atmosphere of discontent in 1930s and in many parts of the country it soon took on the form of no-tax and no-rent campaign. Peasants emboldened by the recent success of the Bardoli Satyagraha (1928) joined the protest in large numbers. In Bihar and Bengal powerful movements were launched against the hated chowkidar tax by which villages were made to pay for the upkeep of their own oppressors.

In Punjab a no-revenue campaign was accompanied by the emergence of Kisan Sabhas that demanded a reduction in land revenue and water rates and the scaling down of debts. The consolidation of left after the formation of the Congress Socialist Party in 1934 acted as a spur to the formation of an all India body to coordinate the Kisan Movement a process that was already underway through the efforts of N.G Ranga and other Kisan leaders. The culmination was the establishment of the all India Kisan Congress in the Lucknow in April 1936 which later changed its name to All India Kisan Sabha. Swami Sahajanand was elected secretary. The first session was greeted in person by Jawaharlal Nehru. A Kisan Manifesto was finalized at the All India Kisan Committee session in Bombay and formally presented to the Congress Working Committee to be incorporated into its forthcoming manifesto for the 1937 elections. The Kisan Manifesto considerably influenced the agrarian programme adopted by the congress at its Faizpur session. The formation of Congress ministries in a majority of the provinces in early 1937 marked the beginning of a new phase in the growth of the peasant movement.

The political atmosphere in the country underwent a marked change: increased civil liberties, a new sense of freedom born of the feeling that our own people are in power a heightened sense of expectation that the ministries would bring a pro-people measures-all combine to make the years 1937-39 the high water mark of the peasant movement. The chief form of mobilization was through the holding of Kisan Conferences or meetings at the Thana, taluqa, district and provincials levels at which peasant demands would be aired and resolutions passed. These conferences would be addressed by local, provincial and All India leaders. During Second World War years the Kisan Sabha continued to play an important role in arranging relief works during Bengal famine of 1943.It also continued its organizational work despite being severally handicapped by its taking the unpopular pro-war stance which alienated it from various sections of the peasantry.

Parth Nath Mukherji has made a study of Naxalbari movement and the peasant revolt in North Bengal in Darjeeling district and the regions are Phansidewa, Naxalbari and Khoribari. There are both tea plantations and paddy cultivation. He analyses the peasant uprising against the background of the communist movement in India. The Communist party of India developed two strands; one which argued that the situation in India was not yet ripe for revolution and the other led by the most articulate group of Siliguri sub division of Darjeeling district under the leadership of Charu Majumdar. Ideological pressures for radicalization of CPI (M) politics were exerted by the Darjeeling District Committee. Even among the radicals there were those who favoured participation in the elections while the others proposed to shun the elections and socialize the masses against it. The former held to the primacy of the land problem and recommended mass struggles to solve it. The Naxalbari peasant movement is related to the Tebhanga Movement of Bengal where the Bengali weavers were exploited. Over a period of time, numerous struggles against such exploitation led to the emergence of Krishak Sabha. But such movements also suffered from various weaknesses. The weakness of the movement was there were two kinds of leadership. On the one hand there was the urban-based leadership, which claimed superior knowledge and status with regard to the manner in which the movement should be conducted. Among the rural leaders there were the indigenous rural leaders like Kanu Sanyal, Panchang Sarker and urban leaders like Charu Majumdar. When most of the rural leaders were in prison the leadership passed into the hands of the urban leaders who were interested in systemic changes rather than a mere just redistribution of the produce. Charu Majumdar shifted the focus from the narrow economic demands to capture of power. He wanted the annihilation of class enemies, which in effect was indistinguishable from secret assassinations. As a result he drove the movement underground.

Ranga Rao made a study of the Peasant Movement in Telengana based on both secondary sources and fieldwork. He places the communist led peasant movement in the wider context of other social movements, which sprang up in Telengana in the beginning of 20th century. The Telugu Literary Movement introduced ideas of renaissance and was against the Nizam's establishment. Under the influence of Indian National Congress and the Arya Samaj the Telengana elite gave a new direction to the activities of the Andhra Mahasabha in the 1930.They mobilized the public for the abolition of forced labour, untouchability and other social evils, They also demanded equal educational and economic opportunities and equal political representation for the Hindus. According to Narayana Reddy it is not enough if economic conditions are ripe foe such a movement. While similar conditions prevailed in Madhya Pradesh and Rajasthan it was the added presence of Nizam as a ruler from minority religious group, lack of civil and religious liberties and lack of correct understanding of the socioeconomic situation prevailing in Hyderabad state by communists that helped a movement to develop. Ranga Rao adds that it was other structural factors like improvement in the economic and social conditions of the people followed by a period of reversal and oppression that made the peasants, rich and poor take part in the campaign of non cooperation against the Nizam's government under the collective leadership of the Congress, the Communist Parties and the Andhra Mahasabha. Many of these movements have also been changed over time and exist today in some form or the other in some places of India.

Bibliography

Adikaram, E. W.: *Early History of Buddhism in Ceylon,* D. S. Puswella, Migoda, 1946.

Agrawala, V. S.: *Shiva Mahadeva: The Great God,* Veda Academy, Varanasi, 1966.

Ahmad, Imtiaz: *State and Foreign Policy: India's Role in South Asia,* Vikas, New Delhi, 1993.

Ahmad, Jamil-ud-din: *Some Recent Speeches and Writings of Mr. Jinnah,* Lahore, Ashraf, 1952.

Aiyar, R. Krishnaswami: *Outlines of Vedaanta,* Chetana, Bombay, 1978.

Archer, W. G.: *The Kama Sutra,* Unwin Hyman, London, 1990.

Ashton, S.R. : *British Policy Towards the Indian States, 1905-1939,* London, Curzon, 1982.

Aurobindo, Sri: *Vyasa and Valmiki,* Acharya Press, Pondicherry, 1956.

Avalon, Arthur and Ellen: *Hymns to the Goddess,* Ganesh and Co., Madras, 1964.

Aziz, Ashraf: *Light of the Universe: Essays on Hindustani Film Music,* Three Essays Collective, New Delhi, 2003.

Bagchi, P. C.: *Studies in Dharmashastra,* University of Calcutta Press, Calcutta, 1939.

Bahadur, K.P.: *The Wisdom of Vedaanta,* Sterling Publishers Private Limited, New Delhi, 1996.

Banerjea, J. N.: *Pauranic and Vedanta Religion,* University of Calcutta, Calcutta, 1996.

Bankimchandra, C.: *Essentials of Dharma,* Sanskrit Book Depot, Calcutta 1979.

Basu, Manoranjan: *Dharmashastra: A General Study,* Shrimati Mira Basu, Calcutta, 1976.

Beaumont, Roger : *Sword of the Raj: The British Army in India, 1747-1947*, Indianapolis, Bobbs-Merrill, 1977.

Benjamin, Joseph : *Scheduled Castes in Indian Politics and Society*, New Delhi, Ess Ess Publications, 1989.

Bhattacharyya, B.: *Nispannayogavali of Mahapandita Abhyakara Gupta*, Oriental Institute, Baroda, 1949.

Borchert, Bruno: *Mysticism: Its History and Challenge*, Samuel Wiser, York Beach, 1994.

Bose, D. N.: *Dharmashastra: Their Philosophy and Occult Secrets*, Kali Press, Calcutta, 1965.

Bowle, John: *The Imperial Achievement: The Rise and Transformation of the British Empire*, Little, Brown, 1974.

Brockington, J. L.: *Righteous Rama: The Evolution of an Epic*, Oxford, London, 1984.

Bromley, D.: *Krishna Consciousness in the West*, Bucknell University Press, Lewisburg, 1989.

Brooks, E.: *The Original Analects: Sayings of Confucius and His Successors*. Columbia University Press, New York, 1988.

Bruhn, Klaus: *The Jina-Images of Deogarh*, MacMillan, Leiden, 1969.

Burke, Mary Louise: *Swami Vivekananda in America: New Discoveries*, Advaita Ashrama, Calcutta, 1966.

Chaudhary, M.: *Partition and the Curse of Rehabilitation*, Calcutta, Bengal Rehabilitation Organization, 1964.

Chaudhuri, Nirad: *Thy Hand, Great Anarch! India: 1921-1952*, London, Chatto & Windus, 1987.

Coomeraswamy, Ananda K.: *Buddha and the Gospel of Buddhism*, MacMillan, London, 1928.

Crawford, Cromwell S.: *Ram Mohan Roy: His Era and Ethics*, Acharya Press, New Delhi, 1984.

Dalton, Dennis : *Gandhi's Power : Nonviolence in Action*, New Delhi, OUP, 2001.

Danielou, Alain: *The Complete Kama Sutra*, Park Street Press, Rochester, 2000.

Dasgupta, Shahana: *Rani Lakshmibai: The Indian Heroine*, Rupa & Company, Calcutta, 2002.

Datta, V.N.: *Sati: Widow Burning in India*, Manohar, New Delhi, 1990.

David, M. D.: *John Wilson and his Institutions*, Mumbai, 1957.

De Bary: *Self and Society in Ming Thought*, Columbia University Press, New York, 1970.

De, Sushil Kumar: *Ancient Indian Erotics and Erotic Literature*, Firma K. L. Mukhopadhyay, Calcutta, 1959.

Deak, Istvan: *The Lawful Revolution: Louis Kossuth and the Hungarians 1848-1849*, Columbia University Press, 1979.

Dhar, Niranjan: *Vedanta and Bengal Renaissance*, Minerva Associates, Calcutta, 1977.

Dikshit, D.P. *Political History of the Chalukyas of Badami*. New Delhi: Abhinav, 1980.

Donat, K.: *Meditate the Tantric Yoga Way*, George Allen and Unwin, London, 1973.

Doniger, W.: *The Rig Veda: An Anthology*, Penguin, New York, 1981.

Duboi, Abbe: *Hindu Manners, Customs and Ceremonies*, Fifth Indian Impression, CUP, 1985.

Dwivedi, M.: *The Principal Upanishads*, Adyar Library, Madras, 1931.

Eaton, Richard M.: *Sufis of Bijapur, 1300-1700: Social Roles of Sufis in Medieval India*, Princeton University Press, Princeton, 1978.

Edwardes, Michael: *Battles of the Indian Mutiny*, London; B. T. Batsford Ltd., 1963.

Erickson, Erik H.: *Gandhi's Truth: On the Origins of Militant Nonviolence*, Norton, New York, 1970.

Farquhar, J.N.: *Modern Religious Movements in India*, Munshiram, New Delhi, 1967.

Fay, Peter Ward: *The Opium War, 1840-42*, University of North Carolina Press, 1975.

Fisher, Michael H.: *The Politics of British Annexation of India - 1757-1857*, Oxford, 1996.

Frauwallner, E..: *History of Indian Philosophy*, Motilal, Delhi, 1973.

Gambhirananda, S.: *Brahma Sutra Shamkar Bhasya*, Adavita Ashrama, Calcutta, 1977.

Gambhirananda, Swami: *Brahma Sutra Shamkar Bhasya*, Adavita Ashrama, Calcutta, 1977.

Gandhi, M. K.: *The Story of My Experiment With Trust*, Washington, Public Affairs Press, 1948.

Garbe, R.: *The Philosophy of Ancient India*, Chicago University Press, Chicago, 1899.

Goradia, Nayana: *Lord Curzon: The Last of the British Moghuls*, New Delhi, Oxford University Press, 1993.

Goudriaan, T.: *Ritual and Speculation in Early Tantrism*, State University of New York Press, New York, 1992.

Gough, A.E.: *The Philosophy of the Upanisads and Ancient Indian Metaphysics*, MacMillan, London, 1882.

Grant, G. P.: *Philosophy in the Mass Age*, Copp Clark, Toronto, 1959.

Grisenold, H.D.: *Insights into Modern Hinduism*, Oxford, New York, 1934.

Growse, F. S.: *The Ramayana of Tulasidasa*, Motilal Banarsidass, Delhi, 1995.

Gurumurthy, S. : *Hindu Heritage, Assimilative, Not Divisive*, Vigil, Madras 1993.

Haich, E.: *Sexual Energy and Yoga*, Aurora Press, New York, 1982.

Hasan, Murhirul: *Legacy of a Divided Nation: India's Muslims Since Independence*, New Delhi, Oxford, 1997.

Hasan, Mushirul: *India's Partition: Process, Strategy and Mobilization*, New Delhi, Oxford UP, 1993.

Heifetz, Hank: *The Origin of the Young God: Kalidasa's Kumarasambhava*, University of California Press, Berkeley, 1985.

Heimann, Betty: *Facets of Indian Thought*, Geroge Allen & Unwin, London, 1964.

Heinsath, Charles: *Indian Nationalism and Hindu Social Reform*, Princeton University Press, Princeton, 1964.

Heschel, J.: *God in Search of Man: A Philosophy of Judaism*, Noonday Press, New York, 1997.

Hirschman, Edwin: *White Mutiny: The Ilbert Bill Crisis in India and the Genesis of the Indian National Congress*, New Delhi, Heritage, 1980.

Hixon, L.: *Mother of the Universe: Visions of the Goddess, Tantric Hymns of Enlightenment*, Quest Books, Wheaton, 1994.

Hopkins, J.: *Kalachakra Tantra Rite of Initiation*, Wisdom Publications, Boston, 1982.

Hopkirk, Peter: *The Great Game: The Struggle for Empire in Central Asia*, Kodansha, 1992.

Hume, R.E.: *The Thirteen Principle Upanishads*, Oxford University Press, London, 1971.

Hutchins, Francis: *Spontaneous Revolution: The Quit India Movement*, New Delhi, Manohar, 1971.

Irene, S.: *Vedic Heritage Teaching Program*. Arsha Vidya Gurukulam, Coimbatore, 1994.

Iyar, K.: *Vedanta: The Science of Reality*, Ganesh and Co., Mardas, 1930.

Iyengar, B.K.S.: *Light on the Yoga Sutras of Patanjali*, Aquarian Press, London 1993.

Jacob, K.: *Religion and Ethics in Advaita*, C.M.S. Press, Kottayam, 1982.

Jafar, Malik Muhammad: *Jinnah as a Parliamentarian*, Lahore, Afzar Publications, 1977.

Jain, Kailash Chand, *Lord Mahavira and His Times*, Saraswati Press, Delhi, 1974.

James, Lawrence: *The Rise and Fall of the British Empire*, St. Martin's, 1997.

James, Robert Rhodes: *The British Revolution, 1880-1939*, New York, Knopf, 1976.

Jean, M.: *Tantrik Yoga*, The Aquarian Press, Wellingborough, 1970.

John, B.: *Mantras: Sacred Words of Power*, George Allen and Unwin, London, 1977.

John, Elsner: *Pilgrimage: Past and Present in the World Religions*, Harvard University Press, Cambridge, 1995.

John, K.: *The Origin and Development of the State Cult of Confucius*, Paragon Book, New York, 1966.

Karmarkar, D.: *Sankara's Advaita*, Karnatak University, Dharwar, 1976.

Kaushik, Asha : *Globalization, Democracy and Culture : Situating Gandhian Alternatives*, Jaipur, Pointer, 2002.

Kaviraj, G.: *Aspects of Indian Thought*, University of Burdwan, Calcutta, 1966.

Kavlekar, K.K. : *Non-Brahmin Movement in Southern India, 1873-1949*, Kolhapur, Shivaji University, 19790

Keith, A.B. : *Rigveda Brahmanas*, Harvard University Press, Cambridge, 1920.

Keith, Arthur Berriedale: *The Religion and Philosophy of the Veda and Upanishads*, MacMillan, Delhi, 1925.

Kishwar, Madhu : *Religion at the Service of Nationalism, and Other Essays*, OUP, Delhi, 1998.

Klaus, K.: *A Survey of Hinduism,* State University of New York Press, Albany, 1989.

Knipe, M.: *Hinduism: Experiments in the Sacred*, Harper, San Francisco, 1991.

Knott, K.: *Hinduism, A Very Short Introduction,* Oxford University Press, New York, 1998.

Kosambi, D. D. : *The Culture and Civilisation of Ancient India in Historical Outline*, London, Routledge and Kegan Paul, 1956.

Kottackal, Jacob: *Religion and Ethics in Advaita,* C.M.S. Press, Kottayam, 1982.

Kuiper, F.B.J. : *Aryans in the Rigveda,* Rodopi, Amsterdam, 1991.

Kuppuswamy, Sastri S.: *Compromises in the History of Advaitic Thought*, Kalyani Press, Madras, 1940.

Louis, Fischer: *Essential Gandhi: An Anthology of His Writings,* Vintage, New York, 1983.

Low, D. A. and Brasted, Howard: *Freedom, Trauma, Continuities: Northern India and Independence,* New Delhi, Sage Publications, 1998.

Maheshwari, Shriram: *Rural Development in India: A Public Policy Approach,* New Delhi, Sage, 1995.

Makhan, L.: *The Ramayana of Valmiki,* Munshiram Manoharlal, New Delhi, 1978.

Mathew, Arnold: *Culture and Anarchy,* The University Press, Cambridge, 1935.

Mayer, A. : *Caste in an Indian Village: Change and Continuity 1954-1992,* Delhi, OUP, 1996.

Mazumder, Sukhendu : *Politico-Economic Ideas of Mahatma Gandhi: Their Relevance in the Present Day,* New Delhi, Concept Pub., 2004.

Mearns, David J.: *Shiva's Other Children: Religion and Social Identity amongst Overseas Indians,* Sage, Walnut Creek, 1995.

Mearns, J.: *Shiva's Other Children: Religion and Social Identity amongst Overseas Indians,* Sage, Walnut Creek, 1995.

Mehra, Parshotam: *A Dictionary of Modern Indian History, 1707-1947*, New Delhi, Oxford University Press, 1985.

Metcalf, Thomas R.: *The Aftermath of the Revolt: India, 1857-1870*, Princeton, Princeton University, 1964.

Mohan, K.: *The Mahabharata*, Munshiram Manoharlal, Delhi 1997.

Mookerjee, Ajit: *Kali The Feminine Force*, Thames and Hudson, London, 1988.

Mookerji, Satkari: *Modern Polity and Vedanta*, Sanskrit College, Calcutta, 1972.

Moon, Penderel: *The British Conquest and Dominion of India*, London, Duckworth, 1989.

Morris-Jones, W.H.: *The Government and Politics of India*, London, Hutchinson, 1971.

Nanda, B. R. : *Gandhi and His Critics*, Oxford University Press, Delhi, 1993.

Neale, Walter C.: *Economic Change in Rural India: Land Tenure and Reform in the United Provinces, 1800-1955*, New Haven, 1962.

Nevile, P.: *Lahore: A Sentimental Journey*, New Delhi, Penguin, 1993.

Oddie, G.A. : *Hindu and Christian in South-East India*, London, Curzon Press, 1991.

Pathak, Dr S.P.: *Jhansi during the British Rule*, Ramanand Vidya Bhawan, Delhi, 1987.

Preston, Diana: *The Boxer Rebellion*, Berkley Books, 2000.

Raimundo Panikkar: *The Vedic Experience: Mantramanjari*, Longman Todd, London, 1977.

Raja, C. Kunhan : *The Taittiriya Sarvanukramani of Yaska*, Madras, 1931.

Ramamurti, A.: *Advaitic Mysticism of Sankara*, Visvabharati, Santiniketan, 1974.

Ranajit Guha: *A Construction of Humanism in Colonial India*, CASA, Amsterdam, 1993.

Renou, Louis: *The Nature of Dharmashastra*, Walker and Co., New York, 1997.

Robson, Brian: *Sir Hugh Rose and the Central India Campaign*, Sutton Publishing Ltd for the Army Records Society, UK, 2000.

Satyapal Verma: *Role of Reason in Sankara Vedanta*, Parimal Publication, Delhi, 1992.

Savarkar, Vinayak Damodar : *The Indian War of Independence* 1857 Rajdhani Granthagar, Delhi, 1988.

Scheftelowitz, Isidor : *Die Kasmirische Rezension von Katyayanas Sarvanukramani,* Zeitschrift fur Indologie und Iranistik, 1922.

Shukla, D. N.: *Vastu-Shastra,* Motilal Banarsidass, Delhi, 1966.

Singh, Birendra Kumar: *Early Chalukyas of Vatapi, circa A.D. 500 to 757,* Delhi, Eastern Book Linkers, 1991.

Smith, Col. J. T. : *Silver and the India Exchanges,* Effingham Wilson, London, 1876.

Strauss, L.: *Political Philosophy,* The Bobbs Merrill Co., New York, 1975.

Swami Vishnu Tirtha: *Devatma Shakti,* Swami Shivom Tirth, Rishikesh, 1962.

Talageri, Shrikant : *Aryan Invasion Theory and Indian Nationalism,* Voice of India, Delhi, 1993.

Tejomayananda, Swami: *Hindu Culture: An Introduction,* Chinmaya Publications, Piercy, 1993.

Thapar, Romila : *Ashoka and the Decline of the Mauryas,* London, Oxford University Press, 1961.

Thompson, Edward: *The Making of the Indian Princes,* Oxford University Press, London, 1943.

Trautmann, Thomas R.: *Kautilya and the Arthasastra: A Statistical Study,* Leiden, Brill, 1971.

Trimingham, J.: *Sufi Orders in Islam,* Oxford University Press, New York, 1998.

Utpat, V.N.: *Riddles of Buddha and Ambedkar,* Itihas Patrika Prakashan, Thane 1988.

Vable, D.: *The Arya Samaj. Hindu without Hinduism.* Vikas Publ., Delhi, 1983.

Vedalankar, Pandit Nardev : *Basic Teachings of Hinduism,* Veda Niketan, Durban, 1978.

Visvantha, K.: *Essentials of Hinduism,* Narosa Pub. House, New Delhi, 1989.

Wendy Doniger: *Siva: The Erotic Ascetic,* Oxford University Press, Delhi, 1998.

Zaidi, A. Moin: *Evolution of Muslim Political Thought in India,* New Delhi: S. Chand, 1975.

Index

□□□